THE
ENTREPRENEUR'S GUIDE

to Patents,
Copyrights,
Trademarks,
Trade Secrets,
& Licensing

Jill Gilbert >>>

BERKLEY BOOKS, NEW YORK

B

A Berkley Book
Published by The Berkley Publishing Group
A division of Penguin Group (USA) Inc.
375 Hudson Street
New York, New York 10014

This book is an original publication of The Berkley Publishing Group.

Copyright © 2004 by Jill Gilbert.
Cover design by Erica Tricarico.
Text design by Julie Rogers.

PRINTING HISTORY
Berkley trade paperback edition / August 2004

Library of Congress Cataloging-in-Publication Data

Gilbert, Jill.
The entrepreneur's guide to patents, copyrights, trademarks, trade secrets & licensing / Jill Gilbert.—Berkley trade paperback ed.
p. cm.
Includes bibliographical references and index.
ISBN 0-425-19409-4
1. Intellectual property—United States—Popular works. 2. Businesspeople—United States—Handbooks, manuals, etc. I. Title.

KF2980.G55 2004
346.7304'8—dc22
2004049437

PRINTED IN THE UNITED STATES OF AMERICA

10 9 8 7 6 5 4 3 2 1

To four especially innovative minds:
Dan, Daniel, Tara, and Julia

Thanks to Vince Polley
of the American Bar Association
Cyberspace Committee.

CONTENTS

Introduction   xi

PART ONE: INNOVATING FOR FUN AND PROFIT   1

CHAPTER 1   The Rise of Intellectual Property Law: Who Owns an Idea?   3

    The Stealing of Ideas Through the Ages   4
    Copyright: The Champion of Artists and Authors   5
    Encouraging Innovation: The Rise of Patent Protection   8
    Testing Trademark Boundaries   10
    Safeguarding Valuable Trade Secrets   11
    So You Have an Idea . . .   12

CHAPTER 2   American Ingenuity in the Twenty-first Century   13

    Intellectual Property Rights As a Bargaining Chip   14
    Co-opting Copyright to Prevent Spam   15
    Piracy on Campus: What's the Matter with Kids Today?   16
    The Music Industry Sings Its Own Technology Tune   17
    Copyright Goes to Hollywood   19
    Wal-Mart Shops Its Litigation Options   19
    Cyber-Jurisdiction   20

PART TWO: TAKING OWNERSHIP OF TRADEMARKS AND TRADE NAMES   23

CHAPTER 3   Making Your Mark: The Basics of Trademark Law   25

The Power and Purpose of a Trademark 26
What Constitutes a Valid Trademark? 27
Legal Basis for Trademark Protection 28
The Basics: How to Acquire Trademark Protection 29
Location! Location! Trademarks and Geographical Factors 32
Not for Logos Only: Categories of Trademarks 33
Trade Dress: The Entire Look 34
Developing a Strong Mark Versus a Weak Mark: Types of Protections 36
Establishing Secondary Meaning 39
Problems with Confusingly Similar Trademarks 40

CHAPTER 4   Maintaining Marks in the Face of Legal Adversity   42

Legal Land Mines: Losing Your Mark Through Misuse 43
Leveling the Playing Field: International Protections 51
Ten Trademark Tips for Selecting and Maintaining a Mark 53

CHAPTER 5   How to Research and Register a Mark from Scratch   57

Preregistration Considerations 58
Researching Your Mark: A Three-Stage Approach 64
The Application Process 69
The Application Form 70
Materials That Accompany the Application: A Checklist 76
What Happens to Applications After You File Them? 79
Rebounding When You're Rebuffed: Responding to a Rejection or Objection 82
Special Issues 83
Wait, There's More: Maintaining Your Registration 85

CHAPTER 6   Trademarks in Cyberspace: The Domain Name Debate   88

Dueling Domain Names 90
Business Regulating Business: The Role of ICANN 90
The Federal Cybersquatting Statute 92
Registration of Domain Name Marks with the PTO 92

PART THREE: CASHING IN ON COPYRIGHTS   95

CHAPTER 7   Critical Copyright Concepts: What's Protected?   97

The Core of Copyright: What's Creative Expression? 99
Only the "Expressive Elements" Get Protection 100
Facts Aren't Copyrightable 101
When Can You Use Facts Compiled in Other Works? 101
The Story Line Versus the Script: What's Protected? 102
Basic Legal Requirements: Originality and Fixation 104
Getting Copyright Protection for Your Work 108
The Rights You Get with a Copyright 110
How Long Do Copyrights Last? 114
Recourse for Rip-Offs: Penalties for Copyright Infringement 115
What's the Real Purpose of Copyright Protection? 118

CHAPTER 8   Limitations on Copyright Protection   119

Limitation #1: The Doctrine of Independent Creation 120
Limitation #2: The Utility Doctrine 123
Limitation #3: The Doctrine of Fair Use 126
Limitation #4: The First Sale Doctrine 139
Cutting into Copyright: How Deep Do the Doctrines Go? 141

CHAPTER 9   Copyright Infringement: Proving It and Defending Against It   142

Proving Your Copyright Has Been Infringed: A Three-Part Test 144
Policing Your Copyright 152
Getting an Alleged Infringer to Stop 153
Getting Permission to Use Someone Else's Work 156
Some Tips for Protecting Yourself Against Infringement Actions 160

CHAPTER 10   Exercising Copyright Caution: Research,
Registration, and Designation   161

The Advantages of Registering, Sooner or Later 163
Filling Out the Forms 166
Using the Copyright Notice 168
Researching Existing Copyrights 169
Supplementary Registration 171
Recording a Change in Copyright Ownership 171

PART FOUR: PRACTICAL PATENT CONCEPTS

173

CHAPTER 11   What Can You Patent?

175

A Contract Between Inventor and Government 177
Constitutional Basis: To Promote "Useful Arts" 177
What Can You Patent? 178
Utility Patents: Concrete Applications Versus Abstract Ideas 180
Design Patents: Inventions of Aesthetic Value 186
Patenting Computer Programs 191
Business Method Patents 192
Biotechnology Patents: Altering Life-Forms 195
Can a Plant Be Invented? 196
What Rights Does a Patent Give You? 197
Limitations on Patent Rights 199

CHAPTER 12   Filing a Successful Patent Application

203

Players in the Patent Process 205
Conducting a Thorough Search for Prior Inventions 208
Filing the Patent Application 211
Some Special Types of Patent Applications 217
Prosecuting Your Patent Application 220
What to Do If Your Application Is Rejected 223
Surviving the Dreaded Patent Interference Process 230
Care and Maintenance of Your Patent 231
How Your Patent Rights Can Be Forfeited 231
Additional Notes About Design Patent Applications 232

CHAPTER 13   Avoiding, Detecting, and Defending
Against Patent Infringement

233

Activities That Constitute Patent Infringement 235
Activities That Aren't Patent Infringement: Unfair Competition 239
Before You Call an Attorney: Is Someone Really Infringing Your Patent? 240
Remedies for Infringement 242
Important Considerations Prior to Filing Suit 244
Statute of Limitations and the Need to Act Promptly 247
Jurisdiction and Venue 247
Your Burden of Proof 249
The New Role of Judges and Juries 249

Arbitration As an Alternative 251
Resolving Infringement Issues Without Litigation 251
Drafting a Complaint for Patent Infringement 252
Stopping Foreign Infringement: The Customs Service 252
Insuring Your Patent 253
How to Avoid Being Sued for Patent Infringement 254
Defending Yourself If You're Accused of Infringement 257

PART FIVE: ISSUES FOR ENTREPRENEURS   261

CHAPTER 14   Trade Secret Protection   263

Why Do We Have Trade Secret Protection? 264
Special Laws Protecting Trade Secrets 265
What Is a Trade Secret? 266
Comparing Patent and Trade Secret Protections 268
Securing Your Trade Secrets 270
Litigating to Protect Your Trade Secrets 273

CHAPTER 15   Getting Your Idea to Market:
Licensing and Other Arrangements   274

Overview: Making It to Market 275
Assignment Agreements 276
Licensing Agreements 276
Manufacturing Agreements 278
Joint Ventures and Other Types of Hybrid Agreements 278
Protecting Proposed Ideas from Being Stolen 278
Third-Party Confidentiality Agreements 279

CHAPTER 16   Software Savvy   280

Bad Laws or Just Bad Patents? 282
The Chronology of Software Patent Cases 283
Critical Software Copyright Cases 287
Patents Versus Copyrights: Which One Works Best? 289
Trade Secret Protections for Software 290
Trademark Protection for Software 292
Software Licensing Agreements 292
Software Piracy Issues 294

CHAPTER 17   Protecting and Promoting Your Web Site   295

Assume Everything Is Protected 296
Get Permission—It's Usually Easier Than You Think 296
Look for Free Materials 297
Don't Link to a Lawsuit 298
Don't Overuse Fair Use 300
Remove Potentially Infringing Material When Notified 300
Disclaim Confusing Affiliations 300
Don't Imitate the Appearance of Another Web Site 301

CHAPTER 18   From Brain to Balance Sheet: Tax Considerations   302

Some Core Tax Planning Concepts 303
IRS Classifications of Licenses: A Trap for the Unwary 307

APPENDICES   311

A. SAMPLE TRADEMARK APPLICATION   311

B. SAMPLE EMPLOYEE CONFIDENTIALITY AGREEMENT   314

C. SAMPLE EMPLOYEE NONDISCLOSURE AGREEMENT   315

INDEX   317

INTRODUCTION ≫≫≫

WHETHER YOU'RE A corporate CEO strategizing your company's future or a college kid wondering just how much trouble you can get into by downloading pirated music, this book has something for *you*. Intellectual property considerations permeate our daily life and color our culture. Intellectual property law has a rich and entertaining history and an exponentially evolving future.

This book is intended to be analytical but informal. It will provide you with the same type of advice you might get over lunch with your lawyer. Of course, individual situations and ideas vary. A single fact about your particular artistic or literary creation or invention can be the basis of a critical legal distinction. If you're seriously concerned about protecting an actual trademark, copyright, patent, or trade secret, you should rely upon this book only as a starting point for your real-life discussions with a living, breathing intellectual property lawyer.

TWO WAYS TO USE THIS BOOK

Readers of this book will generally fall into two categories: those who skim it for what's of interest to them, and those who read it cover to cover. If you're in the first category, you've probably already skipped this introduction to get to the meat of the book. And that's just fine. Each Chapter is intended to be a fairly self-contained treatment of its purported topic, with cross-references to information you may need from other chapters.

If you do read every page sequentially, you'll gain added perspective. The topics are presented in a logical order to help you understand the relationships, distinctions, and development of each area of intellectual property law.

ICONS

This book contains three different types of icons to break the monotony of tiny type and to signal something worth emphasizing. You'll find the following types of icons in this book:

- ⚖ **Lawyer's Note:** This icon identifies a key legal concept that a lawyer might stress in his or her discussions with you.

- **$$ Business Tip:** This icon signals a consideration that may be important to you in planning for your business, working with clients, or in structuring your intellectual property transactions.

- ⊖ **Caution:** Legal distinctions can be subtle, and the technical requirements of the law can be unforgiving. This icon warns you of a detail you should not ignore.

FOOTNOTES AND DOING YOUR OWN FOLLOW-UP RESEARCH

Footnotes break the flow of the text and your concentration, so with few exceptions, they're limited to providing citations to cases, statutes, and full-length articles that will give you more information about the topic being discussed. The footnotes for cases and statutes contain enough information so that you can take them to the reference desk of any law library and ask them to help you locate the full text.

PART ONE

....

Innovating for Fun and Profit

CHAPTER 1 >>>

The Rise of Intellectual Property Law: Who Owns an Idea?

WHO REDUCED THE Bible to written form or invented the wheel? Who thought to use oxen to pull a plow? In modern times, all of these ideas would be owned for a set term of years, entering the public domain only after the term of ownership had expired.

IN THIS CHAPTER YOU FIND OUT:

- What protections are available to artists and inventors

- The origins of copyright, patent, trademark, and trade secret protection

- How intellectual property protections operate in modern times

TAKING ADVANTAGE OF a new court precedent affording patent protection to certain business methods, IBM applies for and receives a patent for its method for determining who gets to use the bathroom next. The patent covers a "system and method for providing reservations for restroom use." In December 2001, IBM's legal team decides to quietly relinquish all of its claims to this particular

patent after a petition is filed challenging the patent on the basis of "prior art."
IBM spokesman Chris Andrews explains IBM "dedicated that patent to the pub-
lic so that we could continue focusing on our high-quality patent portfolio" of tech-
nological innovations.

Patents, copyrights, trademarks, and trade secrets, otherwise known as intellectual property, protect ideas. At the time an idea is spawned, it may be difficult to know its worth. Some of the most significant innovations of this generation, including birth control pills, tampons, personal computers, cell phones, disposable razors, in vitro fertilization, and cloning, initially met with skepticism, hostility, and market resistance.

THE STEALING OF IDEAS THROUGH THE AGES

Intellectual property rights are different than other types of property rights. The ability to exploit them doesn't depend upon possession; their mere disclosure to the public makes them vulnerable to plagiarism and other forms of theft.

In the copyright area, the technology to make copies in printed, photographic, or digital mediums directly impacts an author's or artist's ability to protect against unauthorized appropriation of his or her work. In the patent area, reverse engineering is a common technique for analyzing proprietary technology. Trademarks are subject to dilution and tarnishment in the public eye, and trade secrets immediately lose all of their value if they become known to someone other than their owners.

The development of enforceable laws in each of these areas—copyright, patent, trademark, and trade secrets—has historically lagged behind the technologies that both enhance and threaten them. Changes in intellectual property law are now (and always have been) dictated by increasing levels of technological sophistication that facilitate the stealing of ideas.

COPYRIGHT: THE CHAMPION OF ARTISTS AND AUTHORS

In the first few millennia of the publishing industry, the concept of ownership trumped authorship. Under medieval law, owners of books were paid for lending them out so that they could be reproduced. No one gave any thought to compensating the author.

Somewhere between the fifth and sixth centuries, Chinese merchants progressed from chiseling stone tablets to using paper and carved wooden blocks to printing multiple copies. On the other side of the globe, Greeks and Romans were using slaves as scriveners. From about 500 A.D. to 1500, the world's foremost publishing institution was the Church, which used the free labor of monks to copy books line by line.

Around the fifteenth century, the pace of the publishing industry accelerated. In 1440, Johannes Gutenberg invented the movable type printing press. A gentleman named William Caxton brought it to England in the last half of the fifteenth century. Prior to this time, reproducing books was very expensive and time consuming. Busy with plague, poverty, and social unrest, few had the patience to try. But suddenly, by virtue of Gutenberg's printing press, it was possible to make thousands of copies in a single day.

In 1710, the English Parliament passed the first known statute protecting the rights of authors and publishers. It was entitled *"An Act for the Encouragement of Learning, by Vesting the Copies of Printed Books in the Authors or Purchasers of Such Copies, During the Times Therein Mentioned."*

This statute was remarkable and revolutionary for its time, and not totally unrecognizable from modern-day copyright statutes in its inclusion of the following:

- Acknowledgment of an author's rights

- A twenty-eight-year statute of limitations

- A requirement that authors publicly register their claims

- A requirement that authors donate books to all the major libraries: Oxford, Cambridge, and Scotland

The next milestone for copyright was the United States Constitution which, in 1787, gave Congress the power to grant "to Authors and Inventors the exclusive Right with respect to their respective Writings and Discoveries." It was profoundly significant that a new nation would recognize and encourage ownership rights in creative works.

The first copyright law under the Constitution was passed in 1790. It followed the basic structure of the English copyright law, granting authors the exclusive right to "print, reprint, publish or vend" their works for a period of up to twenty-eight years. It addressed only "maps, charts, and books," and was silent about music.

More significantly, the first Copyright Act provided specific remedies for infringement. Penalties included forfeiture and a fifty-cent fine for every copy created in violation of an author's recognized rights. The act also required that copies of protected works be deposited with the clerk of the district court and the secretary of state.

A major proponent of authors' rights in the 1780s and '90s was Noah Webster, who had published a blockbuster bestseller of the day, *The American Spelling Book 1783*. The book topped the Colonial bestseller list, with more than thirty-thousand copies sold. Webster followed up with another success in 1828, *The American Dictionary of the English Language,* which was the predecessor to our modern-day *Webster's* dictionary. Webster was supported in his advocacy of authors' rights by other prolific journalists of that era: James Madison, George Washington, and Thomas Jefferson.

In 1853, a federal Circuit Court issued a setback to authors' rights, holding that a word-for-word German translation of *Uncle Tom's Cabin* did not infringe Harriet Beecher Stowe's copyright. The court wrote that "[b]y the publication of Mrs. Stowe's book, the creations of the genius and imagination of the author have become as much public property as those of Homer or Cervantes. . . . All her conceptions and inventions may be used and abused by imitators, playwrights and poets."[1]

Fortunately, by the end of the nineteenth century, U.S. courts began to extend protection beyond cases of blatant word-for-word copying. The result reached in the Harriet Beecher Stowe case seems absurd and

---

[1] *Stowe v. Thomas*, 23 F. Cas. 201, 208 (C.C.E.D. Pa. 1853) (No. 13, 514).

cruel by today's copyright standards. Today, movie producers and publishers frequently return unsolicited manuscripts unopened, lest they be accused of appropriating a substantive idea, plot twist, or character into their own work.

Other epiphanies in copyright law over the centuries include protection for:

- Photographs[2]

- Musical recordings (not just the compositions)[3]

- Computer software[4]

- Architectural works[5]

In the 1960s, authors faced another challenge in the evolution of copyright. Chester F. Carlson invented a xerography process in 1938, which was touted as an alternative printing process. Thereafter, Xerox Corporation began marketing the photocopy machine. (To this day, photocopying functions by negatively charging dark parts of page; the positively charged toner powder sticks to the darker portions.)

Xerography remains expensive and has never become a cost-effective alternative to printing. However, concerns about its potential helped spawn the doctrine of fair use, which has proved to be a significant aspect of the comprehensive Copyright Act of 1976. Fair use defines when it's fair to make copies or quote someone else's work in the interests of free speech and to promote intellectual discourse.

Generally, you will not run amuck of the fair use provisions of the 1976 Copyright Act, if you make "isolated and unrelated reproduction" of single copies. This is a controversial phrase, but legislative history seems to suggest it means something less than half a dozen copies. The legislative history also indicates that this exception was intended to permit libraries and archives that make their collections public to make copies to further their collections. However, fair use does *not* permit

---

[2] *Burrow-Giles Lithographic Co. v. Sarony,* 111 U.S. 53 (1884).
[3] Sound Recordings Act of 1971, Pub. L. No. 92-140, 85 Stat. 392.
[4] 17 U.S.C. § 101.
[5] American Ratification of Berne Convention in 1990. Architectural Works Protection Act of 1990.

distribution of multiple copies by an instructor or permit an instructor to send twenty students to the library to make copies.

In the wake of the personal computer, photocopying became as insignificant as papyrus became in the wake of the printing press. In 1998, Congress passed the Digital Millennium Copyright Act. Among other things, this act is aimed at those who "traffic" in devices that circumvent copy-control technologies. It also insulates Internet service providers who meet its requirements from responsibility for infringement by their customers.

Today, copyright not only protects against literal infringement, it prevents copying or other attempts to replicate the general style or overall appearance of a magazine cover or computer screen.

ENCOURAGING INNOVATION: THE RISE OF PATENT PROTECTION

Jerome Lemelson was the third most prolific U.S. patent developer, ranking just below Thomas Edison and Edwin Land (who invented the Polaroid instant imaging camera and founded the Polaroid Corporation). During his lifetime, Mr. Lemelson acquired more than five hundred patents, at one time averaging one about every four months. Mr. Lemelson during his life, and the Lemelson Foundation after his death, have made millions suing or threatening to sue the world's leading corporations for patent infringement and settling such claims for large amounts of money.

Critics of Mr. Lemelson contend his use of the patent process did little to advance technology and that he in fact did not invent many of the technologies he patented. He simply got to the Patent Office first. Mr. Lemelson's former attorney observed, "In many cases, Lemelson didn't patent inventions," says Lieberman. "He invented patents."

The U.S. patent law that Mr. Lemelson found so profitable has its origins in the U.S. Constitution, which authorizes Congress "[t]o promote the Progress of . . . useful Arts, by securing for limited Times to . . . Inventors the exclusive Right to their Discoveries."[6] Our founding fa-

---

[6] United States Constitution, Article I, Section 8, Clause 8.

thers originally contemplated that patent protection would extend only to the functional elements that represented significant innovative discoveries.

However, by 1842, the United States had experienced an unprecedented increase in per capita income and standard of living, and there was a shift from a subsistence agrarian nation to a burgeoning economy with a leisure class. In order to provide "encouragement to the decorative arts," Congress amended the patent statute to cover "new and original designs for articles of manufacture." Today, a wide array of ornamental objects, from display racks to pedestal chairs, enjoy patent protection.

At the turn of the century, plants were deemed strictly a product of nature, and innovations involving the creative hand of man were given no protection under patent law. However, Congress passed the Plant Patent Act of 1930, which extends patent protection to any newly created type of asexually reproducing plant.[7] In 1970, Congress added protection for "distinct" sexually reproducing plant varieties.[8]

Until the mid–twentieth century, patent law didn't provide much protection to the infant pharmaceutical and biomedical industries that now hold patents worth billions of dollars. The Patent Office feared that physicians and pharmacists would use patents to create monopolies on lifesaving technologies. As late as 1945, courts and the Patent Office took the position that "the methods or modes of treatment of physicians of certain diseases are not patentable."[9] Abruptly, and without fanfare, in 1954, the Patent Office and the courts revised this position, approving a patent for a method of injecting medication.[10] This particular patent paved the way for what is now a multi billion-dollar pharmaceutical industry, making possible unprecedented global research and development activity. In 1996, Congress decided the pendulum had swung a bit too far. It created a special exemption for nursing homes, hospitals, and medical schools that infringe pharmaceutical patents.[11]

Software currently represents the greatest challenge to intellectual

---

[7] 35 U.S.C. secs. 161-164.
[8] Plant Variety Protection Act, 7 U.S.C. §§ 2321-2582.
[9] "Ex Parte Brinkerhoff, New Decisions," 27 *J. Pat. Off. Soc'y.* 797, 797 (1945).
[10] See *Ex Parte Scherer,* 103 U.S.P.Q. (BNA) 107 (Pat. Off. Bd. App. 1954).
[11] 35 U.S.C. § 287 (c).

property law this century, with its unique combination of expressive and functional elements. Until the 1980s, both the Patent Office and the courts routinely refused software patent issuance on the ground that all programs basically constituted "mathematical algorithms" and were consequently unpatentable "phenomena of nature."[12]

In 1981, U.S. courts and the Patent Office opened the door to the software industry as they had three-quarters of a century earlier for the pharmaceutical industry. Signaling a major opportunity for software developers, the United States Supreme Court upheld a patent for a software program that regulated the temperature of synthetic rubber inside a mold.[13] Today in the United States, software programs that meet the patent requirements of being novel and nonobvious may qualify for protection. However, many European countries refuse to follow the U.S. example of liberal patent protection for software.

TESTING TRADEMARK BOUNDARIES

Trademark law can trace its origins to well before the mid–nineteenth century, where courts recognized that placing a particular mark on goods caused the public to associate certain characteristics with those goods. Early cases centered on the concept of fraud, finding that an infringer had attempted to pass off his own goods as those of another by deceptive marking.

Early trademark cases recognized only the name of the manufacturer. Made-up names or names indicating geographical origin did not qualify for any protection.[14] In an odd twist, current law now provides that arbitrary, fanciful, made-up names (such as Xerox or Gateway) are afforded the highest level of protection. This is because all of their meaning in the minds of consumers is derived from the marketing and creative efforts of the trademark owner.

An even more amazing expansion of trademark law is the concept of *trade dress*. In 1987, Taco Cabana, a chain of Mexican restaurants in Houston, Texas, sued a rival chain, Two Pesos. Taco claimed that Two

---

[12] See *Gottshalk v. Benson,* 409 U.S. 63 (1972).
[13] *Diamond v. Diehr,* 450 U.S. 175 (1981).
[14] See, e.g., *Fetridge v. Wells,* 4 Abb. Pr. 144 (N.Y. Super. Ct. 1857).

Pesos had deliberately copied its distinctive decor. Taco Cabana claimed that the rival's use of a combination of nonfunctional features such as the layout, color scheme, and a distinctive roof design constituted trademark infringement and a wrongful appropriation of Taco Cabana's trademark appearance. After five years of litigation, Taco Cabana prevailed.[15] This doctrine has since been invoked to protect myriad distinctively dressed objects, including the countless packaged foods, greeting cards, and the uniforms of the cheerleaders for the Dallas Cowboys football team from being used in the movie *Debbie Does Dallas*.[16]

SAFEGUARDING VALUABLE TRADE SECRETS

Trade secrets are business secrets. Unlike patents and copyrights that are granted for a term of years, trade secrets can last forever if they're properly maintained. They can be the most valuable asset a company owns. However, once disclosed, they're lost forever.

After years of research, a company called C&F Corporation developed a process for making and freezing precooked sausage for pizza toppings. The process was a trade secret, and it surpassed other methods for creating precooked sausage, both in terms of price and quality. Pizza Hut agreed to buy a large amount of C&F's precooked sausage on the condition that C&F divulge its process to other Pizza Hut suppliers to assure the availability of backup suppliers. All of the parties entered into confidentiality agreements to protect C&F's trade secret. C&F invested $4.5 million to meet Pizza Hut's needs. Once Pizza Hut's other suppliers learned how to duplicate C&F's results, Pizza Hut demanded drastic price reductions.

Several years later, Pizza Hut provided one of its suppliers, IBP, with C&F's confidential information. Pizza Hut required IBP to sign a confidentiality agreement covering this information. IBP hired a former supervisor in C&F's sausage plant as a production superintendent, then fired the employee five months later, after it had learned the sausage-making process. Two years later, Pizza Hut was buying precooked

---

[15] *Two Pesos, Inc. v. Taco Cabana, Inc.*, 505 U.S. 763 (1992).
[16] *Dallas Cowboys Cheerleaders, Inc. v. Pussycat Cinema, Ltd.*, 604 F.2d 200, 206 (2d Cir. 1979).

sausage topping from IBP. C&F sued both Pizza Hut and IBP. A jury found that IBP misappropriated C&F's trade secrets and awarded C&F $10.9 million in damages.

SO YOU HAVE AN IDEA . . .

No one knows the value of an idea at its outset or exactly how it might be transformed in the marketing process. As you read this book, do so with an open mind as to which protections might best suit your needs, and with the idea that you might need to invoke more than one area of the law to protect the various creative, expressive, and functional implementations of your idea.

CHAPTER 2 ▷▷▷▷

American Ingenuity in the Twenty-first Century

THE TECHNOLOGY OF our generation determines how we spend our time and what's defined as valuable and productive work. It also defines prevailing social norms and moral codes, and dictates what's viewed as dishonest or disloyal behavior in business and personal contexts.

IN THIS CHAPTER YOU FIND OUT:

- How large corporations now use intellectual property rights as bargaining chips

- Various approaches the music industry is taking to combat high-tech piracy

- What happened when Wal-Mart tried to copyright pricing information

- How a Web site can subject you to the jurisdiction of far-flung courts

IN A RECENT campaign to deter software piracy, the Business Software Alliance (BSA) mass-mailed postcards proclaiming: "Nail Your Boss," specifically encourag-

ing whistle-blowing by disgruntled employees. The BSA also announced that it had collected more than $27 million through its litigation and enforcement efforts over the past five years from companies in the United States who had been caught, red-handed, copying software. Law-abiding citizens who wouldn't dream of swiping anything else without paying for it think nothing of borrowing and duplicating copyrighted software for which they have not paid.[1]

Oh, if the founding fathers could see what the constitutional protections "[t]o promote the Progress of . . . useful Arts, by securing for limited Times to . . . Inventors the exclusive Right to their Discoveries" and to grant "to Authors and Inventors the exclusive Right with respect to their Writings and Discoveries" have spawned in a mere two and a quarter centuries.[2]

The Constitution has been stretched to protect technologies that could not have been envisioned even by Benjamin Franklin, arguably the most innovative Colonial mind. Intellectual property issues are as inevitable and integral to the culture of commerce as income tax. The topics in this chapter, presented in no particular order, provide you with a snapshot of how our culture has been altered and shaped in response to an ever-expanding notion of intellectual work product as property.

INTELLECTUAL PROPERTY RIGHTS AS A BARGAINING CHIP

If Parker Brothers were to reintroduce the famous game of Monopoly, it might place squares alongside Boardwalk and Park Place for players to acquire valuable technological patents and licenses in key industries as well as real estate. Players could be sent back a few squares for inadvertently infringing someone else's patent. Most importantly, the new rules would also allow players to trade cards and elect *not* to assert their legal rights against other players, if those players in turn agree to refrain from using their litigation cards.

Large corporations often preemptively patent technologies that they don't have an immediate interest in marketing. Patents, copyrights,

---

[1] Information taken from the Business Software Alliance Web site located at www.bsa.com.
[2] United States Constitution, Article I, Section 8, Clause 8.

trademarks, trade secrets, and even domain names have value as strategic bargaining chips in negotiating with other companies who hold related intellectual property rights. One company may agree not to sue another for patent infringement in exchange for similar forbearance on a technology the company has an actual interest in using.

Microsoft is one example of a company that's constantly negotiating intellectual property rights with other companies in order to offer its product line and keep its competitive edge. In 2002, Microsoft asked the top twenty personal computer vendors which license its operating system to sign an agreement that they would not sue Microsoft for infringement of their patents during the term of their licenses. Many personal computer vendors, including Hewlett-Packard and Gateway, were resistant—even outraged. They claim that by signing such a deal, they would be giving Microsoft free rein over their intellectual property.[3]

AT&T recently filed a lawsuit against Microsoft claiming the software giant infringed on its patent for a technology that allows high-speed transmission of phone calls and video over the Internet. The two companies began licensing negotiations at that point but were unable to resolve the issue. Curiously, Microsoft invested $5 billion in AT&T in 1999. Microsoft has since incorporated the patented technology into its Windows Me, 95, 98, 2000, and NT operating systems. AT&T said it first notified Microsoft of the infringement in April 1999. "The suit speaks for itself," AT&T spokeswoman Cindy Neale said. "We've been in licensing discussions with Microsoft for quite some time. It's obviously a patent that's very important to us."

CO-OPTING COPYRIGHT TO PREVENT SPAM

Spam is the digital equivalent of telemarketing; it is an unwanted side effect of technological advancement. It consists of junk E-mail and unsolicited advertising that wastes time. These spam E-mails often contain deceptive or alluring subject lines calculated to get you to open them.

Poetry and prosecutorial efforts have been merged in the war against spam. A company called Habeas devised a system to embed a

---

[3] IDG News Service, December 1, 2002.

line of copyrighted poetry in E-mails as a code to identify incoming mail as spam free. If spammers co-opt the copyrighted poetry and use it in their own E-mails to get it through the screening device, Habeas contends they can be sued for copyright infringement.[4]

PIRACY ON CAMPUS:
WHAT'S THE MATTER WITH KIDS TODAY?

The Recording Industry Association of America (RIAA) seems to be targeting schools in an ongoing campaign to stamp out music swapping. The industry blames an eighteen-month slump in CD sales on digital piracy.

The U.S. Naval Academy was one of 2,300 colleges to receive a letter from entertainment industry organizations requesting help in cracking down on unauthorized file swapping. In response, on a Thursday afternoon, while students were at class, the academy seized one hundred computers from students who were suspected of having downloaded unauthorized copies of music files over the Internet.[5] An academy spokesman said students found to have downloaded copyrighted material could face penalties ranging from loss of leave time to court-martial and expulsion.

In a similar sting operation, students at the University of Southern California were threatened with a year without computer access if they were busted swapping movies and music on-line. In an E-mail message, school officials warned students that using peer-to-peer file-trading services could force the university to kick students off the network.[6]

Privacy advocates worry about the implications of these aggressive campus crackdowns. The Electronic Privacy Information Center has sent letters to presidents of colleges across the country, asking them to think before they install monitoring tools on university networks. "Monitoring the content of communications is fundamentally incompatible with the mission of educational institutions to foster critical

[4] http://www.wired.com/news/technology/0,1282,54645,00.html?tw=wn_ascii.
[5] *New York Times,* November 26, 2002, http://www.nytimes.com/2002/11/26/technology/26MUSI.html.
[6] *Wired,* September 13, 2002, http://www.wired.com/news/mp3/0,1285,55159,00.html.

thinking and exploration," EPIC wrote. "Monitoring chills behavior and can squelch creativity that must thrive in educational settings."[7] It appears inevitable that policing technology may have unforeseeable impact beyond simply preventing piracy.

THE MUSIC INDUSTRY SINGS ITS OWN TECHNOLOGY TUNE

The music industry succeeded in shutting down Napster, but it has failed to even slow free song swapping. Some 41 million people traded music on-line during the first half of 2002, according to San Francisco–based Odyssey research.[8]

In 2002, music companies unsuccessfully tried to persuade a judge to let them obtain names of Internet file swappers without going to court first. Internet service provider Verizon initially was successful in opposing the music industry's subpoena. Verizon said that since the pirated songs sit on the person's computer rather than Verizon's network, it should not be required to automatically give up the subscriber's name. U.S. District Judge John D. Bates, who heard the case, lamented ambiguities in the Digital Millennium Copyright Act, which was enacted to uphold copyright laws on the Internet while shielding ISPs (like Verizon) from direct liability.[9] On December 19, 2003, the D.C. Circuit Court of Appeals granted Verizon's motion to quash the subpoena and remanded to the district court to vacate its order enforcing the subpoena.

Tired of merely suing pirating Web sites, some recording companies have resorted to technological guerrilla tactics. They've experimented with inundating peer-to-peer computer networks with phony files that have the same titles and number of bytes as popular songs but instead contain annoying music looped to play repeatedly. Madonna created phony swap files with an angry message admonishing those who had attempted to download her music without paying for it. Others have tried

---

[7] "Privacy Group Fights P2P Crackdown," CNET, November 7, 2002. http://news.com.com/2100-1023-964908.html?tag=fd_top.

[8] "Napster or Not, File Swaps Continue," MSN, October 14, 2002. http://www.msnbc.com/news/820292.asp?Osi=-#BODY.

[9] "Verizon Faces Down Music Industry Over File-Swapping," Salon.com, October 4, 2002. http://www.salon.com/tech/wire/2002/10/04/verizon/index.html; (240 F. Supp 2d 24 (D.D.C. 2003)).

to slow down the networks with excessive requests. (There is already at least one U.S. patent application for a method to create impostor files.) Researchers at the University of Washington have concluded that polluting the offending sites with phony files is a more effective strategy than lawsuits.[10]

In another creative attempt to combat music piracy, the rock group Bon Jovi initiated a new, Web-based scheme to discourage pirating of their newly released CD. By entering that code on the group's Web site, fans enroll in a program that puts them "first in line" for concert tickets and allows them to listen to unreleased tracks from the band. "The idea is to make anyone who's file sharing or burning feel like they're missing out by not buying a real copy of the CD," said a media executive representing Bon Jovi.[11]

Peter Gabriel, in a similar attempt to go with the flow of technology rather than fight it, released his album *Up,* as a digital download. Gabriel's album was the first full-length release from such a prominent artist. The on-line album costs $9.99. The CD version in record stores had a list price of $18.98.[12]

On a less entertaining note, the U.S. Department of Justice announced it is prepared to begin prosecuting peer-to-peer pirates. John Malcolm, a deputy assistant attorney general, said Americans should realize that swapping illicit copies of music and movies is a criminal offense that can result in lengthy prison terms. "A lot of people think these activities are legal, and they think they ought to be legal." Malcolm said the Internet has become "the world's largest copy machine" and that criminal prosecutions of copyright offenders are now necessary to preserve the viability of America's content industries. "There does have to be some kind of a public message that stealing is stealing is stealing."[13]

---

[10] "How to Make Morpheus an Endangered Species? Poison Its Habitat," Business2.com, September 2002. http://www.business2.com/articles/mag/0,1640,42874,00.html.

[11] "Can Bon Jovi Foil the Pirates?" *Wired,* September 19, 2002. http://www.wired.com/news/technology/0,1282,55246,00.html.

[12] "Gabriel's Single Has Online Glitch," AP, September 26, 2002. http://apnews.excite.com/article/20020926/D7M9GBP82.html.

[13] "DOJ to Swappers: Law's Not on Your Side," CNET News.com, August 20, 2002. http://news.com.com/2100-1023-954591.html.

COPYRIGHT GOES TO HOLLYWOOD

Robert Moore, an ex-Marine and college dropout, is on the front lines of the legal battle in the dispute between the consumer and the entertainment industry.

Since mid-2001, Moore's company, 321 Studios, has sold more than 100,000 copies of DVD Copy Plus, which allows people to copy DVD movies onto CDs. It includes code that cracks the copy-protection scheme used for most commercial DVD movies. Moore argues, "People already are making DVD copies; we're just making it simpler with a couple of clicks of a button."

Moore is, not surprisingly, bitterly opposed by Hollywood, which believes his company is in violation the Digital Millennium Copyright act. The industry contends that the act bars the picking of electronic locks on copyright works and this is precisely what Moore's innovation does.

Moore's 321 Studios has preemptively sued nine major movie studios in San Francisco federal court, seeking the right to sell its software. Moore requested a ruling that 321's products are legal and don't violate the Digital Millennium Copyright Act. These suits will likely be resolved sometime in 2004.

WAL-MART SHOPS ITS LITIGATION OPTIONS

In November 2002, Wal-Mart intimidated several Internet shopping sites into removing information about its post-Thanksgiving sales by threatening to sue them for copyright infringement. Wal-Mart claimed its pricing information was protected by copyright and could not be republished without its permission. In one letter to on-line retailer Fat-Wallet, Wal-Mart requested that price information be deleted from its "Hot Deals" section. Its attorneys then sent a subpoena to FatWallet asking for "information sufficient to identify the individual who posted the infringing material" as required under the digital copyright law.

Legal experts seemed to concur that invoking a copyright law in this context was questionable. The pricing information posted by FatWallet was a set of facts rather than the sort of creative expression that copyright law protects.[14] A law clinic at the University of California at Berkeley volunteered to represent FatWallet and fight the subpoena. Shortly thereafter, Wal-Mart announced it would not pursue copyright claims against FatWallet.[15] FatWallet subsequently sent Wal-Mart a letter demanding payments for all damages, including costs and attorneys' fees, incurred in addressing the copyright protection claims.

CYBER-JURISDICTION

The global reach of the Internet raises the possibility that you or your on-line business can be subject to the jurisdiction of a court far from where you reside or where your business is physically located. Rules for Internet-based jurisdiction in the United States are just now being developed by U.S. courts.

The emerging standard seems to be that if you maintain an "interactive" Web site on which you take customer orders, you can be sued in any state in which your customers reside. The theory is that you are "present" in the state by reason of doing business with that state's citizens.

$$ BUSINESS TIP: *If you take customer orders over the Internet, you may be subjecting yourself to the possibility of having to defend lawsuits in distant jurisdictions, both in the United States and abroad. To limit this exposure, have customers place orders by telephone or regular mail, rather than on-line.*

A different rule applies to "passive" Web sites, which only advertise or provide information to on-line visitors but on which no actual transactions are conducted. Most courts agree passive Web sites don't provide a basis for jurisdiction. A gray

---

[14] "Internet Sites Delete News of Sales by Big Retailers," *New York Times*, November 21, 2002. http://www.nytimes.com/2002/11/21/technology/21COPY.html.
[15] "Wal-Mart Backs Away from DCMA Claim," CNET, December 5, 2002. http://news.com.com/2100-1023-976296.html?tag=fd_top.

area exists for Web sites that provide some interaction, such as E-mail exchanges.[16]

An international treaty under consideration by the Hague Conference may make Web sites in the United States subject to the laws of forty-eight or more other countries. "The treaty gives nearly every member country jurisdiction over anything that is published on or distributed over the Internet," says James Love of the Consumer Project on Technology (CPT), based in Washington.

Love explains that "[i]n some countries it is permitted to publish leaked memorandums and documents that embarrass governments or corporations, but in other countries this would be considered a violation of copyright laws, as in the U.K. David Shayler case." Shayler is a British citizen who faces charges under the U.K.'s Official Secrets Act for revealing that British intelligence agencies compiled dossiers on Cabinet members.[17]

Love also warns that "[i]n some countries, a failure to obtain permission to hyperlink to a Web page or use a metatag with the name of a business is considered [an] intellectual property [violation], while in other countries it is not."

---

[16] At least one court has held that limited interactivity is not enough to confer jurisdiction, *Hurley v. Cancun Playa Oasis Int'l Hotels,* No. CIV.A. 99-574, 1999 WL 718556 (E.D. Pa. August 31, 1999).

[17] Brian Livingston, "U.S. Web Sites May Fall Under Foreign Jurisdiction," *E-Business Secrets,* September 1, 2002.

PART TWO

....

Taking Ownership of Trademarks and Trade Names

CHAPTER 3 ⪢⪢⪢

Making Your Mark: The Basics of Trademark Law

AMERICAN BUSINESSES—FROM fledgling start-ups to vast multinational corporations—fight ruthlessly and spend billions of dollars each year to develop and protect their trademarks. Inability to protect your marks can cost your company its competitive edge and mean that an otherwise superior product or service line will fail in the marketplace. Trademarks are often the most valuable assets a business owns.

IN THIS CHAPTER YOU FIND OUT:

- What constitutes a valid, protectable trademark

- How to develop a legally strong mark versus a weak mark

- Whether it's necessary to register a mark

- What kinds of words and symbols get trademark protection

- What happens when two businesses are using the same or similar marks

AMERICA ONLINE, AN Internet service provider, spends millions of dollars on an advertising campaign to promote its trademarks, "You've Got Mail," "Buddy List," and "IM." AOL's aggressive advertising makes these words a part of the everyday language of E-mail usage—something most ad agencies can only dream of accomplishing.

In 1998, when the movie You've Got Mail is playing in the theaters, a competitor, AT&T WorldNet, begins using the terms "You Have Mail!," "IM," and "Buddy List" for its Internet services.

America Online files suit in the U.S. District Court in the Eastern District of Virginia alleging trademark infringement. The marks are deemed to be "generic" and unprotectable. The case is thrown out of court on summary judgment.[1]

This chapter shows how even smart, savvy companies like AOL can "miss the mark." By the end of this chapter you'll understand the basic legal standards and strategies for creating and protecting a trademark.

THE POWER AND PURPOSE OF A TRADEMARK

How important is a trademark to the average consumer? There are news stories about armed robberies and even murders committed by teenagers seeking ordinary-looking sneakers bearing the Nike or Air Jordan logo.[2]

On the positive side, the consuming public receives some degree of quality assurance that the products and services they purchase aremanufactured by the company who holds the trademark and are made according to the specifications and standards of that familiar company.

Trademarks are the gears of a free-market economy where consumers choose from competing brands and services. Without them no brand

---

[1] *AOL v. AT&T. U.S.E.D., VA,* Case No. 98-1821-A. (Opinion re Order Granting AOL's Motion for Summary Judgment). This case was subsequently affirmed in part and reversed in part 243 F. 3rd 812 (4th Cir. 2001).

[2] Michael Jordan has publicly expressed shock and outrage at the violence associated with his trademark, stating he would rather pull the product than put teens at risk. Unfortunately, the trademark-oriented violence is not limited to Air Jordans. A Georgetown jacket, Fila sneakers, Mercedes-Benz, Avia high tops, and numerous pairs of Nike sneakers have served as motives for murder. "Your Sneakers or Your Life," *Sports Illustrated,* September 1990.

loyalty or identity could be established. Trademarks serve as consumer shorthand for the unique characteristics of a particular brand. Sometimes they distinguish products that are otherwise indistinguishable.

If you order a Coke or a McDonald's hamburger, you know, with four out of your five senses, what you're purchasing. The trademark conjures the image of the look, taste, texture, and smell of the product. In reality, a Coke may be indistinguishable to your taste buds from any other carbonated, cola-flavored drink, but you may nevertheless order a Coke with your hot dog and fries out of brand loyalty associated with the mark. To The Coca-Cola Company, that loyalty, known as *goodwill*, makes the trademark its most coveted asset.

A Twinkie might taste as sweet by another name, but the trademark itself is now synonymous to the buying public with an elliptically shaped, cream-filled cake. A Twinkie describes a uniquely shaped, if not nutritionally superior, food product. Any company attempting to produce a similarly shaped junk food might find itself defending a lawsuit from Hostess for infringing its trademark design.

Trademark laws protect a company's investment in its products and services and the overall reputation of the company. They make it possible for companies

> ⚖ **LAWYER'S NOTE:**   *Trademarks only protect the words and symbols that identify a product, not the product itself.*

to develop and maintain brand loyalty and goodwill. Trademark regulations also protect responsible companies from being undercut by unscrupulous competitors that attempt to pass off inferior goods and confuse the public as to their actual origin.

WHAT CONSTITUTES A VALID TRADEMARK?

You literally can't get up and brush your teeth in the morning without encountering someone's trademark. By the end of any given day you've likely encountered dozens of trademarks and relegated them to your subconscious. All of these trademarks have a singularity of purpose.

The sole purpose of any trademark is to identify the source of goods and services. A trademark can be as simple as a red triangle or the Nike Swoosh. Any word, symbol, slogan, logo, device, or product design that uniquely identifies a product can be a trademark.

Unlike other types of intellectual property, such as patents and copyrights, trademarks bear no relationship to invention or discovery. In fact, trademarks must *not* have a function other than identifying a product. If they do provide a function, their owners must generally protect the mark as a component of a product's design under patent or copyright laws.

LEGAL BASIS FOR TRADEMARK PROTECTION

Trademarks were used as early as the thirteenth-century when medieval merchants inscribed their unique mark on their goods, and their right to do so was protected by statutes written on parchment.

Modern trademark protections owe their origins to eighteenth-century English common law. Common law is developed by court cases that establish precedents. Courts generally decide new cases based on prior case precedent.

Today, American companies can rely on legal protections based on the following:

- **Common law:** Court precedents interpret federal and state trademark laws and apply them to specific situations. Litigants may rely upon a precedent case if the facts and law discussed in it are relevant.

- **Federal law:** The Lanham Act is the primary federal statute that protects trademarks and regulates related forms of unfair competition.[3] It provides a method for registering trademarks, remedies for infringement, and standards as to what type of material qualifies for trademark protection.

---

[3] Lanham Act, 15 U.S.C. Sec. 1051 et seq.

• **State law:** Most states have statutes regulating the use of trademarks and providing remedies for infringement.

• **Foreign treaties:** Protecting a trademark in a global economy is one of the toughest issues faced by entrepreneurial businesses. Currently, there are several international treaties in force. They afford American enterprises intellectual property rights in more than one hundred nations.

THE BASICS: HOW TO ACQUIRE TRADEMARK PROTECTION

Getting legal rights to a trademark is not as complicated as some lawyers might want you to think it is.

Regardless of whether you're relying on federal, state, or international law, you initially acquire rights to a trademark in two ways: *use* or *registration.*

These methods are overlapping rather than mutually exclusive. If you opt to register first, you still need to document your commercial use of the mark within a specified period. Similarly, if you establish rights to a mark based on prior use, you may later seek federal registration to preempt other parties from using your mark in geographical areas into which you intend to expand in the future.

⚖ **LAWYER'S NOTE:** *Trademarks are used to identify the source of goods and services, not the goods themselves.*

ACQUIRING RIGHTS THROUGH USE

"Use it or lose it" sums up the legal requirements for obtaining legal, proprietary, and ownership rights to your trademark. *Use* is the underlying common law tenet for federal and state trademark ownership rights.

The use requirement is fairly straightforward, with only two commonsense caveats. First, the use must occur in a *commercial* context. Second, you must display your trademark so it's *physically associated* with your product or service, for example, on a label or tag.

To establish ownership rights, your trademark must actually be used in commerce. Simply displaying the mark for the purpose of reserving it, for example, putting it on a business card or brochure, is called *token use*. Token use isn't sufficient to afford you protection. You must engage in actual business transactions. However, once you begin marketing, distributing, and delivering your products to the public in a particular locality, the commercial use requirement is satisfied for that geographic area.

> ⊖ **CAUTION:** *Use of a trademark must be established in the context of actual use in commerce. Token use, without commercial activity, will not establish rights to that mark.*

You must also display a trademark so that it's physically associated with your product. In most cases you do this by affixing a label bearing your trademark to your product. In cases where it's impractical to do this (for example, if you breed jellyfish), you can put the mark on documents physically associated with the sale of the product.[4]

In the case of service marks, the mark need not be physically associated with your service but may be used on your advertising or promotional materials, such as a business card or brochure.

REGISTERING A TRADEMARK

Prior to 1988, businesses faced a miserable dilemma. Federal law wouldn't allow them to register a trademark unless they could prove their prior use of it. This meant they had to spend money promoting a mark and risk associating it with an emerging product or service line without the benefit of registration.

The Trademark Revision Act of 1988 provided that, after November 1989, an applicant could apply to register a mark based upon a bona fide intent to use the mark.[5] For an intent-to-use application, a six-month period to file a statement of use begins with the issuance of a Notice of Allowance. This period is extended in six-month increments

---

[4] 15 U.S.C. Sec. 1127 (provides definition of "use in commerce").
[5] 15 U.S.C. Sec. 1057(c).

for up to thirty months, aggregating up to thirty-six months from the date of the Notice of Allowance.

> ⚖ **LAWYER'S NOTE:** *Registration is based on imminent intent to use. It is not a system of reserving marks for undetermined future use.*

After a proper showing of use in commerce, the U.S. Patent and Trademark Office (PTO) will issue a *Notice of Allowance.* This establishes that the mark has been examined for compliance and has been published for opposition and not successfully opposed. The registration dates back to the application date. Anyone else claiming rights to the trademark must demonstrate their use prior to the application date.

Federal registration has the main benefit of protecting your mark as you expand into wider geographical areas. Federal registration doesn't confer rights in areas where a trademark is already in use, but it's a very effective protection in those areas where no local company has already staked out the mark.

The U.S. Patent and Trademark Office handles federal registrations. This office is normally referred to as the *PTO.*

> ⚖ **LAWYER'S NOTE:** *If the trademark is already being used in several localities, federal registration may not be available or desirable. Similarly, if you plan only to use the mark locally, opting for state registration may save you some money.*

In summary, federal registration gives you rights to a trademark that are superior to claims anyone else may make unless:

1. Someone actually used the mark prior to the effective date of your registration.

2. Someone filed an intent to use application with the PTO prior to the date you filed your application.

3. A company who registered in a foreign country claimed that their application date precedes yours, based on a foreign treaty.

However, if your use in commerce predates another's claim, your claim takes precedence, even if you file your application later.

Chapter 5 explains the trademark registration process in detail and provides you with more information about the advantages and pitfalls of the process.

LOCATION! LOCATION! TRADEMARKS AND GEOGRAPHICAL FACTORS

Most trademarks are so simple, it can't be said that anyone actually invents or discovers them, except in the same sort of context we refer to Columbus as having discovered America. Today, the entrepreneur that is first to use a trademark in a given locality is given the modern-day equivalent to flag planting rights.

As a general rule, the first person to use a trademark in a particular geographic area acquires exclusive rights to it. However, the rights don't extend beyond that geographic area.

Suppose you have been selling Frosty snow cones in Milwaukee continuously for ten years. You acquire rights in the Milwaukee market that can be established by affidavits, testimony, and other evidence of your presence. Even if a huge multinational ice cream company acquires both federal and state registrations to the Frosty mark, you are still free to promote your mark in the Milwaukee area.

Does this seem like an unlikely scenario? It's not. Prior local usage is a sticky issue for large corporations engaged in national and international marketing efforts. The FAQ section of the Twinkie Web site, at www.twinkie.com, offers the following explanation as to why Hostess found it necessary to market the popular Ding Dong snack cake under the name King Don in several localities, despite diligent federal registration:

> When Hostess introduced Ding Dongs in 1967, the advertising campaign included a ringing bell: hence the name Ding Dongs. However, the eastern United States Hostess opted to package the cakes as King Dons to avoid confusion with a competitor's product. Hostess consolidated the King Don and Ding Dong name in 1987, packaging the cakes as Ding Dongs in all regions. Six months later, Hostess decided to go back to using the King Don name in the eastern U.S., again, to avoid confusion with a competing product. But today, the issue has been put to rest and only Ding Dongs are sold nationwide.

NOT FOR LOGOS ONLY: CATEGORIES OF TRADEMARKS

Trademark protections are derived from principles of unfair competition—what businesses can and can't do to gain customer loyalty.

Federal law specifically provides for registration of four categories of marks discussed in this section.[6] It also recognizes a fifth form of trademark protection known as *trade dress,* which is discussed in the next section.

TRADEMARKS AND TRADE NAMES

Don't fall into a common corporate trap of confusing trademarks and trade names. Legally, they aren't the same thing.

A trademark is a mark that identifies the source of goods—cereal, sports cars, or perfumes. This term is often used in a generic sense to refer to all of the types of trademark protection covered in this section.

A *trade name* is the name of a business. Federal law doesn't allow registration of trade names. This is because a trade name doesn't specifically identify the source of specific goods or services, which is the essence of trademark protection. However, a trademark and a trade name may be one and the same, as in the case of the Coca-Cola Company.

> ⊘ **CAUTION:** *Corporate registration does not provide a company with the right to use the corporate name or "doing business as" name as a trademark.*

SERVICE MARKS

Fortunately, the law of trademarks doesn't slight the service-based economy. *Service marks* identify the source of services, such as dry cleaning, transportation, travel agencies, repair, or consulting. In the United States, the rules for determining how service marks qualify for protection are pretty much the same as the rule for trademarks.

---

[6] 15 U.S.C. Secs. 1052-1054.

Examples of service marks include Spring Green lawn service and Blue Cross health insurance. Taco Bell is a service mark for Mexican food preparation services.

Although it seems confusing, a service mark isn't the same as a trade name. McDonald's Corporation is a trade name for a business that prepares products under its service mark, McDonald's.

CERTIFICATION MARKS

Remember the Good Housekeeping Seal? That famous emblem is an example of a *certification mark*.

A certification mark is owned by an entity that uses the mark to signify that certain standards, set by the entity, are met.

Certification marks can signal that certain inspection criteria have been used, the type or quality of materials, or the geographical origin of the product. Federal law requires that the owner of a certification mark be neutral in using the mark and cannot manipulate certification standards for its own marketing purposes. The PTO can cancel a certification mark if an organization fails to exercise proper control over the purported standards or arbitrarily applies its certification requirements.[7]

COLLECTIVE MARKS

A *collective mark* is used by a collective group or organization to identify the goods and services of its members. Collective marks often identify franchises or chains of grocery or retail stores.

TRADE DRESS: THE ENTIRE LOOK

First impressions do count. In fact, they may even be legally protectable. *Trade dress* is the overall appearance of a product. For exam-

---

[7] Section 1064(5) of Lanham Act.

ple, if you design packaging for a jar of jam that looks like homemade preserves, you may find yourself infringing on the trade dress of another jam product that is also packaged to give this overall impression.

A common type of trade dress is called *product configuration*. If the shape or appearance of a product has no function other than identifying the source of the product, it's protectable as trade dress. Examples of protectable product configurations are the ReaLemon lemon juice container that looks like a plastic lemon, and the bottle for Mrs. Butterworth's syrup, which looks like a plump woman in an apron. The popular For Dummies book series with its distinctive yellow cover and standardized format is another example of trade dress.

Trade dress is often associated with services. For example, the Hard Rock Café offers its patrons a distinctive decor and ambiance. Chuckee Cheese pizza parlors offer a combination of games, food products, and entertainment that is instantly recognizable to parents and their young children.

In *Two Pesos v. Taco Cabana, Inc.*[8] a Mexican restaurant appropriated the distinctive decor of its competitor. In *Two Pesos,* the U.S. Supreme Court established the following standards for protectible trade dress:

- The elements of trade dress for which protection is sought must be entirely nonfunctional.

- The trade dress must be inherently distinctive.

The Supreme Court also stated, in *Two Pesos,* that you cannot claim trade dress protection for your business or product if the design or decor is "one of a limited number of equally efficient options available to competitors." Thus, a donut shop with a counter and glass cabinets for viewing freshly baked donuts is probably not inherently distinctive, since there are only so many ways a donut shop can be designed. Even a glass window allowing customers to view the donut-making machine in operation has a function. But a flashy wall mural,

---

[8] *Two Pesos, Inc. v. Taco Cabana, Inc.,* 505 U.S. 763 (1992).

neon-colored countertops, and stools that look like donuts would probably add the element of distinctiveness the court requires to protect the donut shop's trade dress.

DEVELOPING A STRONG MARK VERSUS A WEAK MARK: TYPES OF PROTECTIONS

Looking to save on future legal fees? Consider choosing a strong trademark rather than a weak one.

Some trademarks are legally stronger and easier to protect against infringers. Marks that are easy to defend in the face of misuse or infringement by a competitor are known as *strong marks*. It's generally true that the less descriptive your mark is of the actual product, the stronger your case will be against infringers.

Many savvy and successful companies knowingly and deliberately opt to use a weak mark in the course of their overall marketing strategy. These companies feel that the weaker, more descriptive mark offers the valuable benefit of more quickly educating the consumer. Descriptive marks, like Yellow Pages or Oven Fresh, instantly convey product characteristics.

Terms that serve as trademarks fall into categories based on their relative legal strength. Arbitrary and fanciful marks are afforded the highest degree of protection, while a generic term offers no protection whatsoever.

UNPROTECTABLE GENERIC TERMS

Remember the generic food craze of the 1980s? The companies that sold and distributed these products in their plain green wrappers were able to take advantage of the fact that those terms like *cola, potato chip, fruit cocktail,* and *corn flakes* are generic. This means anyone can use them with abandon. With no way to establish brand loyalty, the market share enjoyed by distributors of generic brands gradually diminished; the craze withered and died.

A generic term is one that has come to be associated with a particular type of product rather than its source. Since the term doesn't identify a product source, the critical requirement for trademark protection, a generic term can never serve as a trademark.

The PTO maintains lists of marks that are considered generic and cannot be registered as trademarks. Table 3-1 contains a sample of some of these terms.

TABLE 3-1: *Some Terms Ruled Generic*

Generic Term	Product
Baby oil	Mineral oil
Aspirin	Acetyl salicylic acid
Escalator	Moving stairways
Hoagie	Sandwich
Honey baked ham	Ham with sweet glaze
Murphy bed	Type of bed that folds into wall
Shredded wheat	Baked wheat cereal
Thermos	Insulated pitcher
Trampoline	Athletic apparatus for jumping

Sometimes a perfectly good trademark term becomes generic because the owners of the trademark allow it to be misused. Aspirin, cellophane, shredded wheat, and escalator are all terms doomed to the trademark graveyard because they've become generic in the public's mind over time. The first section of the next chapter, "Legal Land Mines: Losing Your Mark Through Misuse," explains how this happens to a mark and how to avoid having it happen to yours.

DESCRIPTIVE MARKS

Descriptive marks are often so graphic you can instantly visualize the product upon seeing or hearing the mark. For example, you can't help but visualize the Pizza Hut trademark. And you know just what you'll accomplish with a Dust Buster handheld vacuum upon hearing that mark.

Descriptive marks have the advantage of automatically conveying characteristics of your product. They also have a downside. You must establish *secondary meaning* to protect them.

Secondary meaning is acquired when descriptive terms, such as Light n' Lively or Oven Fresh, become associated with a product over time through widespread use and possibly intensive advertising.

Establishing secondary meaning requires evidence (usually consumer polls and expert testimony) that an otherwise nondistinct term has been bound to a product in the consumer psyche.

The Supreme Court held that a term is inherently descriptive in nature if it's the only way of referring to a particular product. In 1989, Anheuser-Busch Company attempted to trademark the use of LA to refer to its Low Alcohol beer.[9] The court held that Anheuser-Busch's registration application was an attempt to preempt the new low-alcohol beer market. The association of the initials LA with the term "low alcohol" was "inevitable."

SUGGESTIVE MARKS

Suggestive marks are also considered weak marks, although they require some thought and imagination. They don't specifically describe a product or service. They're protectible without a showing of secondary meaning. Examples of suggestive marks are Roach Motel and Sunkist. A suggestive mark provides clues about a product but doesn't specifically describe it.

ARBITRARY OR FANCIFUL MARKS

Arbitrary and *fanciful* marks are the first choice of legal departments everywhere. They're considered the strongest type of mark.

As with suggestive marks, the trademark holder need not show the existence of secondary meaning to acquire rights in the mark. To qualify as an arbitrary or fanciful mark, the mark itself must not suggest the characteristics of the product in any way.

An arbitrary mark can be an ordinary word that isn't normally associated with the product and doesn't in any way conjure an image of the product. For example, Apple is an arbitrary mark for a computer. Trix is an arbitrary name for a cereal, as is Snickers for a candy bar.

---

[9] *G. Heileman Brewing Company, Inc. v. Anheuser-Busch* 873 F.2d 985 (U.S. Court of Appeals, 7th Circuit).

Fanciful marks are a type of arbitrary mark that uses coined or invented words. Arby's is a fanciful mark for a restaurant serving roast beef sandwiches. It's created from the initials for Roast Beef.

It's important to note that simply changing the spelling of a word doesn't make it arbitrary. Misspellings, acronyms, slight phonetic variations, and foreign words are often suggestive rather than arbitrary because they are derived from words with identifiable meanings. For example, Bufferin is considered a descriptive rather than a fanciful term for buffered aspirin. Similarly, IM was considered a generic name for instant messaging rather than an arbitrary trademark, as AOL sought to prove.

ESTABLISHING SECONDARY MEANING

Suppose you want to market a new type of fat-free French fry and call it the Fatless Fry. Your mark, although cute and catchy, isn't distinctive; it's merely descriptive. It's not entitled to trademark protection without a showing of secondary meaning.

If the owner of a nondistinctive mark can prove that the mark has acquired secondary meaning, the mark will qualify to be registered in the Principal Register of the PTO, as discussed in chapter 5.

Proof of secondary meaning usually consists of consumer polls, expert testimony, and snippets of press coverage. However, even without this proof, a nondistinctive mark that's used continuously and exclusively by its owner for a five-year period is presumed, under federal law, to have acquired secondary meaning. This means that if the Fatless Fry manages to sustain sales for five years, it will acquire trademark protection and can be included in the primary register.

⚖️ **LAWYER'S NOTE:** *If you can prove a descriptive mark has acquired secondary meaning, it can immediately receive trademark protection and be registered in the PTO Principal Register. Otherwise, you can get the same protection by registering and then demonstrating exclusive and continuous use for a five-year period.*

PROBLEMS WITH CONFUSINGLY SIMILAR TRADEMARKS

Suppose you're a dedicated veterinarian with an expertise in treating dogs that have psychological barriers to being housebroken. You decide to open a special training clinic, GreatDogs, and sell materials and supplies for dogs that resist being housebroken and risk being put to sleep because of it. You adopt as your logo a silhouette of a dog with one hind leg raised. Much to your surprise, the Greyhound bus company sues you for adopting a mark that's confusingly similar to their trademark logo.

A trademark will be denied registration, and an existing registration may be voided, if the trademark is "confusingly similar" to another mark.

What exactly constitutes confusion? Federal law[10] provides that a mark is confusingly similar if it's likely to cause deception or confusion as to:

- The source of the goods or services connected with the mark

- The affiliation or connection with a company that uses the similar mark

- Whether the mark is sponsored or approved by the entity that owns the allegedly similar mark

Trademarks need not be identical to be confusing. It's enough that they sound alike or give an overall impression of similarity. For example, Blockbuster Video was able to successfully challenge an attempt of a competitor to register the trademark Video Buster. Similarly, The Coca-Cola Company was able to challenge the registration of a mark for Cleo Cola. However, the UNCOLA was not deemed to be confusing.

The similarities and dissimilarities of the goods or services themselves are also a factor. For example, registration was denied for Bell as trademark for computers, because it was deemed confusingly similar to Dell. However, Mrs. Fields cookies was permitted to register its trade-

---

[10] Section 1051 of the Lanham Act.

mark surname despite the previously registered mark of Marshall Field's department stores.

Advertising and sponsorship have evolved. Companies that once sold single product lines now offer diverse goods and services to take full advantage of goodwill associated with their name. For example, Harley-Davidson sells a line of clothing and accessories to capitalize on the goodwill generated from its famous line of motorcycles.

So when all is said and done, will you be able to use your GreatDog logo? Chances are good that you will. Courts usually start with a commonsense inquiry as to whether products and services are similar in the eye of the average consumer. The farther apart the functionality of the products, the less likelihood there is of confusion. It's unlikely that consumers are likely to confuse transportation services with dog training services.

You must be extremely careful to avoid trademarks that are similar to those used on products or services that potentially compete with yours. For example, a dog food manufacturer using the mark Doggie Dinner was successful in opposing the registration of Dog E-Delite for a competing dog vitamin product. The court determined that both products served essentially the same function and even looked alike.[11]

---

[11] *S.E. Mighton Co. v. La Pryor Milling Co.*, 274 F. 2d 676 (Cust. & Pat App. 1960).

CHAPTER 4 ⫸⫸

Maintaining Marks in the Face of Legal Adversity

THE PROBLEM WITH having a profitable trademark is that everyone else seems to want to cash in on its success. While publicity is usually a plus, exposure that dilutes your mark, tarnishes its reputation, confuses consumers, or threatens to make your mark a generic term is a legal and commercial liability.

IN THIS CHAPTER YOU FIND OUT:

- How you can lose valuable rights to your mark through misuse of it

- How to protect your mark's reputation from tarnishment

- About international protections that protect you from knockoffs

- A checklist of factors for maintaining your mark

AL FRANKEN, *A fairly recognizable television satirist who occasionally appears on* Saturday Night Live, *writes a book scheduled for release August 2003. The book is entitled* Lies, and the Lying Liars Who Tell Them: A Fair and Balanced Look at the Right. *The cover depicts Fox News top-rated anchor Bill O'Reilly.*

The book subsequently rises to the number-one spot on Amazon.com. Despite its popularity, not everyone loves it. Fox News files a lawsuit alleging trademark infringement and trademark dilution, and tries to get an injunction to stop the sale of the book.

Fox News had, in 1998, registered "Fair & Balanced" as a federally protected service mark used to identify the source of its television news programs. Fox's attorneys allege that Franken and his publisher use Fox's service mark to "confuse the public as to the origin of the book, and accordingly, boost sales of the book." Fox further contends that because "Franken's reputation as a political commentator is not of the same caliber as the stellar reputations of [Fox's] on air talent . . . any association between Franken and Fox News is likely to blur or tarnish Fox News's distinctive mark . . ."

U.S. District Court Judge Denny Chin denies Fox's motion for a preliminary injunction to block publication, finding that there is virtually no chance that the public will be confused by the use of "Fair and Balanced." Judge Denny opines that Fox viewers are unlikely to conclude that O'Reilly is endorsing a book with his picture and the word LIES stamped all over the cover. The judge refers to the work as a parody. Shortly, thereafter, Fox abandons its lawsuit.

Franken reacts to his legal victory, stating he is "disappointed." Mr. Franken remarks wistfully, "I had hoped it would keep going a few more news cycles."

Public recognition of a mark is essential if the product or service is going to enjoy widespread commercial success. Unfortunately, the very exposure that makes a mark profitable also makes it a target for appropriation and parody.

LEGAL LAND MINES: LOSING YOUR MARK THROUGH MISUSE

The law of trademarks is fraught with peril. Even after successfully registering your trademark, you can fall into several traps that render it less valuable if not entirely worthless. This section tells you how to avoid these legal land mines.

DEATH BY GENEROCIDE

What do aspirin, baby oil, cellophane, shredded wheat, and the game Monopoly all have in common? They're all perfectly good, distinctive trademarks that have become "generocized" over time.

A trademark becomes a generic term when a court or the PTO finds that in the minds of the public the mark has come to represent particular goods or services rather than describing the origin of those goods and services. This is a disaster for a company! All of its prior advertising dollars and marketing efforts are lost.

In order not to become a victim of your own advertising campaign, like the marks in Table 3-1, you must take precautionary measures as to how your trademark is actually used. Sanka coffee, Band-Aid plastic strips, and Xerox photocopies all provide excellent role models in this regard. Xerox sends letters to its customers and shareholders requesting that they use the term *photocopy* in the workplace and to not use the word Xerox as a verb. Sanka calls itself Sanka "brand" decaffeinated coffee—watch for this next time you see a commercial. Johnson & Johnson promotes the use of the generic term *plastic strips* in order to protect its Band-Aid trademark. Kleenex makes sure that its brand name for a tissue is always capitalized and that its advertising materials make clear that it's a registered trademark for disposable paper products.

Here are some cardinal rules of trademark usage:

• **Use the ® symbol to denote a federally registered trademark.** This symbol can be used only in connection with a federally registered trademark and should be used in any materials promoting goods and services covered by the mark.

• **Use the mark as an adjective.** Don't use the mark as a noun or a verb, but rather to describe the source of the goods. ("I'm going to make a Xerox copy" instead of "I'm going to Xerox that.")

• **Don't use the mark as a plural or possessive term.** You won't find Xerox saying, "We sell a lot of Xeroxes" or referring to "Xerox's copies." Instead, you'll see references to a Xerox copy or photocopy machine.

- **Capitalize properly.** Capitalize your mark appropriately, and don't permit it to be merged with other words. For example, don't allow "Kids prefer oscar meyer wieners" instead of "Kids prefer Oscar Meyer wieners."

- **Establish company policies and guidelines.** Establish and enforce clear policies as to how suppliers, distributors, retailers, and promoters should use your mark.

- **Use your mark consistently.** Make sure that your mark is spelled consistently and correctly, and that correct punctuation, such as hyphens, are used. For example, Coca-Cola should not appear as Coca cola.

TARNISHMENT OF A MARK'S REPUTATION: THE *DEBBIE DOES DALLAS* CASE

Your trademark projects and embodies your reputation in the marketplace. Tarnishment of a mark occurs when someone uses it in an unwholesome or distasteful context that adversely affects the reputation of your mark.

The case involving the movie *Debbie Does Dallas* identifies standards for proving when certain uses or public associations tarnish a product's reputation.

In 1979, the Dallas Cowboys were successful in getting an injunction to stop the exhibition of the movie (in every sense of the word). The federal court held that trademark laws are designed to protect a product's reputation, and the strong similarity of the uniform worn by the cheerleader in the movie to the actual uniform worn by the Dallas Cowboys cheerleaders was a form of tarnishment. The court reasoned as follows:

[The] plot, to the extent there is one, involves a cheerleader at a fictional high school, Debbie, who has been selected to become a "Texas Cowgirl." In order to raise money to send Debbie, and eventually the entire squad to Dallas, the cheerleaders perform sexual services for a fee. The movie consists largely of a series of scenes graphically depicting the sexual escapades of the "actors." In the movie's final scene, Debbie dons a uniform strikingly similar to that worn by the Dallas Cowboy cheerleaders and for approximately twelve minutes of film footage engages in various sex acts while clad or partially clad in the uniform.

In contrast, what if a skit appeared on a comedy show such as *Saturday Night Live,* poking fun at the Dallas Cowboys Cheerleaders? Federal law provides that tarnishment doesn't result when a mark is used in any of the following contexts:

• **Noncommercial satire or parody:** The First Amendment protects satire and parody, regardless of how unfunny we view the representation of our marks in this context.

• **Comparative advertising:** Your competitors generally can criticize or represent your mark in their materials, so long as their representations are based on truth.

• **News reporting:** Without this exception, our First Amendment freedoms would be rendered meaningless.

TRADEMARK DILUTION

Think of how the value of status marks like Rolex, Chanel, or Ferrari would diminish if you started seeing them on all kinds of products in every retail store you frequented.

Trademark dilution diminishes the selling power of your trademark. It occurs when a similar mark adversely affects the reputation of your mark, even though it doesn't lead to actual confusion of consumers.

In 1996, federal trademark law was amended to include a special antidilution provision. This statute defines dilution as "the lessening of the capacity of a famous mark to identify and distinguish goods or services, regardless of the presence or absence of (1) competition between the owner of the famous mark and other parties, or (2) the likelihood of confusion, mistake or deception."[1]

---

[1] 15 U.S.C. Sec. 1127.

To obtain relief under the Federal Trademark Dilution Act, you're required to prove:

- Your mark is famous.

- The defendant is making a commercial use of your mark.

- The defendant began using its mark after your mark became famous.

- The defendant's use of its mark diminishes the value and distinguishing power of your mark.

Suppose that you decide to market Dell soda pop. (You choose this mark because Dell is your last name.) Dell is, of course, a famous trademark for computers. The company doesn't manufacture any food or beverage products whatsoever. Nevertheless, you can be enjoined from using your mark if Dell can prove your use of the mark somehow diminishes its value.

How do you know if a mark is "famous"? There's no hard-and-fast rule. Courts determine this on a case-by-case basis, using various facts and circumstances to ascertain the degree of public recognition your mark enjoys. A mark may be famous in one geographical area or locality, even though it doesn't have national recognition.

⚖️ **LAWYER'S NOTE:** *The problem of dilution is closely related to the issue of knockoffs discussed in the next section. The difference is that dilution does not actually confuse the consumer, whereas knockoffs are intended to cause confusion.*

THE PROBLEM OF KNOCKOFFS

You can find fake knockoff Rolex watches on any number of street corners in New York. Technically this is called *passing off* goods and services. It's the intentional effort to create confusion as to the source of goods and services and overlaps with common law concepts of counterfeiting. This is such an obvious legal and ethical no-no that it would scarcely bear a mention if not for frequent dispute over whether there's actually been intent to confuse.

In 1986, Levi Strauss sued another clothier for copying its distinctive back pocket–stitching pattern. The pattern consisted of two intersecting arcs that bisected both pockets. Levi Strauss and Gap Stores had spent millions of dollars on advertisements featuring pictures of the back pockets of Levi's jeans.

Lois Sportswear, the alleged infringer, argued that no confusion could occur because the jeans were clearly labeled. Not so, said the court, and applied several factors intended to provide a real kick in the pants to unscrupulous infringers:

- **The strength of the mark:** The stronger the mark, the more likely the infringement. Recall from the section in chapter 3 on strong marks versus weak marks that a strong mark is one that is either arbitrarily chosen or that has acquired secondary meaning.

- **The degree of the similarity of the marks:** The closer the similarity of two distinctive marks, the greater the likelihood of intent to improperly capitalize on established goodwill. In the Levi case, the stitching that appeared on the back pocket of the jeans was "essentially identical."

- **The similarities of the products:** The Levi case involved very similar pairs of blue jeans.

- **Whether similar trademarks operate in the same market:** The infringer alleged the two brands of jeans were sold in different market segments. Interestingly, the court held that this increased the likelihood of confusion because "a passer-by might think that the jeans were [Levi Strauss's] long awaited entry into the designer jeans market segment."

- **Actual confusion:** Courts will review evidence, such as consumer testimony, relating to actual confusion of the products.

- **Quality of the products:** If the goods are of inferior quality, the trademark owner can claim "debasement" of its reputation. If they're of similar quality, the owner can claim there's a greater likelihood of confusion. A no-win situation for the infringer.

• **The sophistication of the relevant consumer market:** An unsophisticated segment of the consumer market is more likely to be confused by similar trademarks.

MARKS THAT ARE SCANDALOUS, IMMORAL, OR SUGGEST FALSE CONNECTIONS

Some marks are unprotectable based on principle—and federal law. The Lanham Act proscribes registration of marks that are immoral, scandalous, or create false representations.

Scandalous and Immoral Marks

Federal law prohibits registration of "scandalous" marks.[2] But what's scandalous is largely a matter of debate, degree, personal opinion and, ultimately, court precedent.

The PTO has refused to register marks that depict nudity, but it allows registration of marks such as Hustler, Week-End Sex, and Black Tail for adult entertainment magazines. A registration for the word Bullshit, in connection with handbags and wallets, was also reportedly refused.

In one relatively important case, the Old Glory Condom Corp. successfully appealed the Patent and Trademark Office's refusal to register its depiction of an American flag as a trademark for its condoms.[3] The advertising materials read: "We believe it's our patriotic duty to protect and save lives."

The examining PTO officer had determined that "a majority of the American public would be offended by the use of American flag imagery to promote products associated with sexual activity. She argue[d] that the flag is a sacrosanct symbol whose association with condoms would necessarily give offense."

The court disagreed. Citing a prior registration of the trademark Big

---

[2] 15 U.S.C. Section 1052(a).
[3] *In Re Old Glory Condom Corp. United States Trademark Trial and Appeal Board 1993.* 26 U.S.P.Q.2d (BNA) 1216.

Pecker, the court held that the use of the flag as a trademark for condoms "can in no way be considered scandalous."

Marks That Suggest False Connections or Origins

A trademark can't be registered if it suggests a false affiliation with persons, institutions, beliefs, or national symbols. An example of this would be suggesting a tennis shoe has a particular affiliation with a sports team when this isn't the case.

OTHER TRICKY TRADEMARK PROBLEMS

Trademarks permeate our lives, language, and culture. As a result they provide a constant source of material for new legislation, case law and, of course, litigation.

Domain Names

The Internet is a favorite medium for trademark infringers. Domain names are a particular use of your trademark, regulated by a special cybersquatting statute, as discussed in chapter 6.

Trademarking a Slogan: "You've Got Mail"

Trademarking a slogan can be particularly tricky. Slogans are generally used in advertising materials and thus may not get trademark protection, and thus bear a more remote or nonphysical connection to the product. However, a slogan may be registered as a trademark if it functions to designate the source of goods or services.

Interestingly, the slogan "You've Got Mail," as used by AOL, clearly bore a physical connection to the product. Unfortunately, it was deemed to be generic by the court.

Telephone Numbers As Trademarks

Telephone numbers can be protected as trademarks, and a competitor's use of a confusingly similar trademark can be enjoined as both an infringement of the mark and unfair competition. Companies that do a lot of business through telephone orders frequently spend significant advertising dollars promoting telephone numbers such as 1-800-DIAL-Mattress or 1-800-AMI-PREG. Interestingly, courts are sympathetic to the use of telephone numbers as trademarks, even though the numbers may spell out words that are themselves generic terms.[4]

LEVELING THE PLAYING FIELD: INTERNATIONAL PROTECTIONS

Protecting a trademark in a global economy is one of the toughest issues faced by entrepreneurial businesses. Even if you don't market your goods internationally, you can find a foreign infringer at your doorstep. Foreign knockoffs are a headache sometimes facilitated by inexpensive or exploitive foreign labor and individual disregard for U.S. laws.

To protect your trademark in a global economy, you must rely, to some extent, on the laws of each nation in which you market your product. Treaties make this possible. A treaty is an agreement between two or more nations, agreeing to abide by certain standards.

THE PARIS CONVENTION

The principal treaty in force is commonly referred to as the Paris Convention. The United States adopted it in 1887, and currently over 100 countries are parties to its provisions. Should you choose to enter the global market, you can rely upon the following protections:

- **Fair consideration in filing a foreign application:** The Paris Convention provides assurance that foreign applicants for trademark protection will receive the same consideration as domestic applicants.

- **Minimal protection against unauthorized goods:** Although the protections are considerably more difficult to enforce than U.S. remedies, there are some assurances in the treaty to protect against products bearing unauthorized marks.

- **Internationally famous marks:** If you have a mark that achieves national recognition, such as Rolex or McDonald's, the Paris Con-

---

[4] *Dial-A-Mattress Franchise Corp. v. Page,* United States Court of Appeals, Second Circuit 1989, 880 F.2d 675.

vention assures that you won't be forced to compete with locals who try to adopt those marks and capitalize on your goodwill.

• **Priority Rule:** If you file a trademark application in one Paris Convention country, you can use that date as your application date in other Paris Convention countries if you file your application in the other countries within six months.

GATT

The General Agreement on Tariffs and Trade, known as GATT, was amended in 1994 to add a Treaty for Trade-Related Aspects of International Property Rights (TRIPS). TRIPS requires signatory countries to enact laws that comply with minimum standards governing the use of intellectual property.

THE MADRID PROTOCOL

The Madrid Protocol, subscribed to by a number of nations in 1989, is intended to create a method for obtaining international trademark protection. It authorizes the use of a single standardized registration application. In November 2002, the United States passed legislation to adopt the Madrid Protocol in November 2003. The protocol mirrors many of the provisions included in our own Lanham Act.

Some key features of the Madrid Protocol include the following:

• Applicants can base their trademark applications for international registration on a pending national application, rather than having to wait for their national registration process to be completed.

• Each member nation's trademark office has a set period of time, usually eighteen months, to notify the World Intellectual Property Organization (WIPO) of objections to the international registration.

Applications under the protocol may be in either French or English. The list of countries that are currently members of the protocol include

Albania, Algeria, Antigua and Barbuda, Armenia, Australia, Austria, Azerbaijan, Belarus, Belgium, Bosnia and Herzegovina, Bhutan, Bulgaria, China, Croatia, Cuba, Cyprus, the Czech Republic, Denmark, Egypt, Estonia, Finland, France, Georgia, Germany, Greece, Hungary, Iceland, Iran, Ireland, Italy, Japan, Kazakhstan, Kenya, Kyrgyzstan, Latvia, Lesotho, Liberia, Liechtenstein, Lithuania, Luxembourg, Macedonia, Monaco, Mongolia, Morocco, Mozambique, the Netherlands, North Korea, Norway, Poland, Portugal, Russia, San Marino, Serbia and Montenegro, Sierra Leone, Singapore, Slovakia, Slovenia, South Korea, Spain, Swaziland, Sweden, Switzerland, Tajikistan, Turkey, Turkmenistan, Ukraine, the United Kingdom, the United States, Uzbekistan, Vietnam, and Zambia.

USING THE U.S. CUSTOMS SERVICE

The U.S. Customs Service is in a unique position to prevent illegal imports and has procedures in place to protect you against infringement of your trademark by foreign imports. The Customs Service protects trademarks, service marks, trade names, and copyrights that have been recorded with their Intellectual Property Rights Branch (IPRB).

To be eligible to record your mark with the IPRB, you must first register your trademark, trade name, or service mark with the United States Patent and Trademark Office. Approval of your IPRB form usually takes one to two weeks, and you're promptly notified by mail of acceptance or rejection.

Protection is effective from the date your IPRB application is approved and is concurrent in force with the registration of your mark. Customs protection ceases if your trademark registration is canceled, revoked, or expires. (For more information about the trademark registration process, see chapter 5.)

TEN TRADEMARK TIPS FOR SELECTING AND MAINTAINING A MARK

The following checklist for selecting and evaluating a trademark is based upon the principles discussed in this chapter and in the previous one.

TIP #1: SELECT AN EASILY DEFENSIBLE TRADEMARK

Marks that are suggestive but do not use descriptive terms are afforded a high degree of protection. A good way to come up with such a mark is to divide the name of your product into syllables, substituting some of the syllables with random letters, like Motorola or Crayola. Or try marrying random words like Nyquil or Spam (which stands for spiced ham). Best of all, try using a common word in an otherwise unconnected way, such as Apple for computers. Arbitrary marks are afforded the highest degree of protection.

Unfortunately, AOL opted to use some marks that were so descriptive as to be generic. Buddy List describes both the content and purpose of the feature, rather than identifying the source of the product as a trademark is required to do.

TIP #2: RESEARCH YOUR MARK IN THE FEDERAL REGISTERS

Chapter 5 explains how to do this for free on-line. Federal registers are maintained by the PTO, and you can search them to determine if a similar mark is already registered, or if someone has already applied to register it. A competent attorney can also guide you through the process of determining whether any state registrations already exist for marks that may be confusingly similar.

TIP #3: CHECK THE PHONE BOOK AND LOCAL MEDIA FOR PRIOR USE

Remember that rights to a mark can be derived from prior use, as well as registration. Prior users can object to your application or overturn the registration, even after it's granted. Check the phone books and other advertising resources in localities where you plan to use the mark to turn up additional evidence of prior use.

TIP #4: DON'T DESPAIR IF A SIMILAR MARK SURFACES

Even if a similar mark is already in use, it may be possible to use the mark concurrently. Are your goods similar to the ones covered by the prior mark or so entirely different that confusion is unlikely? Is the mark you are considering descriptive or arbitrary and fanciful? If you're considering a descriptive mark for noncompeting goods, you may be able to work out an agreement for concurrent use.

TIP #5: ELIMINATE THE GENERIC, SCANDALOUS AND IMMORAL, AND FALSE CONNECTIONS

Remember that some terms and material can never be trademarks. Eliminate these references from your mark.

Generic terms can never be trademarked. Poor AOL forgot this cardinal rule when it spent millions to promote the terms IM, Buddy List, and You Have Mail, all of which were deemed generic and available for anyone to use.

TIP #6: REGISTER AND DESIGNATE YOUR MARK

Ownership of trademarks is derived from use, but federal registration confers considerable benefits, including the muscle of the U.S. Customs Service. The benefits of registration and use of the ® symbol (both of which are optional) are discussed in detail in chapter 5.

TIP #7: USE IT PROPERLY OR LOSE IT

Remember that rights to a trademark cannot be acquired through registration alone. You must document use of the marks so that your product is associated to them in a commercial context so as to adequately identify the source of the goods.

TIP #8: DON'T ALLOW YOUR MARK TO BECOME GENEROCIZED

Too much exposure can backfire. Don't allow your trademarks to become generocized by allowing the public to use them to refer to the product rather than the source of the product.

TIP #9: DON'T LET OTHERS CONFUSE THE PUBLIC

Police the Internet and your usual marketing outlets for misuse of your mark, and promptly notify the infringer to cease and desist.

TIP #10: CALL UPON THE CUSTOMS SERVICE

In the case of imported goods, notify the U.S. Customs Service, which can impound importations of infringing merchandise.

CHAPTER 5 ⟫⟫⟫

How to Research and Register a Mark from Scratch

RUSHING BEFORE RESEARCHING can subject your business to daunting risks. Before you adopt a mark and attempt to register it, you need to determine whether it's already being used in any market you plan to enter, regardless of whether it's previously registered. If you're attentive to these preliminaries, the registration process itself will be surprisingly smooth and simple.

IN THIS CHAPTER YOU FIND OUT:

- About the costs of complacency when it comes to researching a mark

- How to register the "look" of, as well as the words of, your trademark

- What happens to trademark applications after you file them

- The difference between having your mark entered in the primary versus the supplemental register

TOMMY HILFIGER, A clothing designer, includes in its 1994 spring collection a line of clothing bearing the words Star Class with a red five-pointed star. In preparing to introduce its line, Hilfiger requests from its attorneys a federal trademark search, in the category limited to clothing, for the words Star Class. Hilfiger tells its attorneys that these words are going to be used for clothing with a nautical theme. The search reveals no identical marks. However, Hilfiger's attorneys recommend that Hilfiger conduct a full trademark search of all categories before using the words Star Class. Hilfiger declines to do so.

Only after the International Star Class Yacht Racing Association files suit for trademark infringement does Hilfiger finally agree to do a full search, which easily reveals the prior use of the Star Class mark by the association. Hilfiger continues to sell clothing bearing the allegedly infringing marks, and by the time the case goes to trial, Hilfiger has sold over $3 million worth of clothing bearing the Star Class mark.

Ultimately, the Second Circuit Court finds Hilfiger acted in bad faith by declining its attorneys' advice to conduct a full trademark search. The court states, "Hilfiger's choice not to perform a full search under these circumstances reminds us of two of the famous trio of monkeys who, by covering their eyes and ears, neither saw nor heard any evil. Such willful ignorance should not provide a means by which Hilfiger can evade its obligations under trademark law." Hilfiger is required to pay several million dollars in profits and punitive damages to the plaintiff.[1]

Before you can assert ownership of a trademark or use it in commerce without grave commercial risk, you must research it by all practical means. The costs associated with research are not insubstantial, but they can be minimized by proceeding in logical stages as outlined in this chapter.

PREREGISTRATION CONSIDERATIONS

Some marks are catchy but can prove costly when it comes to trying to establish ownership of them. Carefully selecting a mark can save you

---

[1] *International Star Class Yacht Racing Ass'n. v. Tommy Hilfiger, U.S.A., Inc.*, 146 F.3d 66, 73 (2d Cir. 1998) ("*ISCYRA II*"); *International Star Class Yacht Racing Ass'n. v. Tommy Hilfiger, U.S.A., Inc.*, 80 F.3d 749, 754–55 (2d Cir. 1996).

legal fees in the long run. These funds may be better spent on marketing to create a permanent, legally sound linkage between your mark and your product.

THE COST OF CAPITALIZING ON SUBLIMINAL ASSOCIATIONS

Most businesses strive for a mark that holds the promise of positive subliminal associations. Some companies hire special naming consultants to identify and capitalize on the public psyche. But using terms that have established meanings can be costly when it comes to protecting them and establishing your ownership. Marks with preestablished meanings are the hardest to protect.

The Significance of Secondary Meaning

You can't get trademark protection for descriptive marks without proof that your marketing efforts have caused the public to specifically associate these terms with your product. This type of association between a product and a term used in everyday language is known as *secondary meaning*. The Patent and Trademark Office requires you to provide proof of secondary meaning prior to registering certain types of marks.

As a general rule, the more a term is directly descriptive or already benefits from strong associations in everyday language, the harder it is to protect. For example, terms such as *beautiful* or *best* or *jiffy* have descriptive meanings that were not created by marketing efforts, so it would be unfair to allow a company to claim ownership of the associated meanings.

Degrees of Distinctiveness

Words and logos can be trademarks only if they're deemed distinctive. Potential trademark terms are divided into categories, based on distinctiveness. You need to decide what category your mark falls into prior to registering it so that you can determine if secondary meaning is required, and ultimately, whether your mark can appear in the principal or supplemental register (discussed in this chapter under "Publication: The Principal Versus the Supplemental Register").

The categories of potential trademark terms, from least distinctive to most distinctive are:

• **Generic:** These refer to a general type or category of products, so it would be unfair to allow anyone to establish ownership of them. Words like *modem* and *E-mail* are generic terms.

• **Descriptive:** Descriptive marks contain adjectives that describe the actual characteristics of a product, such as *TimeSaver* or *Diet-Rite* or *FreshSqueezed*. These terms can't be registered until they acquire proof of secondary meaning. It's a common misconception that descriptive terms based on people's surnames, such as Mrs. Fields cookies, are inherently distinctive, but these, too, require proof of secondary meaning. (After all, Fields is a common name.)

• **Suggestive:** Suggestive marks are afforded a higher level of distinctiveness and can be trademarked without proof of secondary meaning. They merely suggest characteristics of a product rather than describe them. Suggestive and descriptive marks can be hard to tell apart. Microsoft is an example of a suggestive mark that suggests software for microcomputers.

• **Arbitrary:** An arbitrary mark uses a term that has no established meaning in connection with the product, such as Apple for computers. These marks are easy to protect, because their association with the product is the result of marketing efforts and not preexisting meanings.

⚖️ **LAWYER'S NOTE:** *Only words that are fanciful, arbitrary, or suggestive are considered distinctive enough to function as trademarks. Descriptive terms can be trademarks or service marks only if they've acquired secondary meaning. Generic terms can never be trademarks.*

• **Fanciful:** These are invented terms, created for the sole purpose of identifying a product or service. Since all of their meaning is derived from such association, it's relatively easy to establish your ownership of the marks.

Table 5-1 provides examples of the various types of terms

and indicates which terms require proof of secondary meaning prior to registration.

TABLE 5-1: *Examples of Descriptive, Suggestive, and Fanciful Marks*

Type of Mark	Proof of Secondary Meaning Required Prior to Registration	Examples
Generic	Not applicable; these terms can never be trademarked	Modem, E-mail
Descriptive marks	Yes	TimeSaver, DietRite, FreshSqueezed
Suggestive	No	Big Kahuna, Gateway, Microsoft
Arbitrary	No	Apple, Pledge
Fanciful marks	No	Dell, Exxon, Nestlé

Sometimes it's difficult to evaluate whether a mark is descriptive, suggestive, or even fanciful; the lines are not always clear. The PTO may ultimately take a different view than you do during the registration process, and it's best to anticipate this possibility when preparing the application.

> **$$ BUSINESS TIP:** *When initially selecting a trademark, try to choose one that's suggestive, arbitrary, or fanciful, rather than descriptive. Fanciful and suggestive marks may be registered without proof of secondary meaning.*

PHONETIC SPELLINGS MAY BE HARD TO PROTECT

Phonetic spellings may be quite creative, but they don't offer the hope of much protection. The trademark office treats all phonetically similar marks and terms as pretty much identical; it ignores differences in the spellings of terms that sound alike. A phonetic spelling of a descriptive term is still considered descriptive. For example, *KoKo* would still be considered a purely descriptive term for *cocoa* and requires proof of secondary meaning prior to registration. Similarly, if your mark has a meaning in a foreign language, it will be deemed descriptive.

REGISTERING THE LOOK OF A TRADEMARK

After picking the perfect trademark term, you may want to give some consideration as to how you actually want the words to appear. Does your mark consist of letters or numbers that have a special appearance?

The famous Coca-Cola logo, with its distinctive white script on a red background, is a good example of how stylized print can be the most recognizable aspect of a trademark image. The trademark statute specifically allows you to protect stylized words, letters, and numbers, and the application directs you to provide samples of the type style needed to register the actual appearance of your mark.

The ability to register and protect the stylized words associated with your mark means a competitor cannot use a mark that emulates the written appearance of your mark but uses a different spelling or word, unless it is a permissible use, such as parody.

CHOOSING STATE OR FEDERAL REGISTRATION

You would be hard-pressed to find a lawyer who tells you *not* to register your trademark. But it's important to remember that registration doesn't protect you against the rights of someone who has previously used your mark or a similar mark in a particular market.

Common Law Considerations

Common law rights to ownership of a trademark derive from the regular and exclusive use of the mark in a particular jurisdiction, not from its registration. A business that has established common law rights can enforce them against you, whether you've registered the mark first or not. Hostess Ding Dongs were marketed as King Dons and Big Wheels in several parts of the country for many years due to conflicting local marks.

Technology Tips the Balance

Technology has tipped the balance in favor of federal registration, since the Internet has created a national point-and-click economy. Federal registration covers all products used in U.S. commerce.

There are some situations, however, when you may wisely opt to register on a state-by-state basis:

• **Marks confined to use within a state's borders are ineligible for federal registration.** This is because the federal government, under the U.S. Constitution, has only the power to regulate interstate commerce and foreign commerce. Commerce that's conducted exclusively within a state's borders, referred to as intrastate commerce, is not subject to federal registration. (An Internet presence can be a good argument, however, that you're involved in interstate commerce and entitled to federal registration.)

• **You may be precluded from using your mark in certain jurisdictions by prior local use.** This may make federal registration unavailable to you.

• **Economics and research costs may favor state registration.** If your product or service will most certainly be confined to local markets, you might want to avoid the expense of a nationwide search for prior use. For example, if you have a small local service, such as a carpet cleaning service, a national trademark search may be overkill.

• **Dual registration may be advantageous where state laws provide more generous protections and rights of recovery for infringement.** If your marketing will be concentrated in a particular state, you may want to see what additional rights its registration process offers you.

Special Advantages of Federal Registration

Federal registration is more than far-reaching. It carries an impressive array of benefits flowing from Congress's right to regulate federal commerce. These include:

• **The right to use the ® symbol:** Only federally registered marks can use this symbol.

• **Priority against subsequent users:** If you opt to register a mark federally, the effective date of your registration is backdated to the date you first used your mark. This date is important for establishing priority of your rights and even applies to subsequent users in foreign countries that are parties to international treaties, which include the United States.

• **Streamlined access to federal courts:** Federal registration confers the right to sue in federal courts. Although owners of unregistered marks may also sue in federal courts, your federal registration serves as a presumption that you own the mark.

• **Generous damages, penalties, and attorney's fees:** If an infringement is deemed willful, you may be entitled to damages equal to three times the amount you can actually prove (called *treble* damages) and attorneys' fees. You may even get criminal damages if actual counterfeiting of your mark has occurred.

• **The right to stop foreign knockoffs and infringing importations:** If your mark is registered in the Principal Register, you can file your registration and invoke the power of the U.S. Customs service to block the importation of infringing merchandise. (Registration with the Customs Service is explained in more detail in chapter 3.)

• **Incontestability:** Marks that have been registered and used in commerce for five consecutive years may be deemed incontesible. This means it becomes very difficult to challenge the mark.[2]

RESEARCHING YOUR MARK: A THREE-STAGE APPROACH

Researching a mark can be time consuming and financially taxing. But it beats defending yourself or your company in a lawsuit for infringe-

---

[2] U.S.C. Title 15 Sec. 339(b) (Lanham Act).

ment. As the *Hilfiger* case demonstrates, failure to conduct a thorough trademark search can be evidence of bad faith, requiring you to give up all your profits plus pay hefty damage awards to a prior user.

You can conduct your research in a cost-effective manner by progressing in logical stages. The first stage of your research should take advantage of the free Patent and Trademark Office (PTO) Web site that enables you to screen federally registered marks and identify conflicts. After this preliminary screening, you can proceed to a more comprehensive fee-based database that allows you to simultaneously research federal, state, and even common law and foreign registrations. If your mark passes these first two screening stages, you're ready to invest in a professional trademark search report.

> **$$ BUSINESS TIP:** *You can cut trademark research costs by proceeding in logical stages and availing yourself of free government resources available on the Internet.*

STAGE 1: CONDUCTING A FREE PRELIMINARY SEARCH

The PTO Internet database, known as the Trademark Electronic Search System (TESS), located at www.uspto.gov, provides a wealth of essential information for any aspiring trademark applicant. This Web site provides free access to records of both federally registered trademarks and pending trademark applications.

Meet TESS

It's surprisingly easy to do a basic preliminary search for the registration status of a proposed mark using TESS. To access the database, follow these steps:

1. Click the trademarks link located at the left-hand side of the USPTO home page.

2. Click the link "Search Trademarks" in the middle of the screen. A screen appears, giving you four types of searches to choose from. In most cases you will want to use a basic search for the trademark

term, or a Boolean search if you know the terms that appear in the mark but not their exact order or placement. (For example, you might enter "real" and "thing" to do a search for the Coca-Cola trademark, "the real thing.")

3. Select the type of search you want to do. (For example, you can elect to do a Boolean search incorporating the words *and* or *or.*)

4. Enter your search term.

5. Click "Submit Query." A list of search results containing your search term or terms appears.

6. Click the result that corresponds to the term you want to search.

7. A screen with information about the status of the mark appears. You can determine the following from the information on this screen:

- **The type of goods or services that are sold under the mark:** Under certain circumstances you can use a similar mark for noncompeting goods and services. (See chapter 3.)

- **The type of the mark:** Whether it is a trademark, service mark, certification mark, etc.

- **The owner of the mark:** The individual entity that owns the mark, as well as their attorney.

- **Whether the application to register a mark has been abandoned:** Abandoned marks are designated as such in the Live/Dead column.

- **Whether the mark is entered into the Principal or Supplemental Register:** Marks entered into the Principal Register are far more difficult to challenge than marks that appear in the Supplemental Register, as discussed in this chapter under "Publication: The Principal Versus the Supplemental Register."

⚖ LAWYER'S NOTE: *Even if an application to register a mark has been abandoned, the mark may still be in use.*

8. Click the Check Status button to disclose the following information:

- **The status of the mark in the registration process:** How far along the mark is in the registration process.

- **The examining office:** The branch of the PTO and the name of the examiner to which the mark is assigned.

Limitations of TESS

Comprehensive as she may be, however, poor TESS has the following limitations:

- **TESS may be incomplete as to recently filed applications:** There is generally a four-month lag between the filing of applications and the time that information about them makes its way into the electronic database.

- **TESS does not include state, common law, or foreign marks:** TESS is limited to marks that are federally registered or for which applications are pending.

In the event that TESS does disclose a prior or pending registration for a similar mark, you can decide whether to take the position that the goods and services sold under your mark are dissimilar and cause no actual confusion. (This concept is discussed in chapter 3.) You can also decide to select another mark since if it already appears in the free preliminary screening, that means there's a conflict.

Other Free Resources

Professional search firms, as discussed below, have a number of resources at their disposal to conduct a full nationwide search for common law marks. However, you can very effectively extend your preliminary screening for conflicting marks without spending a dime by availing yourself of the following:

- **The Internet:** Since most companies, large and small, find it economical to maintain a Web presence, a simple search on the Internet may turn up evidence of prior use of your mark. It's also a good idea to check the domain name registration sites to see if anyone has registered your trademark as a domain name.

• **Trade journals and publications:** Trade journals and publications often maintain their own Web sites and searchable databases.

• **The local press:** Most newspapers maintain Web sites with the capability to do a key word search for your trademark.

STAGE 2: USING A FEE-BASED TRADEMARK DATABASE

Why pay to use a search engine when the government provides you with free access to TESS? There are good reasons. Some of TESS's limitations have already been pointed out, and fee-based search engines include information about:

• Up-to-date information about federal applications

• Phonetically similar terms

• Fragments of your term in other trademarked terms

• Canceled, denied, or abandoned applications

You can locate a number of fee-based search engines on the Internet. The availability of fee-based databases and search engines are constantly changing, with new ones frequently setting up shop. Micropat.com and trademark.com are just two examples of search engines available at the time of the writing of this book.

STAGE 3: OBTAINING A PROFESSIONAL
TRADEMARK SEARCH REPORT

If your trademark passes the preliminary screening stages, it's time to invest in a report prepared by a professional search firm. A professional report contains information about common law and foreign marks, as well as up-to-date information about federal and state registrations. Professional firms have extremely sophisticated techniques and software. You can place a high degree of reliance upon their results; most companies have specific warranties regarding their results.

A standard trademark search report prepared by a professional search firm contains:

- Detailed information about pending registrations and abandoned registrations, as well as about registrations that have been granted

> ⊖ **CAUTION:** *Pay close attention to the warranties, track record, and professional reputation of the professional search firm you select.*

- A survey of registrations in all relevant states

- Information about potentially conflicting, similar, or sound-alike common law marks

- Information about potentially conflicting domain names that operate as trademarks

- Citations and references to relevant court decisions and administrative decisions issued by the Trademark Trial and Appeal Board of the Patent Office

After you receive the report, you can review it carefully with your attorney to evaluate the strengths and vulnerabilities of your mark.

> ⊖ **CAUTION:** Always *review a professional search report with an attorney, who can advise you fully of all of the implications and as to the completeness of the report. While many things in this chapter can be done without a lawyer, interpreting the results of a comprehensive, professionally generated search report probably isn't one of them.*

THE APPLICATION PROCESS

The federal trademark application process has been evolving since the birth of our nation and is well refined. The United States is the world's biggest market, and over 120,000 federal trademark applications are filed annually.

After the tough job of researching your proposed mark, you may be surprised at how streamlined the actual federal registration process has become. In a nutshell, the actual registration process involves three steps:

1. **Filing the application with the PTO:** The standard federal trademark application is not lengthy. Certain supporting materials, discussed in the next section, are required with your application.

2. **Examination of your application by the PTO:** You may be asked to provide additional information to the office to respond to concerns raised during the process.

3. **Publication:** After your application has been approved by the PTO, it must be filed in the *Official Gazette* of the PTO for a requisite time period to allow anyone interested in opposing registration of your mark notice and opportunity to do so within the required time frame.

THE APPLICATION FORM

The trademark application is a surprisingly concise little form, and can even be filed electronically on the PTO Web site located at www.uspto. gov. However, like most legal forms, the questions are surprisingly nuanced with significant legal implications. The standard form, which may be completed and submitted on the Internet, is reproduced in Appendix A, and contains four distinct parts.

SECTION 1: INFORMATION ABOUT THE APPLICANT

The mere task of identifying themselves trips up a lot of applicants. According to the PTO, this simple question is one of the most common bases for rejection of an application.

The "applicant" is the actual owner of the mark and controls the use of the mark in connection with all goods and services offered under it. The owner/applicant can be a partnership, corporation, trust, association, or other legal entity. A common mistake is to list as the applicant the person filling out the application on behalf of an entity such as a corporation or partnership.

SECTION 2: DESCRIBING YOUR MARK

The appearance of your mark may be as important, or more important, than the words. In fact, many trademarks consist entirely of an image and don't have any words. If looks are important, your application should reflect this. In Section 2 of the application, you can select from the following registration options:

- **Typed format:** Selecting this option means your mark can be reproduced in standard type by using a typewriter. You can only use certain punctuation symbols, as indicated on the application form. For example, if your trademark is the word *Exto,* your application would simply state, "the word Exto."

- **Stylized or designed format:** This option allows you to register stylized type, color, and graphic designs. For example, if your trademark was EXTO, using this stylized type, you would state on your application "the word EXTO and design." If you select this option, you're required to submit a computer image file in either JPEG or GIF format.

- **Design marks:** If your mark consists primarily of a graphic design, you need to describe the design with as much specificity as possible. If your mark is a design, like the famous McDonald's golden arches, your application might state "The mark consists of a stylized design consisting of two intersecting golden arches."

Registering only words simplifies both the application process and the research involved in searching for similar marks. The trademark examiner doesn't have to search for trademarks that look similar to yours. How-

⚖️ **LAWYER'S NOTE:** *Registering only the written form of a mark (i.e., the typed format) provides the broadest protection of your mark. It protects all instances of it's use, regardless of accompanying graphics.*

ever, failing to register the stylized type and look of your mark leaves you somewhat vulnerable to competitors who may create marks that look like yours but don't use the specific words you've trademarked.

SECTION 3: IDENTIFICATION OF GOODS AND SERVICES AND LEGAL BASIS FOR FILING

It's a common misconception that every trademark must be unique. In fact, all that's required is that a particular trademark uniquely identifies the goods and services sold under it.

It's not altogether uncommon for two different entities to claim ownership of an identical trademarked term to represent noncompeting goods and services. For example, the TESS database disclosed a number of search results for the term *Pledge*. This overlap is why it's so important for the PTO to determine exactly what goods and services are going to be sold under your mark and to see a specimen of how your mark is actually going to be used to determine if the potential for confusion exists.

The Requirement of a Specimen

A specimen is an actual example of a trademark in use. For example, if you include your mark on articles of clothing you manufacture, you would include a sample or photograph of the embossed portion of the clothing.

What exactly is meant by the application question that asks you to "describe" the specimen? By this question, the office is asking you to describe *how* it's displayed. For example, you might explain, "Applicant intends to use the mark by affixing it to packaging for its software products," or, "Applicant intends to affix the specimen to labels on its line of clothing." If you're applying for a service mark, you might explain that the mark will be used in connection with the advertising of your services. In response to this question, the PTO wants information that may be relevant in determining whether your use can create confusion with any other trademarked product or use.

Identifying the Class of Goods and Services

This is the one section of the application you're actually permitted to leave blank! The PTO will supply this information, if you're not sure of the classification number. (There is no particular reason you *should* know it off the top of your head.)

The purpose of classifying goods and services is to facilitate comparison of marks, to see if granting your application could possibly result in confusion with a similar product. However, it's important not to confuse the term *class* with the term *goods*. Classes are broad categories of goods. If your application is granted, it may preclude others from using it on competing *goods,* but doesn't give you exclusive rights with respect to an entire *class*.

A special issue arises when you're marketing goods and services that span multiple classifications. For example, a hair salon may trademark its logo as service mark. It may also use it on products such as shampoo and hair spray. You can register multiple classifications on one application, but there's a separate fee for each class.

Basis for Filing

This section is the legal meat of the application. To establish a legal basis for your ownership of a trademark, you need to demonstrate that it is or will be *used in commerce*. Remember that rights to a trademark are derived from its use in commerce, and the consequent value it acquires as a result of the public's association with your product.

Prior to 1989, businesses faced a dilemma. Federal law didn't permit registration of a trademark until and unless it was used in commerce. This meant businesses had to invest advertising and promotional dollars in the trademark without any assurance that their attempt to register the mark would ultimately meet with success. Fortunately, the Trademark Revision Act of 1988 provided that, after 1989, businesses could register a mark based on "intent to use." Consequently, there are now four legal bases under which you may register.

Filing on the Basis of Actual Use You're entitled to select this option only if you are already using your mark "in commerce." Actual use in commerce has four specific requirements:

Requirement #1: Commercial Use: The commercial use requirement is met when you expose your mark by placing it on goods, packaging, tags, labels, or displays and documents associated with the goods or services.

Requirement #2: Geographical: Geographically, goods are deemed to be in commerce if they're being sold in more than one state or between the United States and a foreign country. The federal government, under the constitution, has only the power to regulate interstate commerce and foreign commerce. Commerce conducted exclusively within a state's borders is not subject to federal registration.

Requirement #3: Timing: The timing requirement is met only if your goods are *currently* being offered in commerce at the time of filing the application. You are required to provide a statement that the mark is currently being used, such as, "The goods are currently being used in commerce. The trademark was first used on the goods on January 1, 2003, and the goods were placed in interstate commerce in June 2003."

Requirement # 4: Control of the nature and quality of goods and services: It's not uncommon that a mark has been used in commerce prior to the application by someone other than the applicant. For example, the mark may have been used by a predecessor company, if you're buying a business. Or it may have been used by a related company, such as a subsidiary. In this instance, you must include an explanation about the relationship of the applicant to the prior user. You must document that the applicant currently controls the nature and quality of the goods or services. This is an essential requirement for establishing ownership of a trademark.

Filing on the Basis of Intent to Use The intent-to-use application is a blessing for start-up businesses since their owners aren't required to run the risk of investing in an unprotected mark while attempting to establish its use. Once the Notice of Allowance is issued, you have a six-month period to file a statement. This period may be extended in six-month increments for up to thirty months, aggregating up to thirty-six months from the date of the Notice of Allowance.

The intent-to-use application doesn't differ significantly from one for which prior use has already been established. The major differences of which you need to be aware when filing an intent-to-use application are:

- **You don't need to document use in commerce with the original registration application.** Accordingly, you don't need to supply any dates or even provide a specimen with the original registration application.

• **You must file an Amendment to Allege Use form or a Statement of Use form within six months.** The Amendment to Allege Use and Statement of Use forms contain the same information and differ only with respect to the time that they're filed. If you document your use prior to approval for publication in the *Official Gazette* (discussed below), you're required to file the Amendment to Allege Use form. You must file the Statement of Use form after a Notice of Allowance is issued.

Intent to Use Based on Foreign Registration Under certain international agreements, if you qualify, you may file in the United States based on a foreign application or on a registration in your country of origin. The U.S. Trademark application asks you to identify:

> **$$ BUSINESS TIP:** *If you plan to use your mark on several types of goods and services but do not or can not do so on all of them within the six-month period required to establish use, you can file a Request to Divide Out. This form is available on the USPTO Web site at www.uspto.gov.*

• The class of goods and services

• The country of the foreign filing

• The application number and date of the application

The U.S. application must be made within six months of the foreign filing date.

Intent to Use Based on Foreign Application Under certain treaties, the U.S. recognizes the priority of pending foreign applications. The information you are required to provide mirrors that required for applications that have already been granted. There is, however, a duty to provide updated information to the PTO about the pending foreign application.

MATERIALS THAT ACCOMPANY THE APPLICATION: A CHECKLIST

Failing to include the items identified in this section with your application can cause it to boomerang back to you, costing you valuable marketing time.

DRAWINGS AND SPECIMENS

The PTO not only wants to read about your mark, it may want to see drawings and specimens as required to accompany applications on the basis of actual use, but not for applications filed on the basis of intent to use.

Submitting Specimens: What Works and What Doesn't
Drawings and specimens are not the same thing. A specimen is more than simply the image of the mark by itself. A specimen *demonstrates* how you are actually using the mark in commerce. The PTO has identified the following as acceptable specimens:

- Tags and labels

- Instruction manuals

- Containers and packaging that display the mark

- For service marks, acceptable specimens include "signs, photographs, brochures or advertisements that show the mark used in the sale or advertising of the services."

*Un*acceptable specimens for trademarks generally include "invoices, announcements, order forms, bills of lading, leaflets, brochures, publicity releases and other printed advertising material." However, these types of specimens may be used, on occasion, to document use of service marks.

Drawings: Every Application Needs One

Every trademark application must include a "clear drawing" of the mark to be registered. The drawing is required even for marks that consist only of words, using no particular type.

The PTO files this drawing in the USPTO search records and prints the mark in the *Official Gazette* (discussed later in this chapter, under "What Happens to Applications After You File Them?")

> ⬤ **CAUTION:** *Once you submit a drawing of your mark, you cannot make a material change to it.*

If your mark consists of words, letters, or numbers with no particular stylization or design element included in the mark, you should select the "typed" drawing format option on the application. For your drawing, the mark must be typed in all capital letters on an 8½" × 11" piece of paper. The PTO Web page includes the example shown below.

Applicant's Name: A-OK Software Development Group
Correspondence Address: 100 Main Street, Any Town, MO 12345
Goods and Services: Computer services, namely on-line magazine in the field of business management
Date of First Use: January 15, 1995
Date of First Use in Commerce: May 15, 1995
The Mark:

                    THEORYTEC

"Stylized or Special Form"

If the particular style of lettering is important to your mark, or your mark includes a design or logo, select the "stylized or special form" option on the registration form.

You must submit a separate drawing page that contains a black-and-white image.

You aren't allowed to submit a drawing with color or gray shading, even if you use color. Instead, the office directs that you "specify any

Applicant's Name: Pinstripes, Inc.
Applicant's Address: 100 Main Street, Any Town, MO 12345
Goods and Services: Clothing, namely baseball caps and T-shirts
Date of First Use: Intent-to-Use Application
Date of First Use in Commerce: Intent-to-Use Application
The Mark:

PINSTRIPES

color designations in a description of the mark within the body of the application, not on the drawing page (e.g., 'The mark consists of a bird with a blue body and red wings')."

Above is an example of a special form drawing that appears on the PTO Web site.

POWER OF ATTORNEY

The PTO won't talk to just anyone about your application. If you want your attorney to be able to communicate with the PTO, you have to give her written authorization by including a Power of Attorney Authorization with your application. These forms are available on the USPTO Web site at www.uspto.gov along with the application.

THE FEE

Don't forget the check. Fees change periodically, and it's a good idea to check the PTO Web site at www.uspto.gov for latest fee schedule. All filing fees are nonrefundable. You must pay the application fee by credit card or an existing PTO deposit account.

WHAT HAPPENS TO APPLICATIONS AFTER YOU FILE THEM?

What happens to your application once you drop it in the mailbox or file it on-line? This section gives you a heads up on how the processing works and what you can do to expedite it.

THE FILING RECEIPT

Shortly after you've filed your completed application with the PTO, either by mail or on-line at the www.uspto.gov Web site, the office will send a gracious acknowledgment in the form of a filing receipt. You'll receive this document, aptly titled "Filing Receipt for Trademark Application," within a month of your *complete* submission if you file by mail, and via E-mail if you file on-line. The receipt, and more importantly, the filing date for your application, will be delayed if the PTO has to contact you and await additional materials to complete the application.

CHECKING THE STATUS OF YOUR APPLICATION

There are basically two ways that you can proactively track the status of your pending application: by phone or on the Internet. You can call the PTO status line at 703-305-8747 to see where your application is in the processing pipeline. Alternatively, you can access the PTO Web site at www.uspto.gov and click the icon that says "? Status" to check the status of a pending application.

THE NOTICE OF PUBLICATION

Getting your Notice of Publication in the mail is cause for celebration. This event signifies:

- The application has been properly prepared.
- All required accompanying materials have been included.
- The PTO examiner hasn't identified any basis for objection.

On the other hand, the PTO may notify the applicant or applicant's representative that there is an obstacle to the application, such as failing to include all the documentation or the correct fee.

THE CERTIFICATE OF REGISTRATION OR NOTICE OF ALLOWANCE

If you're fortunate enough to receive a Notice of Publication in the mail (instead of an objection, as discussed in the next section), the next phase of the process will take your trademark to the *Official Gazette.* This publication alerts the public to pending registrations and gives them an opportunity to oppose your registration. If your mark is not objected to within the thirty-day time frame specified by statute, and you have already demonstrated your use of the mark in commerce, you receive the coveted Certificate of Registration.

If you've filed an intent-to-use application and not yet filed your Amendment of Alleged use, the Certificate of Registration cannot yet be issued. Instead, you will receive a Notice of Allowance, pending documentation of your use of the mark in commerce. In the unlucky event someone does file opposition, the PTO will hold a hearing of sorts to determine whether the objection has merit.

PUBLICATION: THE PRINCIPAL VERSUS
THE SUPPLEMENTAL REGISTER

How do you put the world on notice that your mark has been federally registered? Where do you go to see if someone else has already registered your mark?

Once your mark has been successfully registered, the PTO publishes it in either the *Principal Register* or *Supplemental Register,* depending on whether the mark is distinctive or nondistinctive. Distinctive marks have either been established or don't require proof of secondary meaning and include suggestive, arbitrary, and fanciful marks. They usually can go directly into the Principal Register. Nondistinctive marks are either descriptive or suggestive, and are relegated to the Supplemental Register until their secondary meaning can be established.

Preferred Positioning: The Principal Register

The Principal Register is definitely where you want your mark to be. Your mark is eligible once it is deemed distinctive.

Being in the Principal Register is considered prima facie evidence (conclusive on its face) that you have exclusive ownership of the mark. This means it's very difficult for anyone else to challenge ownership of your mark. Also, if your mark makes the Principal Register, you can prevail upon the Customs Service to stop the importation of infringing goods, as discussed in chapter 3. A registration appearing in the Principal Register lasts ten years and can be renewed indefinitely for successive ten-year periods for as long as it is used as and functions as a trademark.

The Supplemental Register: Trademark Limbo

In comparison to the Principal Register, the Supplemental Register is a kind of trademark limbo. The supplemental register doesn't offer the prima facie protections of the Principal Register. Instead, it merely exists and serves to give notice of your prior use of the mark to other would-be users.

The Supplemental Register includes descriptive marks, surnames, and marks that reference geographical locations. A supplemental registration, if you maintain it properly, also lasts for ten years. You must file a special affidavit, known as a Section 8 Affidavit, in the fifth year after registration, otherwise the mark is deemed abandoned. You mark may be renewed for successive ten-year periods so long as it is used and functions as a trademark.

Upgrading: Moving from the Supplemental to the Principal Register

Once secondary meaning has been established, the mark is deemed distinctive and qualifies for a spot on the Principal Register. You can petition to move your mark from the Supplemental to the Principal Register after five years or earlier if the mark has acquired secondary meaning.

⚖ LAWYER'S NOTE: As soon as you can establish secondary meaning of a mark appearing on the Supplemental Register (through consumer affidavits, research polls, media reports, etc.), consider a petition to have it moved to the Principal Register.

Marks in either the Principal or Supplemental Register can use ®, which is the federal trademark symbol. Additionally, if your mark has been placed in either register, you are allowed to sue infringers in federal court.

You can check whether an existing mark is in the Principal or Supplemental Register by using the TESS database on the Patent and Trademark Web site located at http://www.uspto.gov.

REBOUNDING WHEN YOU'RE REBUFFED: RESPONDING TO A REJECTION OR OBJECTION

Here's where your attorney earns her fee! Unlike the errors in completing or compiling information, substantive objections to your application raised by the PTO require a more skilled and thoughtful response. For example, the examiner may conclude there's a statutory bar or likelihood of confusion with a previously registered mark. Or the examiner may conclude that a portion of your proposed mark is a generic term, which isn't subject to trademark protection. The PTO examiner may request that you amend the application to cure the problem or may reject the application outright.

AMENDING YOUR APPLICATION

Amendments can be simple to comply with or inordinately troublesome, depending on what the PTO is asking you to do. The PTO can request minor clarifications or changes that materially alter the scope of protection you're requesting. The time frame for completing the amendment is specified in the correspondence. The amount of time to respond to an office action is generally six months.

FIGHTING A REJECTION

Rejections aren't pleasant, but neither are they always fatal. In the event you're notified of a rejection, you have six months to respond. If you fail to file a response, your application will be deemed abandoned.

Sometimes the response is favorably received, and your application continues along the conveyer belt. If, however, after you've filed a response the PTO still doesn't believe your mark can be registered, it will issue a Final Rejection. In the face of a Final Rejection, you have the following options:

- **Appeal to the Trademark Trial and Appeal Board (TTAB):** This type of appeal is made when the objection is *substantive,* or based on trademark law. Examples of substantive objections include lack of distinctiveness or likelihood of confusion.

- **File a Petition to the commissioner:** This avenue is appropriate when you feel the PTO failed to stick to the correct procedures. For example, if the office didn't allow you the correct amount of time to file a response or to submit supplemental materials.

- **Request further reconsideration:** In cases where you feel there's been an error in communication with the PTO, this may be appropriate.

- **Abandon or suspend the application:** If you don't believe that you can overcome the PTO objection, this may be the appropriate course, in certain situations.

- **Amend the application to seek registration on the Supplemental Register:**[3] This is often done when a mark has been ruled descriptive, and the applicant hasn't been able to prove distinctiveness. The application can be amended to seek registration on the Supplemental Register, as opposed to the Principal Register.

SPECIAL ISSUES

Not every registration issue is resolved on the face of the application. This section covers some additional considerations that may occur during the process.

---

[3] 37 C.F.R. Section 2.75.

PROVING SECONDARY MEANING

Marks in the Supplemental Register can't graduate to the Principal Register unless they're deemed distinctive. Fortunately, time alone can serve as proof of distinctiveness. If a trademark applicant can document continuous use of the mark over a five-year period, an otherwise descriptive mark earns a presumption of distinctiveness.

But five years is a long time! If you anticipate that your mark may be deemed descriptive by the PTO, you can include a statement and supporting materials to try to persuade the PTO otherwise. The following is sample statement in support of distinctiveness of a mark:

> The mark has become distinctive as a result of applicant's regular, continuous, and exclusive use of the mark in interstate commerce, as shown by the materials separately submitted with this application.

Materials you might submit in support of your statement of distinctiveness include the following:

- Surveys and affidavits as to public awareness

- Proof of advertising expenditures

- Sample advertising

- Media reports and coverage that would tend to indicate the public's association of your mark with your products and services

COLLECTIVE MARKS AND CERTIFICATION MARKS

A collective mark, as its name implies, is used by a group or association to indicate membership or affiliation, such as the Better Business Bureau or your local Chamber of Commerce. If the group wants to certify that work or products meet the standards of the association, the mark should also be registered as a certification mark. The application process doesn't differ for these types of marks, except that the applicant must identify the following:

- The class of persons entitled to use the mark.

- The relationship of the applicant to the association, group or certifying entity.

- The nature of the applicant's control of the goods and services offered under the mark.

SURNAMES

A trademark that's primarily merely a surname generally can't be registered in the Principal Register without proof of distinctiveness, since secondary meaning is required for a mark that is primarily a surname. This means that surname trademarks, such as Mrs. Fields cookies, are primarily relegated to the Supplemental Register. A mark that consists of or comprises the name or portrait of a living individual can't be registered until you provide the PTO with proof that the person has consented to the mark. Typically, the application for such a mark includes a statement similar to the following: "The name Jill Gilbert identifies a living individual whose consent is on record."

DOMAIN NAMES

For many businesses, the most important trademark they own is their domain name. Domain names are not trademarks unless they are used as trademarks. But when they are, domain names are special types of trademarks. They are discussed separately in chapter 6.

WAIT, THERE'S MORE: MAINTAINING YOUR REGISTRATION

Getting a Certificate of Registration for your mark is certainly cause for celebration. But remember, you still have significant ongoing legal obligations to keep your newly registered mark in force.

SECTION 8 AFFIDAVIT: CERTIFICATION OF CONTINUING USE

In order for your registration to remain effective for the statutory ten-year period, you must file a document known as a Section 8 Affidavit between the fifth and sixth years following your registration. Basically, this affidavit is a statement attesting to the fact that the mark is still used in commerce.

Although this seems like a long way off at the time of registration (because it is), it's important to mark this date on your calendar so you don't miss it. You can find a copy of the Section 8 Affidavit form on the USPTO Web site located at www.uspto.gov.

SECTION 15 AFFIDAVIT: REQUEST TO HAVE YOUR MARK DECLARED INCONTESTABLE

If you've continuously used your mark in commerce for five years and can prove it, you should file a Section 15 Affidavit. You can even file this affidavit at the time of your registration, if you have been using the mark continuously for five years prior to registering it.

RENEWING YOUR REGISTRATION AFTER TEN YEARS

Your registration lasts for ten years, and if you don't renew it within the proper time frame, you run the risk of having to repeat the registration process. However, since actual legal ownership results from use of the mark, inadvertently allowing your mark to expire may cause you inconvenience more than anything else.

A registration may be renewed in the year period preceding its ten-year anniversary with a grace period of six months after expiration. There is a surcharge for renewals made during the grace period.

USING THE TRADEMARK ® SYMBOL

In addition to filing lots of paperwork to maintain your mark, you are expected to properly designate it. It's your obligation to place the public on notice of your registration. You should display the ® symbol with your mark if you don't want to go to the trouble of using cumbersome words like "Registered with the U.S. Patent and Trademark Office." Failure to display your mark in a way that reasonably puts the public on notice can limit your recovery in an infringement action (see chapter 4).

CHAPTER 6 >>>>>

Trademarks in Cyberspace: The Domain Name Debate

A PHENOMENON OF the mid-1990s was the persistent failure of huge corporate legal departments to recognize the need to register and protect their trademarks as domain names before everyone ranging from teenage hackers to the corporations' largest competitors appropriated them. Fortunately, the commercial interests of every business that ever hired a lobbyist were in perfect alignment, and Congress quickly passed legislation to remedy the problem. The international business community has also reacted to protect themselves from this threat.

IN THIS CHAPTER YOU FIND OUT:

- What cybersquatting is and why it's such a vilified practice
- What domain names you can and cannot register with the PTO as trademarks
- The role of ICANN in international domain name disputes

IN 1996, KAPLAN Educational Centers, a marketer of SAT prep courses, sues its archrival, Princeton Review, over a domain name dispute. Princeton has registered the domain name Kaplan.com. Kaplan argues that this move violates laws of trademark infringement and constitutes unfair competition. An arbitration panel agrees, deciding that Princeton Review must relinquish all rights to the Kaplan.com name, and transfer it to Kaplan.[1]

In 2000, an international arbitration panel finds that the use of the domain name walmartcanadasucks.com is not a domain name confusingly similar to the Wal-Mart trademark and refuses to invalidate the use of the domain name.[2] Another arbitration panel upholds the uses of the domain name michaelbloom bergsucks.com as protected free speech.[3] And yet another panel refuses to invalidate the domain name fucknetscape.com on the basis of similarity to the Netscape trademark, finding it "inconceivable" that anyone logging on the Web site would think it had any connection with the trademark owner.[4]

Reverend Jerry Falwell is unable to stop a parody/comedy site making fun of him from using the domain name www.jerrryfalwell.com.[5] However, another organization, the People for the Ethical Treatment of Animals (PETA) is successful in invalidating the registration of the peta.org used for a parody on the PETA acronym: People Eating Tasty Animals.[6]

Planting your flag on the uncharted territory of cyberspace is exhilarating. But can you lay claim simply because you got there first? When it comes to domain names, someone who has neither registered a particular term as a trademark nor used it on the World Wide Web may actually have superior rights.

---

[1] This arbitration decision is discussed in "The Intellectual Property Law Server, Remedies in Domain Name Disputes, A Canadian Perspective," by George A. Wowk. Published October 29, 1997, in Intellectual Property Law Server, www.intelproplaw.com.

[2] WIPO Case No. 2000-1104 (November 23, 2000).

[3] *Bloomberg L.P. v. Secaucus Group*, NAF file No. 97077 (June 7, 2001).

[4] *America Online v. Jonathon Investments*, WIPO Case No. D2001-0918 (September 14, 2001).

[5] *Falwell v. Cohn*, WIPO Case No. D2002-0184 (June 3, 2000).

[6] *People for the Ethical Treatment of Animals v. Doughney*, 263 F. 3rd 359 (4th Cir. 2001).

DUELING DOMAIN NAMES

Domain names are valuable and unique assets that can be held by only one owner. There can be only one www.affiliated.com on the Web, even if several entities have trademarks and trade names that include the term *Affiliated*. Disputes over whether the use of a domain name by one business infringes on the established trademark rights of another have become commonplace.

BUSINESS REGULATING BUSINESS: THE ROLE OF ICANN

Registering your domain name is the first step in the cyberspace flag-planting process. Two regulated organizations have historically managed the domain name system.

Network Solutions, Inc., more commonly known as InterNIC, formerly acted as a clearinghouse for domain names, to keep track of which domain names were already taken. InterNIC didn't have the resources to monitor new applications for conflicts with existing trademark registrations, but it refused to register domain names that are blatantly infringing existing trademarks. For example, it revoked Sprint's registration of mci.com, shortly after issuing it. InterNIC concluded that Sprint could not possibly have a legitimate purpose or claim to the MCI moniker.

InterNIC has now ceased to manage the domain name system. Domain names have come to be regulated largely by individual contracts entered into with private, ICANN-approved, for-profit domain name registering companies.

The Internet Corporation for Assigned Names and Numbers (ICANN) was formed by entrepreneurs and private domain name registration companies to create order out of what was certain to become a tangle of litigation and chaos.

ICANN is a not-for-profit corporation formed by a broad coalition of the Internet's business, technical, academic, and user communities. Amazingly, ICANN has been recognized on an unprecedented global level by the United States and other governments as the entity to coordinate the technical management of the Internet's domain name system and allocate IP address space.

ICANN has created a formal Uniform Dispute Resolution Policy (UDRP) under which you can bring a complaint to resolve domain name disputes. This policy governs all generic top-level domain names and many of the country-code top level domain names. You can review these policies and even file a complaint on the ICANN Web site located at http://www.icann.org. ICANN's policies strongly favor trademark holders in domain name disputes.

If you file a UDRP complaint with ICANN, your case will be decided by an arbitration panel from one of the ICANN-accredited arbitration services (such as WIPO or NAF). As of the writing of this book, this system has generated more than 7,500 arbitration proceedings since January 2000, involving greater than 12,000 disputed domain names.

To prevail in an ICANN arbitration proceeding, you must show:

1. The domain name is identical or confusingly similar to a trademark or service mark in which you have rights.

2. The person using the domain name has no rights or legitimate business interest in doing so.

3. The person registered and using the domain name is doing so in bad faith.

One of the disadvantages of a UDRP arbitration proceeding is that you cannot receive damages. UDRP remedies are limited to cancellation or transfer of ownership of the offending domain name. However, it's very economical to bring an action, and generally disputes are resolved very quickly, sometimes in a matter of a few weeks, which can be important to your business. The average time frame for receiving a UDRP decision is fifty-two days.

THE FEDERAL CYBERSQUATTING STATUTE

Cybersquatting, that nasty practice of registering a domain name that contains a trademark of another company, is usually done for the purpose of extracting funds from the company or capitalizing on its goodwill. To curtail this practice, Congress has passed special legislation entitled the Anticybersquatting Consumer Protection Act (ACPA).[7]

Unlike the UDRP (which can only cancel registrations), if you file a full-blown lawsuit under the ACPA, a court deciding the case can award statutory damages of up to $100,000 per domain name. In really egregious cases of cybersquatting, courts can also award attorney's fees.

To prove you've been a victim of cybersquatting, the statute requires that you establish:

1. Your mark was distinctive or famous at the time of the domain name registration.

2. The registered domain name is identical or confusingly similar to your trademark.

3. The alleged squatter has "bad faith intent to profit from that mark."[8]

This statute even deals with the problem of foreign entities that attempt to register domain names that infringe on your mark. Relief includes cancellation of the domain name registration.

REGISTRATION OF DOMAIN NAME MARKS WITH THE PTO

Predictably, the Patent and Trademark Office has received a growing number of applications for marks that consist of domain names. Although domain name applications are generally subject to the same re-

---

[7] The Anticybersquatting Consumer Protection Act is codified at Section 43(d) of the Lanham Act, 15 U.S.C. Sec. 1125(d).

[8] 15. U.S.C. Sec. 1125(d)(1).

quirements as other trademark applications, the PTO has identified several issues especially pertinent to domain name mark applications.

DOMAIN NAMES DON'T AUTOMATICALLY QUALIFY AS TRADEMARKS

In 1998, the PTO issued a decision stating that an attorney named Eilberg was not entitled to trademark protection for the domain name www.Eilberg.com because the term was not used as a unique identifier of the attorney's legal services.[9] The PTO found that even though the attorney's name also appeared on his business card, it didn't serve the function of a trademark. The PTO reasoned:

> [T]he asserted mark, as displayed on applicant's letterhead, does not function as a service mark identifying and distinguishing applicant's legal services and, as presented, is not capable of doing so. As shown, the asserted mark identifies applicant's Internet domain name, by use of which one can access applicant's Web site. In other words, the asserted mark WWW.EILBERG.COM merely indicates the location on the Internet where applicant's Web site appears. It does not separately identify applicant's legal services as such. *Cf. In re The Signal Companies, Inc.*, 228 USPQ 956 (TTAB 1986).

ADVERTISING ISN'T A SERVICE

The PTO Web site admonishes that some applicants have tried to register their domain names, arguing that their site provides the service of "providing information about [a particular field]." The PTO will not accept an application that attempts to register a domain name as a service mark when "specimens of use make it clear that the Web site merely advertises the applicant's own products or services."[10] In other words, businesses that create a Web site for the sole purpose of adver-

---

[9] See *In re Eilberg*, 49 USPQ2d 1955 (TTAB 1998).
[10] See *In re Reichhold Chemicals, Inc.*, 167 USPQ 376 (TTAB 1970); TMEP §1301.01(a)(ii).

tising their own products or services cannot register a domain name used to identify that activity as a service.

SURNAMES

Surnames are often used as domain names by attorneys, consultants, and other service providers. Surnames must meet special requirements to be registered as trademarks as discussed in chapter 5.

DESCRIPTIVENESS

A domain name can't be registered with the PTO if it's purely descriptive or generic. Descriptiveness won't preclude registration as a domain name, but neither the UDRP or ACPA standards offer you protection from cybersquatting, infringement, or confusing similarity if you're using a generic or purely descriptive term.

> **$$ BUSINESS TIP:** *The first company to register a common dictionary term that is not generic or purely descriptive often prevails in domain name disputes provided the company has a legitimate interest in the domain name and there is no evidence of bad faith.*

PART THREE

······································

Cashing In on Copyrights

CHAPTER 7 >>>>

Critical Copyright Concepts: What's Protected?

HAS ANYONE IN Hollywood been sued with more regularity than Steven Spielberg? It's amazing how many creative minds conceive story lines involving extraterrestrial beings, sharks snacking on sunbathers, and amusement parks with live dinosaurs.[1]

Fortunately for Mr. Spielberg, copyright law doesn't protect ideas and imaginings of the masses—only the "fixed," tangible expression of ideas. All aspiring writers cum litigants who sue Mr. Spielberg for copyright infringement must prove that significant portions of their actual manuscripts are substantially similar or equivalent to the successful motion picture, not merely about similar subjects.

---

[1] There are a number of reported cases involving Steven Spielberg movies. *Litchfield v. Spielberg*, 736 F.2d 1352 (9th Cir. 1984); *Zambito v. Paramount Pictures Corp.*, 613 F. Supp. 1107 (E.D.N.Y), aff'd 788 F.2d 2 (2d. Cir. 1985); *Williams v. Crichton*, 84 F. 3d 581 (2d Cir. 1996); *Chase-Riboud v. Dreamworks, Inc.*, 987 F. Supp. 1222 (C.D. Cal. 1997).

IN THIS CHAPTER YOU FIND OUT:

- What materials you can and cannot copyright

- How to control the use of your own original work product

- What you can safely and fairly use from the works of others

- What rights a copyright holder has

- How to get copyright protection for your work

- How long a copyright lasts

- About damages and penalties for infringement

URANTIA FOUNDATION IS an organization whose members believe in the teachings of nonhuman spiritual beings. These teachings are delivered through revelations made to a patient of a Chicago psychiatrist, Dr. Sadler. The psychiatric patient has assembled teachings in a book that the foundation duly copyrights and formally registers.

The foundation learns that one of its members, Kristen Maaherra, is distributing a computerized version of the book on disk.

The foundation sues Maaherra in the District Court of Arizona for infringing its copyright. Maaherra contends that the foundation's copyright is invalid because copyright laws do not protect works authored by nonhumans. The district court rules in favor of Maaherra, and the foundation appeals.

The appellate court opines the "threshold issue in this case is whether the work, because it is claimed to embody the words of celestial beings rather than human beings, is copyrightable at all." Ultimately, the appellate court holds the foundation is entitled to copyright protection because humans have "compiled" the teachings of the divine beings, and compilations qualify as original, copyrightable work under the law.[2]

As this case illustrates, copyrights protect a wide range of creative expression from a universe of sources. This chapter provides you with an overview of the legal bounds of protectable creative expression.

---

[2] *Urantia Foundation v. Maaherra*, 114 F. 3d 955 (9th Cir. 1997).

THE CORE OF COPYRIGHT: WHAT'S CREATIVE EXPRESSION?

It's not uncommon for multiple keen minds to independently come up with the same ingenious ideas or discoveries. But it's unlikely that two creators will express their ideas in exactly the same way. This is precisely why copyright law was never developed to protect ideas. Copyright protects the creative *expression* of ideas. It's not enough in a copyright infringement action to prove similarity of ideas; the litigant must prove that meaningful portions of the creative expression have been used without permission.

Ideas, concepts, methods, and processes are not subject to copyright protection. The current copyright statute clearly states, "In no case does copyright protection for an original work of authorship extend to any idea, procedure, process, system, method of operation, concept, principle, or discovery, regardless of the form in which it is described, explained, illustrated or embodied in such work." Ideas, processes, methods, and concepts are the purview of patent protection, while the works that express them are protected by copyright.[3]

> ⚖ **LAWYER'S NOTE:** *Copyright law recognizes that great minds think alike. The essence of copyright law is that it protects expression of ideas, not the ideas themselves.*

A recipe for chicken soup isn't subject to copyright protection. It's a method or process for creating the soup. Anyone is free to reproduce a list of ingredients and proportions for this popular dish. However, a written, descriptive work containing detailed textual instructions and original photographs of the soup is subject to copyright protec-

> ⚖ **LAWYER'S NOTE:** *The first step in determining whether material is of a type that can be copyrighted is whether it constitutes some form of expression. The law makes a clear distinction between what constitutes expression and what is an idea, process, method, concept, system, principle, or discovery that may be better suited to patent protection.*

---

[3] 17 U.S.C. Sec. 101 et. seq.

tion. Similarly, facts about a historical figure are not copyrightable, but a biography expressing them may be copyright protected.

ONLY THE "EXPRESSIVE ELEMENTS" GET PROTECTION

One of the most important copyright cases ever decided involved a field we don't usually associate with creativity: bookkeeping.

Baker v. Selden,[4] decided in 1879, is quoted in many recent decisions involving software. *Baker v. Selden* is the landmark case that attempted to draw the line between ideas and expression.

In *Baker v. Seldon*, the court considered an attempt to copyright accounting forms that are the basis of the double entry bookkeeping system. This well-known method is based on a system of debits in one column, offset by credits in the other. It's still used today, although it's more commonly implemented with a computer than a pencil. The litigation centered on some of the commonly used forms included in an accounting textbook. The textbook illustrated the forms and explained how to use them.

The court held that the textbook describing the method could be copyrighted, since it was an expression of ideas. No one could use the book without permission. However, the blank accounting forms and the accounting method itself could *not* be copyrighted because they were unprotectible ideas or processes.

This case has long since been cited for the proposition that copyright sifts out and protects elements of expression, separating them from other unprotectable elements that may be included in a work. In 1976, Congress clarified and codified the idea/expression distinction. Section 102(b) of the 1976 Copyright Act precludes copyright of "any idea, procedure, process, sys-

⚖️ **LAWYER'S NOTE:** *Many works contain both creative expressions, which are covered by copyright, and unprotectable information. Third parties can use the unprotected portions of the work without infringing on any copyright.*

---

[4] 101 U.S. 99 (1879).

tem, method of operation, concept, principle, or discovery."[5] In other words, copyright protects only the expressive, creative elements of a work and none of its functional aspects.

FACTS AREN'T COPYRIGHTABLE

Universal Studios has a long history of setting precedent in the copyright area. Fortunately for the studio, its lawyers usually manage to prevail.

In 1980, a writer named Hoehling sued Universal Studios for incorporating certain elements of his script into a motion picture screenplay.[6] It seems that Mr. Hoehling had come up with an interesting, original theory that the *Hindenburg,* a famous passenger-filled airship that burst into flames and crashed in 1937, was sabotaged.

The court in Mr. Hoehling's case determined that while Hoehling's book was a protectable work as a whole, certain facts, aspects, and ideas were not subject to copyright protection. Had the story been a work of total fiction, rather than an interpretation of historical facts, the lawsuit might have had a different outcome.

WHEN CAN YOU USE FACTS COMPILED IN OTHER WORKS?

You can copy your local telephone directory with impunity. This is because it's merely a listing of facts. Copyright case law dictates that no one can have a monopoly on facts or information. Otherwise, freedom of speech and press would be severely curtailed by copyright laws.

Authors can copyright only what they create. In *Feist v. Rural Telephone Services,*[7] the court held that listings in a telephone directory were not protectable because they represented listings of factual data. The court rejected a "sweat of the brow" standard pursuant to which the phone company argued that it had expended considerable effort and resources to compile the listings.

---

[5] 17 U.S.C. Sec. 101.
[6] *Hoehling v. Universal City Studios, Inc.,* 618 F.2d 972 (2d Cir.).
[7] 499 U.S. 340 (1991).

Subsequent courts have held that compilations of unprotectable elements, such as facts, may be protectable if the selection or arrangement exhibits sufficient creativity and originality.[8]

$$ BUSINESS TIP: *You can use the factual data contained in copyrighted works without obtaining specific permission. However, you are not entitled to copy a creative compilation or original method of expressing such facts.*

However, in *Feist,* the Supreme Court held that a mere alphabetical ordering does not rise to the level of a protectible arrangement. Hence no protection for phone books.

THE STORY LINE VERSUS THE SCRIPT: WHAT'S PROTECTED?

Judges deciding copyright cases have read thousands of books, plays, and manuscripts that allegedly infringe on other books, plays, and manuscripts.

Judge Learned Hand was considered by many to be the most brilliant judge ever sitting on the bench.[9] He's credited with some of the most prescient opinions ever written. (Any first-year law school student knows the name of Learned Hand.) However, it appears that even the renowned Judge Hand had trouble figuring out where to draw the line between ideas and expression; his two major decisions in this area seem to many lawyers to be contradictory.

In *Nichols vs. Universal Pictures Corp.,*[10] Judge Hand considered whether a motion picture, *The Cohens and the Kellys,* infringed on a hit play, *Abie's Irish Rose.* Both plots involved the intermarriage between Jewish and Catholic families and the ensuing animosity and reconcilia-

---

[8] See, e.g., *Atari Games Corp. v. Nintendo,* 975 F.2d 832 (Fed. Cir. 1992). (The arrangement of elements on a program interface may be copyrightable if they are sufficiently original and not dictated by function.)

[9] Judge Learned Hand (1872–1961) was a judge of the U.S. District Court for New York's Southern District (1909–1924) and of the federal Second Circuit Court of Appeals (1924–1951). He has often been referred to as the "tenth justice of the Supreme Court." During his distinguished career, Hand authored more than 2,000 opinions, which were often quoted in Supreme Court opinions and elucidated some of the nation's most important legal standards.

[10] 45 F.2d 119 (2d Cir. 1930).

tion of the families of the bride and groom. In *The Cohens and the Kellys,* Judge Hand held that "A comedy based on the conflicts between Irish and Jews into which the marriage of the children enters, is no more susceptible of copyright than the outline of *Romeo and Juliet.*"

Judge Hand's opinion in *Nichols* would certainly appear to clarify the standard, if not for the fact that he reached a seemingly opposite conclusion in a subsequent case six years later. In *Sheldon v. Metro-Goldwyn Pictures Corp.,*[11] Judge Hand got to watch the 1932 movie, *Letty Lynton,* starring Joan Crawford and Montgomery Clift. He had to decide whether the movie, produced by Metro-Goldwyn Pictures, infringed on yet another popular play having a similar story line. After viewing the flick, Judge Hand decided there was "parallelism" of the characters and events that made the movie substantially similar and thus an infringement of the copyrighted play.

> **$$ BUSINESS TIP:** *Since a general concept (such as plot or story line, or idea for a software application) is not entitled to copyright protection, it's a good idea to think about the detail in which you discuss your works in progress with potential competitors.*

Both the movie, *Letty Lynton,* and the play, *Dishonored Lady,* were based on actual historical events—an 1857 murder case in which the defendant, Madeline Smith, was acquitted of poisoning her former lover. In this case, Judge Hand decided that there was sufficient "parallelism" to constitute copyright infringement, despite the historical basis of both plotlines.

In yet another case, *Peter Pan Fabrics Inc. v. Martin Weiner Corp.,*[12] twenty-four years later, Judge Hand himself confessed the extreme difficulty of what constitutes an idea versus expression:

> The test for infringement of a copyright is of necessity vague. In the case of verbal "works" it is well settled that although the "proprietor's" monopoly extends beyond an exact reproduction of the

---

[11] 81 F.2d 49 (2d Cir. 1936).
[12] 274 F.2d 487 (2d Cir. 1960).

> **$$ BUSINESS TIP:** *A general idea for a story or plot is not copyrightable. However, if a script too closely resembles the twists and turns of the plotline of a copyrighted script, it will be deemed to infringe. Similarity of manuscripts is determined on a case-by-case basis.*

words, there can be no copyright in the "ideas" disclosed but only in their "expression." Obviously no principle can be stated as to when an imitator has gone beyond copying the "idea." And has borrowed its "expression." Decisions must therefore inevitably be ad hoc.

BASIC LEGAL REQUIREMENTS: ORIGINALITY AND FIXATION

If creativity knows no bounds, how does one define the scope of the law covering creativity?

The scope of exactly what is covered by copyright and how it is protected is in a constant state of evolution. The reach and parameters of copyright law change with each new technology, whether it is movable type printing presses, sound recordings, or the Internet.

Copyright has a specific constitutional basis. The first copyright statute was passed in 1790 and applied to books, maps, and charts. In the past 214 years, this statutory protection has stretched, evolved, and metamorphosed into protection sufficient to cover things our forefathers literally could not have imagined, such as digital recordings and software.

The current copyright law covers books, dramatic and choreographed works, music, sound recordings, photographs, sculpture, architecture, movies, computer programs, and other modern day forms of expression.[13]

The copyright statute decrees:

Copyright protection subsists, in accordance with this title, in original works of authorship fixed in any tangible medium of expres-

---

[13] 17 U.S.C. Secs. 101–107.

sion, now known or later developed, from which they can be perceived, reproduced, or otherwise communicated, wither directly or with the aid of a machine or device.

Throughout the historical development of copyright, two criteria have remained constant. Copyrighted works must be both original and "fixed" in a "tangible medium of expression."

DEFINING ORIGINALITY: WHY IS ENGRAVING DIFFERENT THAN A PHOTOGRAPH?

The originality requirement is actually pretty low, once you've established that your work is expressive rather than utilitarian or factual. Sometimes the element of originality isn't even apparent to the naked eye (or ear).

In 1951, the Second Circuit Court of Appeals was called upon to decide whether an engraving of a famous painting, Gainsborough's *Blue Boy* was sufficiently original to be copyright protected.

Alfred Bell & Co. was an engraving company that made special mezzotint engravings of works of several paintings by old masters, such as Gainsborough. Another company, Cantalda Fine Arts, made lithograph prints of the engravings, since they could not gain access to the original paintings through the museum.

Cantalda probably figured the lithograph was, after all, just a copy of a copy of a painting that was in the public domain. (Public domain works include those for which copyright protection has expired.)

Alfred Bell & Co. sued Cantalda Fine Arts Company, claiming copyright protection for its engraving of the *Blue Boy* painting.[14]

Ultimately, the Court of Appeals held that the engravings were entitled to copyright protection. Engraving was viewed as a skilled craft that required numerous creative decisions; no two engravings were identical. For example, techniques of pulling the engraving tools across the paper determined how closely the engraving emulated the texture of the original painting.

---

[14] *Alfred Bell & Co. v. Cantalda Fine Arts, Inc.*, 191 F. 2d 99 (2d Cir. 1951).

The *Alfred Bell* court held that originality, for purposes of federal copyright law, means that "the particular work 'owes its origin' to the 'author.' No large measure of novelty is necessary." The court went on to explain:

"A copyist's bad eyesight or defective musculature, or a shock caused by a clap of thunder, may yield sufficiently distinguishable variations. Having hit upon such a variation unintentionally, the 'author' may adopt it as his and copyright it."

In the *Alfred Bell* case, it's important to recognize that the *Blue Boy* painting itself was in the public domain. The public domain is a term for creative works that may be used freely by the public, usually because the term of the copyright protection has expired. This is why the only issue of the case was whether the engraving met the standard for originality and not whether it was an infringing work.

The threshold for originality established by the *Alfred Bell* case has been left intact by subsequent decisions over the past fifty years. In 1999, Bridgman Art Inc. sued Corel for reproducing its photo transparencies of public domain paintings held by a number of museums.

True to the standard enunciated in the *Alfred Bell* case, the court held for Corel on the issue of originality. The court held that Corel had not infringed Bridgman's copyright, because the photographs of works of art could not be the subject of any copyright protection. The court held there was no element of creativity in simply taking a straight-on photograph of a public domain work of art.[15]

⚖️ **LAWYER'S NOTE:** *Once a creator has established that his or her work constitutes a protectable form of expression, the standard for establishing originality is relatively liberal.*

THE REQUIREMENT OF FIXATION

"How do I protect my sighting of Elvis?"

This is one of the Frequently Asked Questions listed on the Web site for the U.S. Copyright Office.

The Copyright Office provides the following answer:

---

[15] *Bridgeman Art v. Corel, Inc.,* 36 F. Supp. 2d 191 (S.D. N. Y. 1999).

Copyright law does not protect sightings. However, copyright law will protect your photo (or other depiction) of your sighting of Elvis. Just send it to us with a form VA application and the $30 filing fee. No one can lawfully use your photo of your sighting, although someone else may file his own photo of his sighting. Copyright law protects the original photograph, not the subject of the photograph.

The reason that the Elvis sighting must be memorialized is the statutory requirement that a work must be "fixed" in some sort of tangible form in order to be protected. The fixation requirement is met when the sighting is memorialized by a photograph.

The copyright statute provides:

A work is "fixed" in a tangible medium of expression when its embodiment in a copy or phonorecord, by or under the authority of the author, is sufficiently permanent or stable to permit it to be perceived, reproduced, or otherwise communicated for a period of more than transitory duration. A work consisting of sounds, images, or both, that are being transmitted, is "fixed" for purposes of this title if a fixation of the work is being made simultaneously with its transmission.

To our forefathers, the statutory requirement of fixation in a "tangible medium" likely would have involved quill pens or laborious movable type printing. To our generation, it involves PCs, images, and text accessed on the Internet and mega bookstores with massive distribution outlets.

Congress, in enacting the 1976 version of the federal copyright law, was well aware that the term *fixation* would mean different things in different technological eras. The Conference Committee charged with drafting the new law specifically commented on the scope of what might constitute fixation presently and in the future under the act. The committee stated, "[I]t makes no difference what the form, manner or medium of fixation might be—whether it is words, numbers, notes, sounds, pictures, or any other graphic or symbolic indicia, whether embodied in a physical object in written, printed, photographic, sculptural, punched, magnetic or any other stable form."

Congress wisely recognized the need for copyright law to keep up with new technology. The committee expressly included within the scope of works meeting the fixation requirement "those capable of perception directly or by means of any machine or device 'now known or later developed.'" This language would seem to include even the most innovative technologies science fiction writers can envision.

⚖ LAWYER'S NOTE: *Copyright law specifically recognizes technologies that do not yet exist but that may exist in the future and be capable of recording and fixating creative work products.*

GETTING COPYRIGHT PROTECTION FOR YOUR WORK

What exactly do you need to do to get copyright protection for your work? Absolutely nothing!

COPYRIGHT PROTECTION IS AUTOMATIC

Copyright protection is free, and it's automatic. The Web site for the U.S. Copyright Office, located at www.copyright.gov, explains, "Your work is under copyright protection the moment it is created and fixed in a tangible form so that it is perceptible either directly or with the aid of a machine or device."

USING THE © SYMBOL

These formalities are now optional, since copyright protection is truly automatic. This wasn't always the case.

Prior to 1989, to secure copyright protection in the U.S., authors had to place a copyright notice on published copies. The notice, as you may recall, consisted of the word or abbreviation for the word *copyright* or the symbol ©. These requirements were liberalized by the 1976 revision of the Copyright Act and abandoned altogether in 1989 to fall into line with European nations.

As a condition of joining the highly desirable Berne International Copyright Convention, the U.S. had to abandon all formal requirements for copyright protection. European countries did not require formal registration, and the U.S. insistence on formalities was perceived as inequitable. Europeans wondered why Americans should be afforded instant rights in their countries, while they had to comply with seemingly complex

CAUTION: *While registering and designating your work with the © symbol are now optional formalities, these measures are strongly recommended to expand and protect your rights, as discussed in chapter 10.*

formal registration requirements to be afforded similar protections in the United States. The presumed unfamiliarity with American laws and institutions also furthered the perception that European writers and artists were subject to a U.S. home court advantage when it came to obtaining protections.

Currently, in the United States, registration is considered optional, because it doesn't affect your rights in work that's subject to copyright. However, the registration process becomes very important if you actually want to sue someone.

The law provides that in order to bring an action for copyright infringement, you need to comply with the registration process. Section 411 of the 1976 Copyright Act specifically provides that registration is a prerequisite for bringing an infringement action. The basic registration currently costs $30, and the forms are available on-line. This optional registration process is covered in more detail in chapter 10.

Courts vary in their positions as to whether the copyright registration process must be completed, or merely initiated, before a lawsuit will be entertained. In some circuits, merely filing an application is sufficient. Further, the statute provides that if your application is rejected, you can still sue by serving proper notice on the copyright office.

THE RIGHTS YOU GET WITH A COPYRIGHT

Copyright protection is a great deal in life. Not only is it free and automatic, it confers an impressive array of benefits.

Once your work is eligible for copyright, it's entitled to a range of rights conferred by U.S. statutes and international treaties. The economic value of the following rights, of course, depends upon the commercial viability of the work itself.

MAKING COPIES

The exclusive right to profit from copies of your own work product is the essence of copyright protection. The original copyright statute, passed in 1790, dealt only with "reprinting." Today, the law confers upon the copyright holder the exclusive right to "reproduce" the copyrighted work, regardless of the method or medium.

DISTRIBUTION

The drafters of the original copyright statute did not envision the huge global distribution networks we take for granted today; they certainly could not have had Amazon.com or Blockbuster video in mind.

The Copyright Act of 1790 recognized the exclusive right to "publishing and vending." The current federal statute confers "exclusive rights . . . to distribute copies of phono records of the copyrighted work to the public by sale, or other transfer of ownership, or by rental, lease or lending."

This broad distribution right, which includes the right to import and export works to other countries, is subject to a very significant limitation called the first sale doctrine, which is discussed in chapter 8.

DERIVATIVE WORKS

Derivative works are creative works that are derived from *other* creative works. An example of a derivative work is a screenplay based on a novel. Derivative works, made with proper authorization (or based on public domain works), acquire their own separate copyright protection. For example, a translation of a novel can be copyrighted separately from the original work. However, if the translator failed to obtain appropriate permission to the original work, there would be no copyright protection. The creator of the derivative work could be enjoined from distributing the derivative work on the basis of copyright infringement.

The current copyright statute grants the copyright holder the exclusive right to make a "translation, musical arrangement, dramatization, fictionalization, motion picture version, sound recording, art reproduction, abridgment, condensation or other form in which a work may be recast, transformed or adapted."

PUBLIC PERFORMANCE: DO GIRL SCOUT CAMP SING ALONGS VIOLATE COPYRIGHT?

If you hold a copyright to a type of work that's normally performed, such as music or drama, you have the right to control who performs it. Copyright protection extends to performance of a tune at a wedding, music played in an elevator, and even Girl Scout sing alongs.

The origin of this right is an interesting case involving a 1920s hit song called "Sweethearts" from an opera by Victor Herbert. Mr. Herbert was strolling down the street and happened to hear an orchestra playing his work in a sidewalk café. Although Herbert had received handsome royalties from theatrical presentations, he wasn't getting a penny from the restaurant orchestra.

Mr. Herbert decided to test the limits of copyright protection and filed suit against the restaurant. The restaurant argued the performance was not for profit, since it didn't charge a separate cover charge for the music. Mr. Herbert took his case all the way up to the Supreme Court and ultimately prevailed.[16]

Courts subsequently had no trouble finding a wide variety of public performances were "for profit," even though the music might be merely incidental or even coincidental to the main performance. In 1922, the court held that music accompanying a silent movie was subject to copy-

---

[16] *Herbert v. Shanley*, 242 U.S. 591 (1917).

right. Copyright protection was extended to music in bars and shopping malls. Music played on the radio was supposedly distributed for free, but arguably its sponsors expected to profit.

This line of judicial reasoning had unintended consequences over the next five decades. The Copyright Act of 1976 inexplicably dropped the reference to "for profit" from the statutory language, adding instead a list of specific exemptions intended to cover specific types of not-for-profit performances. In a public relations fiasco, the American Society of Composers, Authors and Publishers (ASCAP) sent letters to the Girl Scouts and summer camps across the country, asking them to pay modest fees for music performed at the camps.[17] After an explosion of negative publicity, ASCAP quietly withdrew its request.

PUBLIC DISPLAY

Analogous to the right of public performance is the right of public display. This right was specifically recognized by the Copyright Act of 1976, which places strict limitations on what purchasers may do with copies of art they've purchased. The act provides that purchasers of such work may display artwork "either directly or by the projection of no more than one image at a time, to viewers present where the copy is located."

In plain English, this means that you may display your purchased copy of a work in a public forum, but you cannot make multiple copies for display or broadcast the image or sound to other locations without the permission of the copyright owner.

ATTRIBUTION AND INTEGRITY

Just because someone acquires other rights to your copyrighted work doesn't mean they're permitted to represent the work as their own. The work should still be attributed to you, the original creator.

The United States specifically recognized the rights of attribution

---

[17] See, e.g., "The Birds May Sing, But Campers Can't Unless They Pay Up," by Lisa Bannon, *The Wall Street Journal*, August 23, 1996.

and integrity in 1990, to con-
form with similar rights already
afforded in European countries.

⚖️ **LAWYER'S NOTE:** *The right of attribution is the right to have your name associated with your work, and it exists independently of other rights you may transfer or assign.*

The right of integrity is the
right to avoid having your work
demeaned by use in a manner
that compromises its integrity.
For example, if you have painted
a portrait of a public figure, it might undermine the integrity of your
work if someone were to display the image of the subject's head atop a
naked torso.

The rights of attribution and integrity in the United States are fairly
limited, extending only to certain works of fine art that exist in single
copies or in signed, numbered, limited editions of less than two hundred
copies.

SOUND RECORDING AND BOOTLEGGING

Benjamin Franklin, one of the original drafters of the copyright statute,
never attended a rock concert, let alone had the opportunity to download Napster. So it's not surprising that live musical performances were
not extended copyright protection until 1994.

In 1994, as part of its treaty obligations as a member of the World
Trade Organization, Congress passed a special provision protecting
performers against unauthorized bootleg tapes of their performances.
The performers themselves have the right to record and distribute
recordings of their performances.

THE RIGHT TO ENCRYPT AND ENCODE

The Digital Millennium Copyright Act, passed in 1998, helps copyright
holders help themselves.

If copyright holders protect their work by using special computer
code to prevent unauthorized access, it is illegal for third parties to circumvent that protection. Copyright holders can also embed information that allows them to identify their work and track unauthorized
usage. The act makes it illegal to circumvent these protections.

HOW LONG DO COPYRIGHTS LAST?

Artists found a political friend in the late Sonny Bono.

Sonny Bono, holder of a number of copyrights to hit songs of the early '70s, proposed some legislation that clearly reflected his own concerns and those of his fellow artists.

The Sonny Bono Copyright Term Extension Act, signed into law on October 27, 1998, generally extended the duration of copyright protection an additional twenty years. Additionally, the 1976 Copyright Act makes a sharp distinction between works created before and after 1978.

WORKS CREATED AND PUBLISHED AFTER JANUARY 1, 1978

For works created after January 1, 1978, copyright protection lasts for the life of the author plus an additional 70 years. For jointly created works, the term lasts for 70 years after the last surviving author's death. For anonymous and pseudonymous works and works made for hire, the term is 95 years from the year of first publication or 120 years from the year of creation, whichever expires first.

FOR WORKS CREATED BUT NOT PUBLISHED PRIOR TO 1978

For works created but not published or registered before January 1, 1978, copyright protection lasts for the life of the author plus seventy years, but in no case will it expire earlier than December 31, 2002. If the work is published before December 31, 2002, the term will not expire before December 31, 2047.

PRE-1978 WORKS

For pre-1978 works still in their original or renewal term of copyright, the total term is extended to 95 years from the date that copyright was originally secured. The status of public domain works was not affected by the Sonny Bono Act.

RECOURSE FOR RIP-OFFS:
PENALTIES FOR COPYRIGHT INFRINGEMENT

Not all surprises are pleasant. There's nothing more disconcerting to an artist, writer, or designer than seeing their hard work in a place they never expected to find it or intended to put it. And worse yet, someone else (whom they probably don't even know) may be making money off his or her efforts.

What can you get in a court of law if it happens to you?

DAMAGES: ACTUAL AND STATUTORY

The remedy of choice for most aggrieved copyright holders is money. Courts can go about awarding monetary damages in two ways: actual or statutory.

ACTUAL DAMAGES

Actual damages are on losses actually incurred such as lost sales, lost value of the copyright, and so forth. You must prove you incurred them. This can be messy, since if you knew what they were, they wouldn't be "lost."

STATUTORY DAMAGES

Statutory damages need not be specifically proved. Section 504 of the 1976 Copyright Act provides:

> [F]or all infringements involved in the action, with respect to any one work, for which any one infringer is liable individually, or for which two or more infringers are liable jointly and severally, in a sum of not less than $750 or more than $30,000 as the court considers just.

Section 504(c) (1) of the act provides that in cases of willful infringement, the court may increase the damages award beyond the

$30,000 limit, up to $150,000. *Willfulness* means the infringer has acted with "actual knowledge or reckless disregard for whether its conduct infringed upon the plaintiff's copyright."[18]

It's interesting to take a look at how the courts apply this statute. In *Universal Studios Inc., v. Ahmed*[19] the court had to decide the amount of statutory damages to award to Universal Studios for unauthorized videotapes of the movie *Jurassic Park II* that the defendant was selling less than a week after the movie hit the theaters. The court had no problem finding the defendant's conduct willful based on the circumstances. But this didn't mean the court automatically awarded damages in excess of $20,000, which was the limit then in effect. Instead, the court said that in the absence of an evidentiary hearing, a plaintiff was required to present sufficiently detailed affidavits to permit the court to apply the appropriate factors in awarding damages in excess of $20,000.

Universal Studios argued that it should receive $50,000 for each unauthorized tape. The studio's logic was "that the average price of a movie ticket is $7.50 . . . [and] each [counterfeit] film could be viewed on a daily basis by 25 (or more) people times 365." The studio argued the resulting loss would be "$60,937.50 for each one copy of the film in a year."

The court decided this was a stretch and interpreted the amount in the statute to apply to each work infringed, not each individual copy of the tape. It held Universal could recover $50,000 jointly, from all of the codefendants, and not a separate award from each infringing defendant. The court quoted Congressional hearings for the statute, in interpreting Congressional intent. "A single infringer of a single work is liable for a single amount . . . no matter how many acts of infringement are involved in the action, and regardless of whether the acts were separate, isolated, or occurred in a related series. . . ."[20] Thus, it would appear to be the law of the land that, when it comes to copyright infringement, it's one damage award per customer, no matter how many copies or codefendants.

[18] *Original Appalachian Artworks, Inc. v. J.F. Reichert, Inc.,* 658 F. Supp. 458, 464 (E.D. Pa 1987).
[19] United States District Court, E.D. Pennsylvania 1993, 29 U.S.P.Q.2D (BNA) 1775.
[20] H.R. Rep. No. 1476, 94th Cong. 2d Sess. 161.

INJUNCTIONS

An *injunction* is a court order directing a party to stop doing something, such as selling merchandise that infringes on a copyright. The copyright statute authorizes both temporary and permanent injunctions.[21]

> ⚖️ **LAWYER'S NOTE:** *Statutory damages provide from $750 to $30,000 per work infringed, or up to $150,000 if the infringement is shown to be willful.*

To obtain a *preliminary,* or *temporary* injunction against an infringer pending the outcome of a trial, you're required to prove likelihood that you will ultimately be successful on the merits of your lawsuit for infringement. You must also show that you will be irreparably harmed if the court doesn't order the infringers to stop what they're doing. As a practical matter, the courts will issue an order for a preliminary injunction if you can show you have met the basic evidentiary standards to show infringement (called a prima facie case).[22]

If you're successful at trial, the court will issue a permanent injunction if there is a threat of continued violations by the defendant.

SEIZURE OF THE INFRINGING MERCHANDISE

> **$$ BUSINESS TIP:** *Even a temporary injunction can be a real legal coup; the disruption it causes can be all it takes to drive the infringer out of business.*

Copyright law also allows you to go in and seize infringing merchandise, subject to a court order. The statute provides:

At any time while an action under this title is pending, the court may order the impounding, on such terms as it may deem reasonable, of all copies or phonorecords claimed to have been made or used in violation of the copyright owner's exclusive rights, and of all plates, molds, matrices, masters, tapes, film negatives, or other

---

[21] Se. 502(a).
[22] *Bourne Co. v. Tower Records, Inc.,* 976 F.2d 99, 101 (2d Cir. 1992).

articles by means of which such copies or phonorecords may be re-produced.[23]

As the statute indicates, it's up to the court to specify what can be seized, who gets to grab it, and what to do with it once it's confiscated.

WHAT'S THE REAL PURPOSE OF COPYRIGHT PROTECTION?

Technology is clearly the tail that wags the copyright dog. Copyright is an area of law that is under constant construction.

The Supreme Court attempts to apply existing law to a new technology, and the American public often deems the result of applying the present law to new technology imperfect or even undesirable. Congress has historically stepped in to change the law and pass new legislation calculated to protect creators while leaving the horizon wide open for future advancements.

---

[23] 17 U.S.C. Sec. 503.

CHAPTER 8 >>>>

Limitations on Copyright Protection

IT USED TO be that an infringer had to go to a lot of trouble to copy someone's work and distribute it. Now, all it takes is a mouse click to create a mass mailing, and it costs virtually nothing to publicly display your work on a Web site. Someone can even parody or criticize your work, your business, or your persona on a Web site, mass E-mailing, or in a traditionally published format. Such an appropriation may be deemed "fair use." Copyright infringement is difficult to police in an electronic age, and concepts of free speech and fair use may legally trump your right to control your copyrighted work product.

IN THIS CHAPTER YOU FIND OUT:

- What to do if someone claims they thought of your idea first
- What constitutes "fair use" of copyrighted material for educational purposes
- Why works that are purely "useful" can't be copyrighted

- Why it may not be copyright infringement if you publicly spoof or make fun of someone's work

- Why you can rent a movie DVD and not a music CD

IN 1998, A dramatic sequel of sorts, involving the epic novel Gone With the Wind, *published more than fifty years before, is played out in the courtroom of the Eleventh Circuit Court of Appeals.*

The plaintiff, SunTrust, is the trustee of the estate of Margaret Mitchell, and as the legal representative, holds the copyright to Gone With the Wind.[1] *The defendant, Alice Randall, is the author of a book called* The Wind Done Gone, *which admittedly uses scenes and characters from* Gone With the Wind.

Ms. Randall's publisher, Houghton Mifflin, also a defendant, argues that the doctrine of fair use protects The Wind Done Gone *because it's a parody of* Gone With the Wind *and a critique of* Gone With the Wind's *depiction of slavery and the Civil War era American South. Ms. Randall explains it was necessary to appropriate characters, plot, and major scenes for the first half of* The Wind Done Gone. *The court rejects the defendants' argument and rules that the* Gone With the Wind *copyright has been infringed and that the defendant must pay substantial damages from the sale and publication of the book.*

Copyright laws are intended to champion creativity but are subject to limits intended to walk a tightrope between fostering innovative expression and creating monopolies on ideas.

LIMITATION #1:
THE DOCTRINE OF INDEPENDENT CREATION

Movie producers generally return unsolicited manuscripts they receive in their morning mail unopened. They want to avoid as many copyright infringement claims as possible, recognizing that any hit movie is inevitably going to produce some claims of infringement. Even unsuccessful claims cost time and money to defend.

---

[1] *SunTrust Bank v. Houghton Mifflin Co.*, 136 F. Supp. 2d 1357, 1364 (N.D. Ga. 2001), vacated, 252 F.3d 1165 (11th Cir. 2001).

The doctrine of independent creation protects work that is independently developed but turns out to be coincidentally similar to copyrighted work. Independent creation is often a core defense in infringement suits.

More than one aspiring writer has decided, independently, to portray the life of Sally Hemings, the slave with whom Thomas Jefferson is said to have had an affair and several illegitimate children. So long as each of these writers develops their manuscripts independently, they are entitled to copyright protection. Sally Hemings's historical persona is not subject to copyright protection. However, each completed manuscript is an expression of that idea, and as such, is copyrightable work.

> **$$ BUSINESS TIP:** *If you ever decide to write a screenplay, locate a reputable literary agent to contact the movie production companies on your behalf. Otherwise, your manuscript is likely to be returned unread.*

Because of the doctrine of independent creation, the movie producer who returns an unread manuscript is in a much better position to defend against an infringement action should he or she produce a movie having a vaguely similar plotline. The idea of a cute alien befriended by a child is an *idea* for anyone to pursue. The completed manuscript is an expression protectable by copyright law.

THE ISSUE OF ACCESS

The return of unopened manuscripts would seem a bit paranoid, if not for the fact that access is a factor upon which many court decisions turn.

The doctrine of independent creation is usually a pretty successful defense if the defendant who is being sued can prove he or she didn't have access to view the work that's allegedly been copied. On the other hand, if the alleged infringer did have access to the copyrighted work, it's a more difficult defense upon which to prevail.

Even if a later work is substantially similar to a previously copyrighted work, the effective presumption is that such works were independently created. A finding that the works are so similar that it's implausible they were independently created can rebut this presumption.

INDEPENDENTLY INSPIRED OR BLATANT KNOCKOFFS?

If you take a black-and-white photo of the Grand Canyon or a redwood forest, are you infringing on Ansel Adams's copyright? If you photograph your infant in cute costumes resembling flowers and vegetables, are you infringing Anne Geddes's copyright, since she is famous for such photos? Maybe so, depending on your access to the prior work and the level of similarity of distinctive, creative aspects of the photo.

In 1982, a photographer named John Duke Kisch took a photograph of a woman holding a musical instrument (a concertina) and standing in front of a mural at a famous nightclub, the Village Vanguard, in New York. The angle at which the photo was shot and the lighting were very distinctive.

In 1985, another photographer, Perry Ogden, decided to photograph a different musician, holding a saxophone, in front of the same mural using the same angle and lighting. Ogden argued that the photos were different: his photo depicted a male performer holding a saxophone. The Kisch photo depicted a woman with a concertina. The court held, however, that the similarity of the angles, lighting, and the use of the same corner of the nightclub was an unmistakable effort to reproduce the effect of the Kisch photo, resulting in a decision of infringement.[2] The court found for the plaintiff and assessed damages.

ACCESS TO POPULAR SONGS: THE ESSENTIAL MUSICAL KERNEL

In 1962, the Chiffons had a popular radio hit entitled "He's So Fine." Eight years later, George Harrison hit the top ten charts with "My Sweet Lord." Then he got hit with an infringement suit.

When you listen to the two songs, the similarities are so apparent you wonder why someone didn't take poor George aside in the recording studio and suggest to him there might be a problem. The reviewing court concluded that the copying was probably unconscious and inadvertent. However, it was, unmistakably, copying.

Each song consisted of three notes repeated four times ("He's so

2 *Kisch v. Ammirati & Puris, Inc.* (S.D.N.Y., 657 F. Supp 380) (1987).

fine" or "My sweet Lord") followed by a series of five notes repeated three or four times ("Don't know how I'm gonna do it" or "I really want to see you"). Although the repetitions had a varied number of beats, the court found that these differences were because "different words and number of syllables were involved. This necessitated modest alterations in the repetitions or the places of beginning a phrase, which, however, has nothing to do whatsoever with the essential musical kernel that is involved."

The court seemed to base its decisions on the overall impact of the songs. The court found some notes had greater impact than others and that these formed the "essential musical kernel."[3] Harrison was forced to pay damages to the plaintiff and continuing royalties for the right to publicly perform the song.

LIMITATION #2: THE UTILITY DOCTRINE

The most useful innovations of our time are not subject to copyright protection—precisely because they are useful. The concept of utilitarian function, as it has been dubbed by some legal and academic commentators, prevents the copyright of any functional aspects of an expressive work. Only the expressive aspects can be copyrighted.

WHY CAN'T YOU COPYRIGHT USEFUL THINGS?

Giving protection to ideas would allow a copyright holder to enjoy a virtual monopoly on a topic. It would also allow people who express or memorialize methods and processes to circumvent the relatively lengthy and rigorous patent process (described in part 4 of this book). Allowing the first person who expresses methods, processes, facts, and ideas to copyright them would confer exclusive rights without regard to who actually figures out how to implement the methods or processes in practical ways society can use.

---

[3] *Bright Tunes Music Corp. v. Harrisongs Music, Ltd.*, 420 F. Supp. 177 (S.D.N.Y. 1976) aff'd, *ABKCO Music Inc. v. Harrisongs Music, Ltd.*, 722 F2d. 988 (2d Cir. 1983).

The doctrine of utility also makes a lot of sense when you consider the relatively low standard of what's afforded protection under copyright law and the high standard of "novelty" that applies in patent cases.

WHEN THE DOCTRINE APPLIES

The doctrine of utility most often comes into play when the subject of the copyright is a pictorial or sculptural work. This is an area where it's particularly hard to separate expressive artistry from functionality. The statute, in a clear-as-mud fashion, specifically addresses the difference between protectible expression and unprotected functionality:

> "Pictorial, graphic, and sculptural works". . . shall include works of artistic craftsmanship insofar as their form but not their mechanical or utilitarian aspects are concerned; the design of a useful article, as defined in this section, shall be considered a pictorial, graphic or sculptural work only if, and only to the extent that, such design incorporates pictorial, graphic, or sculptural features that can be identified separately from, and are capable of existing independently of, the utilitarian aspects of the article.[4]

The doctrine of utility can have strange applications when it comes to designs involving drawings or plans—for example for a dress, a building, or the pedestal chair shown in Figure 8-1.

Drawings and plans are copyrightable; no one can copy them since the drawings are creative works or are clearly expressions of an idea. However, it may *not* be infringement for someone else to simply produce the *items*, if the items themselves are useful and not necessarily creative.

---

[4] 17 U.S.C. Sec. 101 and Sec. 113.

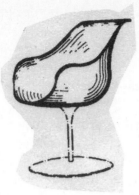

FIGURE 8-1: *Eero Saarinen pedestal chair: Is it functional or expressive?*

BLURRING THE LINE BETWEEN THE USEFUL AND THE EXPRESSIVE

The line between patent and copyright protections is supposed to be clear-cut, but it's not. Attorneys' arguments as to why one and not the other applies can be as creative as the material they're hired to protect.

The doctrine of utility has been the subject of considerable criticism in the United States, because European countries don't specifically have statutes to invoke it. This gives European competitors an advantage in foreign markets, because their designs may be more fully protected.

Congress has passed two specific copyright exceptions to the doctrine of utility. In 1990, legislation was passed to protect architectural works, and in 1998, boat hull designs were specifically afforded protection. This means that these types of works can now be copyrighted, even though it's not possible to separate their functional and artistic elements.

More importantly, the line seems to be moving in from the patent side, with patent law beginning to encroach on what has previously been the exclusive domain of copyright. As explained in chapter 11, certain ornamental aspects of a design can now be patented. Mr. Saarinen received a design patent on his pedestal chair in 1958, which afforded him the exclusive right to produce the chair, and the right to collect damages from the manufacturers who had been producing the infringing chairs[5] Design patents have subsequently been used to pro-

---

[5] U.S.P.T.O. Des. 181,945 (January 21, 1958).

tect ornamental aspects, ranging from bottles to belt buckles to architectural configurations.

LIMITATION #3: THE DOCTRINE OF FAIR USE

Copyright laws are intended to promote creativity, not to foreclose future creations by granting minimonopolies on ideas. Fair use is a safe harbor for artists and innovators that allows them to use portions of protected materials in specific ways. It protects users from getting slapped with a copyright suit exercising their First Amendment rights.

THE FAIR USE STATUTE

Fair use is a culmination of two centuries of case law that Congress rolled into Section 107 of the Copyright Act of 1976.

This statute is incredibly flexible or incredibly vague, depending on your perspective and how you want to invoke it. The term *fair use* is never specifically defined. Instead, it's sort of parameterized by a listing of examples of uses that may be permissible, followed by a list of factors to help you decide whether the examples apply.

The relevant text of the statute is as follows (with emphasis added):

§ 107. LIMITATIONS ON EXCLUSIVE RIGHTS: FAIR USE

Notwithstanding the provisions of sections 106 and 106A, the fair use of a copyrighted work, including such use by reproduction in copies or phonorecords or by any other means specified by that section, for **purposes such as criticism, comment, news reporting, teaching (including multiple copies for classroom use), scholarship, or research**), is not an infringement of copyright. In determining whether the use made of a work in any particular case is a fair use the factors to be considered shall include—

(1) the purpose and character of the use, including whether such use is of a **commercial nature or is for nonprofit educational** purposes;

(2) the **nature of the copyrighted** work;

(3) the **amount** and substantiality of the portion **used** in relation to the copyrighted work as a whole; and

(4) the **effect** of the use upon the **potential market** for or value of the copyrighted work.

The fact that a work is unpublished shall not itself bar a finding of fair use if such finding is made upon consideration of all the above factors.

THE FOUR FACTOR TEST: INTERPRETING THE FAIR USE STATUTE

The four factors outlined in the fair use statute above are a legal litmus test the courts use to determine what is and isn't fair use.

Sometimes an alleged infringer can make a pretty good case on some of the factors but will fall short on one or two others. Courts have the discretion to decide how much weight to give each factor and which factors carry the most weight.

The following guidelines for considering each factor are derived from the cases discussed in this chapter.

• **Noncommercial use is favored.** Copying and using a work for commercial purposes is more likely to be viewed as an infringement than copying and using the same work for noncommercial purposes, such as copying a cartoon to make your kid a T-shirt.

• **Creativity is protected more than factual work.** The more creative a work is, the greater the protection it enjoys. The more factual the work, the less protection it receives.

• **Both the amount and significance of copied material count.** Not only the amount of copying but the significance of the particular material copied is a factor. For example, co-opting the opening line from a *Tale of Two Cities* or *Moby-Dick* may be viewed as significant. Similarly, a few key lines of computer code from a lengthy program can be a major transgression if it's an essential algorithm.

• **Destroying the value of copyrighted work is frowned upon.** A parody or commentary is generally fair use, but associating Mickey Mouse with drug use or prostitution may tarnish the value of the original copyrighted work. This factor may weigh against the argument that co-opting the cartoon is fair use.

HUSTLER MAGAZINE V. THE MORAL MAJORITY: APPLYING THE FOUR FACTORS

In a maneuver showing more legal savvy than taste, *Hustler* magazine sued the Moral Majority, ironically playing the role of an aggrieved plaintiff. Although the interesting arguments brought by *Hustler* ultimately did not prevail, the case resulted in a very thoughtful judicial decision applying the four statutory factors and some pretty provocative dissents.[6]

In 1983 *Hustler* magazine published a parody featuring the Reverend Jerry Falwell, the well-known fundamentalist minister. The parody featured the Reverend Falwell describing the "first time" he had sex as occurring in an outhouse with his mother and saying that he always gets "sloshed" before sermons. At the bottom of the page in small print was the disclaimer, "ad parody—not to be taken seriously."

In an outraged response to the parody, the Moral Majority, Inc., an ultraconservative political lobbying group, sent out two mailings signed by Falwell. The first mailing went out to about 500,000 of the organization's members. The mailing described the parody and contained an impassioned plea for contributions to fund a lawsuit against *Hustler* to help Falwell "defend his mother's memory." The second mailing went out to 29,600 major donors and included "a copy of the parody with eight of the most offensive words blackened out."

Three days after the second mailing, Old Time Gospel Hour, a corporate sponsor, mailed a similar solicitation to 75,000 supporters including a complete copy of the parody. The organization received about $620,000 within about a week.

Realizing the impact that the parody had on his supporters, Falwell

---

[6] *Hustler Magazine, Inc. v. Moral Majority, Inc.*, 796 F.2d 1148 (9th Circuit 1986).

decided to display the parody on one of his nationwide television sermons. The amount of donations received from the broadcast was never disclosed. *Hustler* promptly sued the Moral Majority for copyright infringement.

The district court found in favor of the Moral Majority, and the appellate court affirmed, carefully applying the four factors outlined in Section 107 of the Copyright Act.

Factor #1: Purpose, Character, and Commercial Nature

There was no question the Moral Majority distributed copies of *Hustler*'s work with an intent to profit from a financial appeal. The court noted that the Moral Majority did in fact profit handsomely as the result of its appeal, raising almost a million dollars.

However, the court went on to find that "even though commercial purpose is a factor that weighs against fair use, the characteristics are at least equally important in making a fair-use analysis." Although the primary purpose of reproducing the parody was to raise money, the court recognized that the Moral Majority also "used the copies to rebut a personal attack on Falwell and make a political comment on pornography. There was no attempt to palm off the parody as that of [the Moral Majority]. In fact, the very opposite is true." The court held that "Section 107 expressly permits fair use for the purposes of criticism and comment," precisely as the Moral Majority had used it.

Factor #2: The Nature of the Copyrighted Work

This is perhaps the vaguest of the four factors identified in the statute. The *Hustler* case sheds light on it.

The *Hustler* court appeared to interpret this factor to mean that the "scope of fair use is greater when 'informational' as opposed to more creative works are involved." The court gave this particular point to *Hustler,* finding that verbatim copying of what was a creative work— *Hustler*'s parody of Falwell—enjoyed less fair-use consideration.

Factor #3: Amount or Substantiality of the Portion Used

There was no question in the *Hustler* case that the defendant copied the entire work of parody.

Hustler's clever legal team quoted precedent stating, "[T]his court has long maintained the view that wholesale copying of copyrighted material precludes application of the fair use doctrine."[7] The court found for *Hustler* on this point as well.

Factor #4: Effect upon the Potential Market or Value

Did the Moral Majority's use of the *Hustler* parody diminish its value? The effect on the potential market value was probably the toughest of the four factors to apply in this particular case.

The court noted that "the parody was first published September 27 and was off the news stands before the defendant's first mailings in November. Thus, the republication did not diminish the initial sales . . . the effect on the marketability of back issues of the entire magazine is de minimis. . . ." The court found there could be no loss of potential sales because it was unlikely the Moral Majority or viewers of the *Old Time Gospel Hour* could be counted among *Hustler*'s readers.

Conclusion: The Moral Majority Prevails (Just Barely)

The court held in favor of the Moral Majority despite finding that the reprinting of the parody was a commercial use and that it had been copied wholesale. The court found that there simply was no unfair exploitation of *Hustler*'s work, giving great weight to its own finding that the commercial value of the work had not been diminished.

As an aside, the Reverend Falwell later sued *Hustler* for libel and infliction of emotional distress. This case went all the way to the Supreme Court. *Hustler* prevailed in the civil suit.[8] The magazine prides itself as a champion of First Amendment freedoms and probably didn't suffer from the publicity.

GOOD LEGAL FUN: STANDARDS FOR FAIR USE IN PARODY

Copyright can definitely take a joke.

Although the statute doesn't specifically protect parody, courts have uniformly held that humorous adaptations are a form of "comment" and "criticism." However, the line is tough to draw between permissi-

---

[7] Citing *Marcus v. Rowley,* 695 F 2d 1171, 1176 (9th Cir. 1983).
[8] *Hustler Magazine v. Falwell,* 485 U.S. 46 (1988).

ble parody and definitely unfunny infringement. Courts have generally declined to articulate a clear test, instead opting for a case-by-case basis applying the statutory factors. This approach leaves satirists and their attorneys to speculation.

Although it's tough to generalize, courts seem to allow as much copying as is necessary to make the spoof work. Courts favor works that draw recognizable caricatures rather than copying images wholesale from the parodied work. Also, context appears to be an important factor to the courts in determining whether a parody has a tendency to diminish the value of the copyrighted work, which is the fourth factor cited in the statute. For example, *MAD* magazine is rarely sued because the context is clearly a spoof, and rarely is the magazine outrageously offensive in its style. For example, *MAD* has previously co-opted Disney characters without being sued. However, when another publication, an underground magazine, duplicated Disney characters in a parody that made references to sexual and drug-related activities, Disney sued to enjoin them on the basis of copyright infringement and won.[9]

The following are some examples of parody courts have found acceptable:

• *MAD* magazine lyrics sung to the tune of famous songs.[10]

• A spoof of a *Vanity Fair* cover that featured an Annie Leibovitz photo of a naked, hugely pregnant Demi Moore. In the spoof, a picture of Leslie Nielson was shown naked and pregnant on fake magazine covers.[11]

• A parody of the song "Pretty Woman" by the musical group 2 Live Crew that contained sexually explicit lyrics.[12] The court held that the commercial character and the excessive borrowing employed by the parody didn't outweigh its fair use purpose.

Not every parody has been deemed fair game. A parody using Dr. Seuss–style artwork solely to illustrate a story of the OJ Simpson trial

---

[9] *Walt Disney Productions v. Air Pirates*, 581 F.2d 751 (9th Cir. 1978).
[10] *Berlin v. E.C. Publications, Inc.*, 329 F2d 541 (2d Cir. 1964).
[11] *Leibovitz v. Paramount Pictures, Corp.*, 137 F 3d. 109 (2d Cir. 1998).
[12] *Campbell v. Acuff-Rose Music Inc.*, 510 U.S. 569 (1994).

was deemed infringement.[13] The work appropriated must be at least in part a target of the parody.[14]

CRITICISM AND COMMENTARY: THE L. RON HUBBARD CASE

No one enjoys criticism. And criticism can be especially stinging when someone co-opts portions of your own work product to criticize you.

Criticism is considered a fair use, subject to the four-factor test articulated in the *Hustler* magazine case. Not even even a church is immune to criticism. In 1990, the Second Circuit Court of Appeals had to take a look at a book called *A Piece of Blue Sky: Scientology, Dianetics and L. Ron Hubbard Exposed,* about the founder of the controversial Church of Scientology.[15]

The author was a former, disenchanted member of the church "convinced that the church was a dangerous cult, and that Hubbard was a vindictive and profoundly disturbed man." The author referred to Hubbard as an "arrogant, amoral egomaniac" and a "power hungry petty sadist." To buttress his criticisms, the author borrowed liberally from Hubbard's work, reproducing entire passages.

The court held that "biographies in general, and critical biographies in particular fit 'comfortably within'" the boundaries of fair use. It noted that "the scope of fair use is greater with respect to factual than non-factual works." In applying the four-factor test, the court found it "unthinkable" that an unfavorable biography would diminish the commercial viability of the L. Ron Hubbard works referenced within. Nor was it persuaded that the author had appropriated so much of Hubbard's work that the substantiality factor of the test would justify, in and of itself, an injunction to prevent publication of the unfavorable biography.

In short, courts give a wide berth to commentary and criticism. Courts will not offer relief to copyright holders in situations where someone has properly attributed the work to the copyright holder but hurt his or her feelings.

---

[13] *Dr. Seuss Enters, LP v. Penguin Books USA Inc.,* 109 F.3d 1394 (9th Cir. 1997).
[14] *Campbell v. Acuff-Rose Music Inc.,* 510 U.S. 569 (1994).
[15] *New Era Publication International vs. Coral Publishing Group,* 904 F.2d 152 (2d Cir. 1990).

FOR THE PUBLIC GOOD: SCHOLARSHIP AND RESEARCH

Copyright law is designed to promote advancement, not people. It's intended to provide incentives for production of creative works that benefit society as a whole. For this reason, artistic advancement seems to have been given a lot of leeway at the expense of holders of specific copyrights.

The Sony Betamax Case

In 1976, Universal Studios and Walt Disney sued Sony Corporation for copyright infringement, alleging that some "individuals had used Betamax video tape recorders to record some of [their] copyrighted works." Universal Studios and Disney limited their legal strategy to suing Sony and declined to sue any individual users of the emerging Betamax technology.[16]

What a dilemma for the courts! To rule in favor of a device so obviously used to circumvent the rights of copyright holders was to strike a blow to an emerging technology that consumers would clearly find useful (and fun).

The court stretched the law like flubber to create a precedent that would work for the situation. The court insisted that viewers were simply "time shifting" by making copies to view in time slots consistent with their schedule. Sony argued it intended that the technology be used for legitimate purposes. The courts would not hold the manufacturers responsible for other unsavory uses, however foreseeable those illicit uses might be.

Painting with an even broader brush to protect the emerging technology, the court stated, "Even unauthorized uses of a copyrighted work are not necessarily infringing. An unlicensed use of the copyright is not an infringement unless it conflicts with one of the specific exclusive rights conferred by the copyright statute."

Unsuccessful in the courts, the movie industry prevailed upon Congress. It enjoyed mixed success. Initially it sought both legislation that would require a license fee for home use and a prohibition on the renting of videotapes (the latter being an exception to the first sale doctrine

---

[16] *Sony Corp. of America v. Universal Studios, Inc.,* 464 U.S. 417 (1984).

discussed below). The industry received neither of these concessions but does receive royalties for each copy rented.

Instead, Congress included some limited concessions for the industry in the Digital Millennium Copyright Act of 1998. As of July 1, 2000, video recorder manufacturers were required to include a special chip in their recorders that would recognize a copy protection system many movie manufacturers were including in their tapes.

In any event, the video recorder proved to be an unexpected boom rather than a bust for the movie industry. Many movies now make far more from their video release than in the theater.

Reverse Engineering of Copyrighted Material

Another interesting case shows just how far courts will bend copyright principles to protect emergent technologies.

Important precedent emerged as the result of a technology used primarily by kids: the competitive video game market.[17] Sega made the popular Genesis game system played by millions of kids. In order to assure that only its licensees could sell cartridges compatible with its system, Sega implanted a special code.

The defendant, Accolade, reverse engineered Sega cartridges to learn the secret codes that would make its cartridges compatible with the Sega system. This involved producing printouts of the object code, which was a series of zeros and ones read by the computer, and then the source code written by programmers to create the object code. (The process of reverse engineering is discussed more fully in chapter 11.)

Accolade didn't copy any of Sega's actual games, only enough code to make its own games compatible with the Sega system. Sega sued for copyright infringement over what actually amounted to about twenty to twenty-five bytes of code. Sega initially won its suit in the district court, which issued a preliminary injunction to ban the sale of the Sega-compatible games manufactured by Accolade. On appeal, the decision was reversed, and the court held in favor of Accolade based on principles of fair use and public policy grounds.

Dissolving the preliminary injunction, the court held that reverse engineering was a legitimate activity if it was the only way to obtain access

---

[17] *Sega v. Accolade*, 977 F.2d 1510 (9th Cir. 1992).

to those elements of the code that were not protected. The court stated "disassembly of copyrighted object code is, as a matter of law, a fair use of the copyrighted work if such disassembly provides the only means of access to those elements of the code that are not protected by copyright and the copier has a legitimate reason for seeking such access."

The court defended its novel interpretation of the fair use statute to permit reverse engineering on public policy grounds. The court described the public's interest as follows:

> Accolade's identification of the functional requirements for Genesis compatibility has led to an increase in the number of independently designed video game programs offered for the use with the Genesis console. It is precisely this growth in creative expression, based on the dissemination of other creative works and the unprotected ideas contained in those works, that the Copyright Act was intended to promote. . . . [Sega's] attempt to monopolize the market by making it impossible for others to compete runs counter to the statutory purpose of promoting creative expression and cannot constitute a strong equitable basis for resisting the invocation of the fair use doctrine. . . .

Recording Music with MP3

In 1992, Congress passed the Audio Home Recording Act, which applies specifically to audio home recording devices. It requires manufacturers of digital audio recorders and digital audiotape to pay royalties of 2 to 3 percent to the artist and authors.

In 1999 the Recording Industry Association of America (RIAA) sued Diamond Multimedia Systems in connection with its manufacture of a device called the RIO.[18] The RIO is a portable music player that allows a user to download and listen to music files recorded in a special format known as MP3. The MP3 format allows files to be compressed and transferred across the Internet.

The RIAA requested a preliminary injunction, arguing that the Internet distribution of files would encourage the pirating of copyrighted

---

[18] *RIAA v. Diamond Multimedia Systems*, 180 F. 3d 1072 (9th Cir. 1999).

material. The 9th Circuit court denied RIAA's request for an injunction, stating the RIO device didn't qualify as a "digital audio recording device" under the Audio Home Recording Act.

The court reasoned that the RIO did not allow direct recording of a digital music transmission, only of MP3 files. In language that was very reminiscent of the Sony Betamax case, the RIO court stated the "RIO operation is entirely consistent with the Act's main purpose—the facilitation of personal use . . . the RIO merely makes copies in order to render portable or 'space shirt' those files that already reside on the user's hard drive."

Going Too Far: The *Napster* and *Aimster* Cases

Not every emerging technology receives the sympathy of the courts as "creative expression." Napster and its progeny Aimster are clear examples of emerging technology judges easily found crossed the copyright line.

Napster began suddenly as a teenage craze trading music files on the Internet and swelled to 60 million users of all ages. Napster was sued by several record companies charging that Napster violated copyright laws by allowing millions of users to download and swap protected music for free.

In March 2002, Napster was directed to comply with an earlier court order directing it to stop the transfer of copyrighted material. The order directed the large recording companies that had sued Napster to provide Napster with lists of songs they wanted removed from the system. Napster installed software to block select titles from being transferred through its system, but users quickly found ways to defeat it. For example, the software blocked identified song titles, but users could still search for misspelled or abbreviated versions of those same song titles. Ultimately, Napster was unable to function under the terms of the court order.[19]

But the marketplace had spoken, articulating a demand and a huge potential for inexpensive, easily downloadable music. In May 2002, German-based Bertelsmann AG agreed to buy Napster's assets for $8

---

[19] *A & M v. Naptster,* 114 F. Supp. 2d 896, (N.D. Cal 2000) (granting injunction); affirmed in part 239 F. 3d 1004 (9th Cir. 2001).

million. One of the terms of the contract was that Napster would seek bankruptcy protection, which would ultimately enable it to become a wholly owned unit of Bertelsmann. The media company has invested more than $85 million in Napster since October 2000.

Napster went off-line on December 14, 2001, to test a new version of its software. Napster is now back with a flashy, new Web site at www.napster.com boasting "Napster 2.0 It's Back (and legal)." It has developed a new pay service, which it claims complies with the terms of the court's order and will respect the copyrights of owners and artists, offering downloadable tracks for 99 cents and albums for $9.95.

After the legal demise of Napster, several imitators and wanna-bes emerged, including MusicCity.com and Aimster. These systems used a peer-to-peer system in which the music files resided on users' hard drives, rather than a central server as was the case with Napster. Aimster leveraged the popularity of AOL's Instant Messenger by allowing users to trade music files with people on a list of users they compiled. (Aimster users did not have to be AOL subscribers.) As anyone could have predicted, Aimster was promptly sued by the music companies and the RIAA.

In November 2002, U.S. District Court Judge Marvin Aspen granted an all-encompassing preliminary injunction against Aimster. The court had, two months earlier, granted the record companies' request for a preliminary injunction. In that prior ruling, the court described the Aimster system as "a service whose very *raison d'etre* appears to be the facilitation of and contribution to copyright infringement on a massive scale."[20]

After issuing its opinion, the court asked for proposals from the parties as to the language for a permanent injunction. The record companies and music publishers submitted a proposal. Aimster did not submit its own proposal, arguing that it was impossible to filter out infringing recordings. The court adopted the record companies' and RIAA's proposal in full. The court ordered Aimster to:

- Immediately prevent its users from uploading and downloading copyrighted works, or shut down its operations until it could

---

[20] *In Re Aimster Copyright Litigation,* slip op. 14265 (N.D. Ill. September 4, 2002).

- Employ known technological measures to prevent copyright infringement

- Keep the court updated on its continuing efforts to prevent infringement.

Following the Aimster decision, RIAA president Gary Rosen noted that "Chief Judge Aspen considered every argument presented by defendants and stated that Aimster 'managed to do everything but actually steal the music off the store shelf and hand it to Aimster's users.'" Rosen concluded, "This decision helps to support the continued development of the legitimate on-line music market for fans, which is, of course, our goal in all of our on-line enforcement activities."

News Reporting

Technological advancement is not the only area where the public interest overrides the right of the copyright holder. The public's right to know is another trump card over copyright.

In 1963, Abraham Zapruder took perhaps the most extraordinary home movie in history. He managed to film the clearest, most explicit footage of the Kennedy assassination. Zapruder immediately copyrighted the film and sold it to Time, Inc.

Subsequently, a man named Josiah Thompson made unauthorized drawings of frames in the film to illustrate his book *Six Seconds in Dallas*. When Time, Inc. sued for copyright infringement, the court held that the overriding public interest rendered the renditions of the captured, copyrighted images fair use.

The court found an overriding interest "in having the fullest information available on the murder of President Kennedy. Thompson did serious work on the subject and has a theory entitled to public consideration. While doubtless the theory could be explained with sketches . . . the explanation action made in the Book with copies is easier to understand. The Book is not bought because it contained the Zapruder pictures; the Book is bought because of the theory of Thompson and its explanation, supported by Zapruder pictures."[21]

---

[21] *Time, Inc. v. Bernard Geis Associates*, 293 F. Supp. 130 (S.D.N.Y. 1968).

Fair Use and Unpublished Works

Some critics of the *Zapruder* case feared that it would curtail copyright protections by giving a free ride to anyone desiring to use copyrighted material of arguably historical significance. However, in a subsequent case, the Supreme Court upheld a copyright holder's right to profit from the *first* publication of his or her work.

The Supreme Court held that fair use did not give *The Nation* magazine the right to publish an excerpt from President Ford's book, *A Time to Heal,* prior to the book's publication. Since Ford's book was already scheduled for publication, the court held the public interest in seeing the material would be served without *Nation* magazine's preemption.[22]

The court stated that "if every volume that was in the public interest could be pirated away by a competing publisher . . . the public [eventually] would have nothing worth reading."

LIMITATION #4: THE FIRST SALE DOCTRINE

The first sale doctrine is part of the current Copyright Act, which states "the owner of a particular copy of phonorecord lawfully made under this title, or any person authorized by such owner is entitled, without the authority of the copyright owner to sell or otherwise dispose of the possession of that copy or phonorecord."[23]

THE FIRST SALE DOCTRINE AND THE DIGITAL AGE

Generally, if you legitimately acquire a specific copy of a book, a videotape, or a piece of art from the owner, you have the right to do as you wish with it. No one is exactly sure how the first sale doctrine will survive the digital age and what transformations it may undergo.

In the past, if you lent a book to a friend, only one of you could read it at a time. However, if you buy a digital book or movie, you could po-

---

[22] *Harper & Row Publishers v. Nation Enterprises,* 471 U.S. 539 (1985).
[23] 17 U.S.C. Sec. 109(a).

tentially share and distribute copies you've made with a number of people. The first sale doctrine was never intended to cover sharing among multiple users. As of the writing of this book, Congress has been silent as to how the first sale doctrine extends to digital sharing.

EXISTING LIMITATIONS ON THE FIRST SALE DOCTRINE

This general rule is subject to many limitations, some of the most significant of which are the following:

- **Attribution and integrity of visual works:** Generally a purchaser of a work cannot pass it off as his or her own work product or use the work in a way that degrades the integrity of the artist's work, for example, by distorting or mutilating it. U.S. law provides rights of attribution and integrity to certain statutorily defined "works of visual art."[24]

- **Audio works:** In 1984, the music industry successfully lobbied Congress to pass a statutory exception to the first sale doctrine that precluded the rental of music recordings. Presumably, such rentals would lead to unauthorized copies. (Particularly since many of the rental companies were also selling blank tapes to facilitate such copying.) The movie industry was unsuccessful in getting a similar provision passed for video rentals.

- **Computer Software:** In 1990, the computer software industry persuaded Congress it should be allowed the same treatment as the sound recording industry. The software industry now has its own statutory ban on rentals, carving out another exception to the first sale doctrine.

It's an odd twist of fate and lobbying irony that the video rental amendment did not pass, while the music and software amendments sailed through Congress. But in the end, the movie industry profited nicely from the sales of videos. Profits from video releases often exceed the money made on the movie release.

---

[24] 17 U.S.C. 106A.

The movie industry also subsequently won an important victory impacting the right of first sale in the context of movie viewing. In 1984, the U.S. Court of Appeals for the Third Circuit held that the copyright holder's right of public performance prohibits a business from *publicly* playing a movie.

Maxwell's Video Showcase was a business that had individual booths in which customers could view rented videos on a large theater-type screen. The court held that "showcasing a video at Maxwell's is a significantly different transaction than leasing a tape for home use." Thus, public performance remains the exclusive right of the copyright holder and limits what a purchaser can do under the first sale doctrine.

CUTTING INTO COPYRIGHT: HOW DEEP DO THE DOCTRINES GO?

With all of the exceptions and doctrines limiting the rights conferred by the copyright statute, you may wonder what a creator is left holding at the end of the day. The next chapter provides insight into bringing a successful action for infringement that doesn't run afoul of the doctrines discussed in this chapter.

CHAPTER 9 ›››

Copyright Infringement:
Proving It and Defending Against It

WHILE YOU HOPE your work will turn a tidy profit, it's disconcerting to find the profit being turned for someone else. Since it's hard to spawn an idea in this world that isn't somehow inspired by someone else's idea, our legislature and judiciary have spent two centuries trying to mark the line.

This chapter clarifies the criteria for determining when there has been a copyright infringement of your work and what you can do if it happens to be your work that's been infringed. It also provides you with insights as to how to steer clear of accusations that you've infringed the works of others.

IN THIS CHAPTER YOU FIND OUT:

- What constitutes copyright infringement

- How to defend your copyright without litigation

- How to avoid allegations you've infringed the works of others

- How to stay on the fair side of fair use

IT'S THE NEW millennium, and it appears that the law is powerless to stop a technology that circumvents the rights of thousands of songwriters and musicians. Over 80 million users are thumbing their noses at copyright law and using Napster and other popular programs to make bootleg copies of all the free music they can download.

The program is based on technology that allows registered users to search each other's computers and swap music. There's no centralized database to seize or shut down, and Napster is only the program that enables users to swap. The actual music is stored on tens of thousands of systems registered with Napster.

The Recording Industry Association of America sues Napster for copyright infringement, easily winning on the obvious facts of the case. The United States Court of Appeals for the Ninth Circuit holds that Napster is liable for "vicarious" copyright infringement where it fails to affirmatively use its ability to patrol its system and preclude access to potentially infringing files listed in its search index.[1]

As soon as a federal court shuts Napster down, half a dozen variations of the music swapping service spring up. The music industry is stunned and helpless. There seems to be no way to track the rampant abuse, let alone stop it.

MSNBC reports in October 2002: "The music industry succeeded in shutting down Napster, but it has failed to even slow free song swapping.... Some 41 million people traded music on-line during the first half of 2002 ... [and] the increasing popularity of CD burners and portable digital music devices [is] opening up another hole."[2]

Ultimately, it appears it will be technology, and not the law, that comes to the rescue of the music industry. A secure format for music is currently being developed that will prevent copying of music over the Internet. The Digital Millennium Copyright Act, already in place, makes it a crime to circumvent these protections. The industry itself will develop and introduce new marketing strategies that make it more advantageous to own an original copy of the CD (see chapter 2).

---

[1] *A&M Records Inc. v. Napster Inc.*, 9th Cir., No. 01-15998, March 25, 2002.
[2] On-line report by MSN located at www.msnbc.com/news/820292.asp (October 14, 2002).

PROVING YOUR COPYRIGHT HAS BEEN INFRINGED:
A THREE-PART TEST

It's yours, and you know it! You recognize your own work when you see it.

You're surfing the Web and see it on someone else's site. Or you happen to be reading a magazine article on a topic that interests you, and you see words or images that are all too familiar. Or you see it on the stage—someone *else's* stage. But how do you prove it?

PART #1: DOES THE WORK QUALIFY FOR COPYRIGHT PROTECTION?

Not every creative work product qualifies for copyright protection.

As was explained in chapter 7, there aren't any required formalities to invoke copyright protection for qualifying works. But here's the catch: the work you want to protect must be of a type that legally qualifies for copyright protection. Generally, your work must be:

- Original and fixed in a tangible form

- Expressive rather than factual (except that an original compilation or arrangement of factual material can sometimes qualify for copyright)

Does It Meet the Basic Requirements for Copyright Protection: Originality and Fixation?

To qualify for copyright protection, your work must be an "original [work] of authorship fixed in any tangible medium."

The standards of originality are pretty low, having even been extended to a reproduction of an old painting, when the court found that creative decisions made in the course of the engraving technique satisfied the burden of originality.[3]

The concept of fixation is one that's constantly evolving with technology. To our founding fathers it meant printed copy. The first copy-

---

[3] *Alfred Bell v. Cantalda Fine Arts, Inc.*, 191 F.2d 99 (2d Cir. 1951).

right statute, passed in 1790, covered books and maps. Today it can be computer code, an artistic element of a visual design, or a digitized sound pattern.

Is It Expressive Rather than Functional?

Copyright protection is free and automatic. Since copyright law protects the creative and expressive aspects of a work, it makes sense that the protections are spontaneous for qualifying works.

However, if your work is deemed functional, you are required to apply for patent protection. The copyright statute specifically provides protection for "works of artistic craftsmanship insofar as their form but not their mechanical or utilitarian aspects are concerned. . . ."[4]

Patent protection is superior to copyright protection in several respects. If you have a patent, you have a virtual monopoly on your technology and are protected from competition from inventions that serve the same function. This is the case even if the functionally similar item was independently developed. Copyright provides no protection from similar works that may have been inspired by your work or for works that are strikingly similar but fall short of actual copying.

To receive a patent, you must prove that your work is truly original, functional, and nonobvious. In the application process, you must undertake the complicated analysis of and distinguishing its function and design from similar patented works and works in the public domain. (Chapter 12 explains this process in detail.)

Are the Expressive Elements Distinct from Ideas and Facts?

Many stories involve plotlines where children of parents from rivaling ethnic or political groups fall in love, and there is a tragic end to their romance. *Romeo and Juliet* and *West Side Story* are two of the most notable scripts based on this idea. Copyright doesn't allow anyone to have a monopoly on facts or ideas. It only protects *expression* of facts and ideas.

Similarly, facts cannot by copyrighted. That's why telephone books aren't subject to copyright protection. Names and addresses are merely compilations of factual information. Courts have rejected the sweat-of-

---

[4] 17 U.S.C. Sec. 101 and Sec. 113.

the-brow argument that the labor involved in compiling factual information justifies copyright protection.[5]

An author researching historical facts does not receive copyright protection that precludes others from using those very same facts in other works, no matter how difficult the information was to gather. It does, however, protect someone from plagiarism of the work in which the facts are expressed, such as a biography.

Is It in the Public Domain?

What isn't protected by copyright (or other intellectual property laws) is fair game and free for everyone to use. This wonderful stuff is called *public domain*.

Works may fall into the public domain for the following reasons:

- **Expired copyright:** Once a copyright expires, it falls into the public domain.

- **Forfeited copyright:** If the owner of a copyright doesn't comply with required formalities, like filing for a renewal extension, the copyright can fall into the public domain.

- **Dedicated works:** Sometimes authors want their works to be freely available to the public and for this reason don't seek or invoke copyright protections. For example, some books include a computer CD with works that the authors invite purchasers to use for free.

- **Government works:** Your tax dollars at work! Any work created by a U.S. government employee in his or her official capacity, such as an article, report, or research document, is in the public domain. This means that you can use it without fear of violating a copyright. This rule does not apply to works created by state and local government employees, so you must still seek permission to reproduce or otherwise use those works.

---

[5] *Feist Publications, Inc. v. Rural Telephone Service Co.*, 499 U.S. 340 (1991).

- **Never protected:** Countless works are in the public domain simply because their authors never sought protection or had no copyright protection available to them at the time.

How do you find out if a work is in the public domain? The copyright office, unfortunately, doesn't maintain lists of works in the public domain. Private companies perform public domain searches for a fee. You can locate a number of these companies on the Internet.

PART #2: HAS THE WORK BEEN COPIED?

Even schoolchildren know the basic moral precept that copying someone else's work is wrong. When an adult is accused of copying another adult's work, it's more complicated to prove the copying took place. To prevail in an action for infringement, you must demonstrate both that the copied work is substantially similar to your protected expression and that the copycat had access to your work.

Is the Work Substantially Similar?

Similarity is often in the eye of the judge and jury. It's a subjective test rather than an objective one, absent a clear case of verbatim copying.

Courts have generated some arguably inconsistent results over the past century, particularly in the area of evaluating similarity of works of fiction. Judge Learned Hand held that copyright did not protect a movie about a Catholic-Jewish interfaith marriage when another movie, involving a similar plotline and very similar characters, was released. On the other hand, Judge Hand found a play involving the same historical event as a prior movie to be an infringing work.[6] Both dramas were based on the trial of a woman named Madeline Smith, who had poisoned her lover in 1857 but was acquitted of the crime. Judge Hand was convinced that in this blurry case, creative expression rather than mere historical facts had been sufficiently appropriated to infringe the plaintiff's copyright.

Evaluating similarity of musical works also has been no picnic for

---

[6] *Nichols v. Universal Pictures Corp.*, 45 F.2d 119 (2d Cir. 1930); *Sheldon v. Metro-Goldwyn Pictures Corp.*, 81 F. 2d. 49 (2d Cir. 1936).

the courts. It's altogether possible to create a similar effect using entirely different notes in a song. Courts have also held that even though the majority of a song may be distinct, the copying of key notes or chords may be so significant to the work that copying a minimal portion constitutes infringement.

Did the Copier Have Access to the Original Work?
Even if two works are substantially similar, the doctrine of independent creation allows for the possibility of mere coincidence. Two people may simply have the same copyrightable idea at the same time, and their expression of the idea may be suspiciously similar.

For this reason, a plaintiff bringing an infringement action must demonstrate that the alleged infringer had a reasonable possibility of access to their work product. With popular songs that have constant radio play, this isn't difficult to prove.

On the other hand, for unsuccessful or unpublished works, the issue of access may be more difficult. In 1978, a relatively unknown songwriter sued the Bee Gees for copyright infringement, claiming their hit song "How Deep Is Your Love" was substantially similar to his song "Let It End." "Let It End" had been performed publicly but was never released as a record or sold in sheet music form. Initially, a jury found that the two songs were so substantially similar they couldn't have been written independently. But the judge set aside the jury's verdict because there was simply no evidence or a reasonable possibility that the Bee Gees had heard "Let It End."[7]

PART #3: IS IT FAIR USE?

Fair use allows you to use copyrighted material for limited purposes without getting into trouble. It's a set of exceptions built into current copyright law to further public interest.

If you want to sue someone for copyright infringement, you must not only prove that they've copied your copyrighted work, you must rebut any argument that their usurpation of your material constitutes fair

---

[7] *Selle v. Gibb*, 741 F. 896 (7th Cir. 1984).

use. Fair use is an *affirmative defense* the defendant can offer for copyright infringement.

Fair use involves a four-part test based on factors specifically set forth in the copyright statute. To analyze whether a particular use of a work is fair use, you need to ask yourself four questions.

Factor #1: What Is the Character of the Use?

In a sense transformative use is more likely to be deemed a fair use. The user must somehow add value, intellect, or commentary to the work that's used. Copying for the sake of copying is not the type of use the statute condones. For example, in a parody, the transformative element is humor. In news reporting, the transformative element is commentary. Use of photographs in a distinct aesthetic arrangement or compilation may also be sufficiently transformative.[8]

Not-for-profit educational use trumps commercialism in the land of fair use. The Copyright Act states that "fair use of a copyrighted work . . . for purposes such as criticism, comment, news reporting, teaching (including multiple copies for classroom use), scholarship, or research is not an infringement of copyright."

In a pivotal precedent, *Universal Studios, Inc. v. Sony Corp.*, the Supreme Court held that the home videotaping of free over-the-air television broadcasts was fair use, so long as the intended use was personal and not commercial.[9]

Table 9-1 lists several types of uses and the level of fair use protections they receive. Uses in the left two columns tip the balance in favor of fair use. The uses on the right tend to tip the balance in favor of the copyright owner.

This table is only a guide and must be considered in the context of all of the remaining factors of this test, rather than as a presumptive classification of accuracy:

---

[8] *Sandoval v. New Line Cinema Corp.*, 973 F. Supp. 409 (S.D.N.Y. 1997).
[9] *Universal Studios, Inc. v. Sony Corp.*, 464 U.S. 417 (1984).

TABLE 9-1: *Levels of Protection for Various Types of Use*

Highest Level of Fair Use Protection	Frequently Entitled to Fair Use Protection
Nonprofit	Criticism
Educational	Commentary
Personal	News reporting
	Parody

Factor #2: What Is the Nature of the Work Used or Copied?
The Supreme Court has stated, "[C]opying a news broadcast may have a stronger claim to fair use than copying a motion picture."[10]

The copying of factual information is far less likely to result in an action for infringement than copying the creative elements of someone else's work. This makes sense when you consider that copyright isn't intended to confer a monopoly on facts or ideas.

Copying and distributing factual, scholarly, and scientific information promotes the free spread of ideas and the creation of new scholarly and scientific works. This is the essence of the fair use exception.

Factor #3: How Much of the Work Has Been Used or Copied?
How much copying constitutes infringement? This is an amorphous standard. It's not just how much you copy but how and where it appears.

It seems a few significant notes or chords of a popular song have been held to be infringement, while large passages of other works have been held to have been fair use. In 1997,[11] a Los Angeles television station broadcast a couple of minutes of a videotape of a man named Reginald Denny. Mr. Denny was a white truck driver who was in the wrong time and wrong place following the Rodney King verdict, and he was dragged from his truck and beaten by a hostile African American mob. The television station had previously been denied permission to broadcast the tape but obtained portions of it from another television station. The court held that the partial broadcasts of the critical aspects of the beating, although factual and newsworthy, constituted the "heart" of the videotape.

---

[10] *Universal Studios, Inc. v. Sony Corp.*, 464 U.S. 417 (1984).
[11] *Los Angeles News Service v. KCAL-TV Channel 9*, 108 F.3d 1119 (9th Cir. 1997).

Factor #4: What Effect Will the Use Have on the Market for the Original Work?

This final factor asks, "Is the owner losing money because of this use?" It looks to whether the copying commercially competes with the original or avoids payment for permission (royalties) in an established market.

This factor takes into consideration such factors as whether:

> ⚖ **LAWYER'S NOTE:** *Not-for-profit uses are viewed more favorably than commercial uses. For example, a nonprofit educational institution might possibly be permitted to copy an entire article from a journal for students in a class as a fair use, but a commercial copy shop might need permission for the same copying.*[12]

- **The original is available or out of print:** If the original is out of print, a strong argument can be made that the copyright holder is no longer profiting from it. It can even be argued that using or quoting portions of the work can revive interest in the original work.

- **The granting of permission has an economic value for which people are willing to pay:** Is it conceivable that anyone is willing to pay for permission? Will the potentially infringing use undercut the profits of the permission holders who've legitimately acquired their rights?

- **Copyright owner is unidentifiable:** Sometimes it's simply not possible to find out who created a work. This is the case with a lot of funny, clever things that get circulated by E-mail. If you can't find or identify the copyright holder of something widely disseminated after diligent inquiry, that's a pretty good indication that he or she isn't currently profiting. This argument is weaker, of course, if the work isn't being widely distributed.

In 1984, a famous sculptor, Jeff Koons, decided to create a sculpture from a well-known photograph that was in a number of museums and printed on a note card. Three of the sculptures were sold to collectors for a total profit of about $367,000. The court held that the sculpture

---

[12] See, generally, chapter 7.

violated the photographer's copyright, heavily emphasizing the fact that the photographer had the right to profit from all conceivable derivative uses.[13]

On the other hand, some fairly blatant copying is considered fair use, even though the intent is clearly to undermine profits. Copying a magazine cover or product's packaging for purposes of comparative advertising is permissible. For example, it is permissible to show a competitor's box of laundry detergent on a commercial purporting to compare the competitor's cleaning power to yours. Comparative advertising doesn't undermine the need for the product.

POLICING YOUR COPYRIGHT

An ounce of prevention is worth a pound of copyright litigation. Copyright is business, and like any good businessperson, a copyright holder must look after his or her own interests.

Good practices for policing your copyright include the following:

- **Periodically check the Internet for infringing works.** Use search techniques and use key words likely to disclose unauthorized use of your copyrighted material.

- **Register your copyright.** In 1988, Congress prospectively dispensed with all formalities for copyright protection. Although the protection is now automatic for any original work that's in a fixed medium of expression, the optional registration process adds to your enforcement arsenal. If you even *think* you might ever need to sue to protect your copyright, register it. And if you do opt to sue, you'll need to bring your certificate of registration with you to court in order to recover statutory damages and attorney's fees. The registration process is covered in detail in chapter 10.

- **Put potential infringers on notice.** The copyright notice is no longer legally necessary to protect your rights, since Congress has

---

[13] *Rogers v. Koons*, 960 F. 2d 301 (2d Cir. 1992).

dispensed with all of the formalities. However, it clears up misunderstandings and may make someone think twice about misappropriating. You'll find a copyright notice at the beginning of this book and in just about every other one you own.

GETTING AN ALLEGED INFRINGER TO STOP

Imitation is the sincerest form of flattery—and the surest source of liability when it comes to copyright. What are your options when you think someone is ripping off your ideas?

ATTEMPT TO RESOLVE IT ON YOUR OWN: WRITING A CEASE AND DESIST LETTER

Sometimes problems are cleared up by some simple communication. A letter, rather than a lawsuit, might be in order if:

- The culprit copying your work isn't turning an enviable profit at your expense.

- You suspect the alleged infringer is relatively unsophisticated about the nuances of copyright law.

- You suspect that the publisher or Web site owner is unaware that someone on his or her staff has plagiarized your work; a simple cease and desist letter might make them aware of a source of liability they'll be eager to get rid of as expeditiously as possible.

A cease and desist letter should include:

- Information as to where you saw or encountered the infringing work.

- Identification of your copyrighted work and an explanation that you own the copyright. (If your copyright is registered, include the date of the registration and the registration number.)

- An explanation that you believe infringement has occurred.

- A request that the infringer cease their unauthorized use and/or compensate you for it.

A sample of this type of letter is shown below.

Sample Cease and Desist Letter

January 8, 2003

Ms. Marilyn Kayros, Publisher
Culinary Treasures Magazine
345 Corporate Drive
Urban, WI 54321

Dear Ms. Kayros:

I recently purchased the January issue of Culinary Treasures Magazine *and found a significant excerpt from my article "Olive Oil on Everything." The excerpt was reprinted without my permission.*

I hold the copyright for this article, which was previously published on my Web site, www.foodtalk.com.

Because permission to reproduce my work has not been obtained, I request that you cease distributing any more copies of your December issue containing my article. Alternatively, I demand that you compensate me in the amount of $1,000 for the continued use of my work.

Please respond to this letter within ten days.

Sincerely,
Jill Gilbert

GOING TO COURT

If you don't get the response you want from a polite letter, it may be time to take off the gloves and sue.

Who Can Sue and Who Can Be Sued?

A legal owner of a copyright can sue anyone who infringes it, as plaintiff. The defendants may be anyone who is involved in the infringement or who profits from it.

When Can You Sue Someone?

The civil statute of limitations for copyright infringement is three years. This means that you must have your *complaint* (which is the legal document that begins the litigation process) filed within three years from the date the infringing work was published, displayed, or distributed.

What Can You Get If You Sue Someone?

If your lawsuit is successful, a court may provide any of the following remedies:

- **Injunction:** The court can order the infringer to stop publishing or distributing the infringing work.

- **Actual damages and the profits the infringer has earned:** You are entitled to be compensated for money you lost as a result of the infringement, or, in some cases, as to any profits the infringer made off your work (you are entitled to the infringer's profits to the extent they do not duplicate amounts assessed for your own lost profits).

- **Attorney's fees:** Sometimes a court may agree to award you attorney's fees and the costs of going to court. (Your copyright must be registered prior to the commencement of the infringement for you to be eligible for this protection).

- **Statutory damages:** This type of damages is a little perk provided by the statute to encourage use of the optional registration process. These damages are awarded under the statute without you having to prove the actual amounts of your loss. This simplifies the litigation process considerably. The amounts of the statutory damages vary, depending on whether the infringement was inadvertent or willful.

The remedies and requirements for obtaining them are discussed in more detail in chapter 7.

GETTING PERMISSION TO USE SOMEONE ELSE'S WORK

Warning: Giving credit and putting material in quotation marks is not enough! Even the most gracious (even gushing) attribution of work in which you credit the original author may not be enough to avoid trouble. If you incorporate significant portions of the work, you may find yourself facing a threat of litigation. Whether the threat is credible or not, it's ultimately cost effective to err on the conservative side: always get permission in writing.

> **$$ BUSINESS TIP:** *Getting written permission avoids threats of litigation that may have no purpose other than to force you to pay something to settle the dispute.*

Getting written permission is a two-step process. First, you have to figure out who owns the copyright and has authority to grant you permission. The second step is actually drafting the written request to be signed by the copyright holder.

FINDING THE COPYRIGHT OWNER

Tracking down the rightful owner of a copyright can be tricky, but fortunately the Internet simplifies the hunt.

Books and Journal Articles
If you know who the author or publisher of copyrighted material is, you can contact them directly. You need to allow a reasonable time, sometimes as much as a few weeks, for a response. This can be frustrating and inefficient, if you have need to obtain permissions for a lot of different materials.

If the work is part of a book or a journal article, you can streamline the process. Contact the Copyright Clearance Center (CCC) located at www.copyright.com. The CCC is a nonprofit, central clearinghouse established in 1977 by publishers, authors, and users, which acts as agent for the publisher and grants permissions for a fee. CCC's electronic database allows you to search for the work and computes the applicable fee. Your fee is then remitted to the copyright holder.

CCC represents close to 10,000 publishers and has approximately 2 million registered works. If the work you want to use is registered with the CCC, you can sometimes get permission immediately. If it's not registered, the Copyright Clearance Center will locate the copyright holder and will usually respond within twenty-four to thirty-six hours.

For larger companies, CCC also offers an annual license fee arrangement. A corporate user can obtain the right to photocopy copyrighted materials registered with the CCC for internal use.

Musical Works

If you want to perform a musical work, you can most likely obtain permission through the Web site of cooperative music licensing organizations such as the American Society of Composers, Authors and Publishers (ASCAP). This site is located at www.ASCAP.com. ASCAP currently represents and licenses performance rights for about 140,000 artists.

ASCAP was founded in 1914 by a group of composers and their attorneys. The purpose of the organization was to collectively enforce the copyrights of all of its members. Generally, for a single fee a user can license the rights to perform all ASCAP works for one year. ASCAP has a complicated allocation system for paying the participating artists, depending upon how often their particular work is accessed. It provides an efficient system for compliance for the hundreds of thousands of musicians who perform its registered works each year.

A competitor of ASCAP is Broadcast Music, Inc. (www.bmi.com), representing over 300,000 artists. If you are looking for rights held by European artists, a good alternative source is the Society of European Stage Authors and Composers, located at www.sesac.com.

News Archives

If the work you need to use is from a newspaper or other news organization, check the World Wide Web. Many of the largest news organizations have placed archives of their back issues on-line, along with instructions for obtaining permission from the organization.

Plays

The rights for most plays and musicals are held by play publishing houses. To obtain the rights to produce a play or musical, determine which play publishing house has the rights to the play you wish to produce. Each company usually maintains a catalogue of royalty fees for each work. The royalty structure may vary, depending on the type of organization seeking performance rights.

DRAFTING YOUR REQUEST

When you're getting permission to use a copyrighted work, you don't want to scare the copyright holder off with a ten-page form full of legal jargon. You just want to ask for what you need in a straightforward manner and secure legally binding permission to use it.

Your signed, written permission form must incorporate the following information:

- Name of the copyrighted work and where it appears

- Your name

- The purpose for which you intend to use the work, including the name of your work in which it will appear

- A request that permission be granted to display the work wherever your work may appear (For example, if you're writing a book that may eventually be electronically published, you want to be sure to get permission covering electronic publication of your book.)

Sample Permission Request

Ms. Marilyn Kayros
Culinary News
1234 Paper Drive
Article, WI 53209

Re: Legal/Journalistic Permission to Reprint Photograph

Dear Ms. Kayros:

I am currently writing a book, *Storing Sangria,* that will be published by Gourmet Press, Inc. in June 2003.

I am requesting permission to reprint the photograph of the sculpted crystal carafe appearing on page 2 of your May 2002 newsletter, and the text that appears in the caption.

I request permission to use this photograph in all subsequent editions and printings of *Storing Sangria,* as well as in any electronically published versions of the book.

If this proposed use is acceptable to you, please sign one copy of this letter and return it to me. (A second copy is provided for your records.)

Sincerely,
Jill Gilbert

I authorize the use and distribution of the material described in this letter for the uses identified. I represent that I am either the owner of all rights to such material, or authorized to consent on behalf of the copyright holder.

_____   _____
Ms. Marilyn Kayros   Date

⚖️ **LAWYER'S NOTE:** *Although a signed release is best, you can also get permission verbally, and follow up with a written confirmation letter.*

SOME TIPS FOR PROTECTING YOURSELF AGAINST INFRINGEMENT ACTIONS

Ignorance of the law is no excuse in an infringement action. Even inadvertent infringement carries penalties.

To avoid being sued for infringement, follow these preventative practices:

- **Obtain written permission whenever possible.** If there's any doubt whatsoever that your use of the copyrighted material may fall outside the scope of fair use, err on the safe side and get the copyright holder's consent in writing.

- **Have a policy for material posted on your Web site.** Post notice on your Web site directing anyone who believes an infringing work has been posted on your site to contact you (rather than sue you) immediately. State that it's your policy to remove all infringing material.

- **Give credit where credit is due.** Attribution is essential when appropriating small amounts of copyrighted material.

- **Proceed cautiously with parody and criticism.** Use only as much of the original work as is necessary to make your point. Paraphrase and make reference to the work when possible, rather than directly quoting or copying. Less is more when it comes to making an argument for fair use.

- **Paraphrase rather than quote.** Copyright protects expression rather than ideas. Quoted material is protected expression, whereas ideas are not. Unprotected ideas in a work may be used freely, but copyrightable expressions may not.

CHAPTER 10 ⟩⟩⟩

Exercising Copyright Caution: Research, Registration, and Designation

THE LEGAL LORE that mailing a copy of your work to yourself gives you copyright protection is a myth. Mailing a copy to yourself (even if it's certified) doesn't do much, except possibly help to establish the date the work was created. But then again, everyone knows envelopes are easily steamed open. Fortunately, the registration procedures that can preserve your rights aren't a whole lot more complex.

IN THIS CHAPTER YOU FIND OUT:

- *Whether it's worthwhile to register your copyright*

- *How to research who owns copyrights to other work*

- *How and where to get copyright forms*

- *How and when to display the © symbol*

FLIPPING FROM CHANNEL to channel on your television the last few Christmas seasons, you may have noticed the absence of It's a Wonderful Life. The holiday mainstay isn't appearing on every single channel; you can actually watch something else if you really want to.

It's a Wonderful Life is now being run just once a year on NBC. You can't even get extra showings on premium cable stations.

This is because a company named Republic (formerly NTA) is asserting that it still owns the rights to the film's music. Although the film itself passed into the public domain after the initial twenty-eight-year term, the rights to the music were copyrighted separately and renewed. Republic sold the exclusive rights to air the music contained in the film to NBC in 1997 after informing all the other networks, in a Scrooge-like fashion, that they were in violation of its copyrights.

Republic's claims of a separate registration and renewal are true but may not be definitive. The musician, Dimitri Tomikin, signed a contract to Capra/Liberty, the film's producers, assigning rights to the music. It may be that those rights belong to Capra/Liberty and their successors (the public). But then, who is going to pay an attorney to argue for free public access? One of the Bailey kids is reportedly angry that Republic went after him for using still shots in his It's a Wonderful Life calendar, and has publicly vowed to wage a legal challenge to Republic, but so far no holiday litigation sequel is airing.[1]

Registration isn't a mandatory copyright requirement; it's a form of optional insurance.

Not every work you produce may justify taking the time and money to register its copyright. However, works in which you've invested substantially or that offer the promise of significant financial returns warrant the added protection of registration. This chapter takes a look at the advantages of obtaining a registration certificate, and of using the ® symbol.

---

[1] This information was reported in an article by David B. Hayes, in a newsgroup called alt.movies.silent (October 22, 1997).

THE ADVANTAGES OF REGISTERING, SOONER OR LATER

There's no rush to register. In fact, you can register anytime within the life of the copyright. However, your claims can be more difficult to document and some protections can be lost if you don't file your registration within specified time frames.

REGISTRATION ESTABLISHES A PUBLIC RECORD OF THE CRITICAL CREATION DATE

The date you create a work is legally significant, because copyright protection is automatic once your work is memorialized in a fixed, tangible form. Registration beats the self-addressed envelope for establishing the date that you created your work. No one can accuse you of steaming anything open.

REGISTRATION IS REQUIRED TO FILE A LAWSUIT FOR INFRINGEMENT

Registration provides the keys to the courthouse. Before you can file a lawsuit for copyright infringement in every U.S. jurisdiction, for a work of U.S. origin, you have to apply to register it. You can do this on the eve of filing your lawsuit, since you can register any time within the legal copyright term. (Copyright terms are discussed in chapter 7.) However, as the following sections of this chapter explain, your remedies may be enhanced by registering more promptly.

REGISTRATION WITHIN FIVE YEARS ESTABLISHES A PRESUMPTION OF VALIDITY FOR CERTAIN FACTS

If you register within five years of publication, your registration will establish certain facts in court you would otherwise have to go to the expense of proving. The court will presume validity of your copyright and of the facts stated in the registration certificate.

REGISTRATION WITHIN THREE MONTHS IS REQUIRED FOR STATUTORY DAMAGES AND ATTORNEY'S FEES

If you registered before the infringement or it started within three months after publication of your work, you can collect statutory damages as well as attorney's fees if you prevail in an infringement action. Otherwise, you're limited to recovering your actual damages.

$$ BUSINESS TIP: *Registering your work may make it easier to find an attorney willing to handle your case on a contingency basis, rather than requiring you to pay an expensive hourly rate up front. Registration permits statutory damages of up to $150,000 if a willful infringement is found, and also enables you to recover attorney's fees and costs from an infringer.*

Actual damages are losses you must prove you've incurred, such as lost profits. If you qualify for *statutory damages,* a court can award them without specific proof you've incurred them. They range from $750 to $150,000 per work infringed, depending upon whether the infringing act is deemed "willful."[2] (See chapter 7.)

REGISTRATION PROTECTS AGAINST IMPORTATION OF INFRINGING WORKS

Registration provides a powerful weapon against foreign knock-offs. You can record your registration with the U. S. Customs Service for protection against the importation of infringing copies.

To get this perk, you must register with the Intellectual Property Rights Branch (IPRB) of the Customs Service and present documentation showing you've already registered with the U.S. Copyright Office.

Approval of an IPRB application usually takes one to two weeks, and you're promptly notified by mail of the acceptance or rejection of your application. Protection is effective from the date your IPRB application is approved and remains in force as long as your copyright registration is in force.

---

[2] 17 U.S.C. Sec. 504(c).

REGISTRATION SATISFIES THE MANDATORY DEPOSIT REQUIREMENT

Registration kills two birds with one formality. While registration is now optional, there's a mandatory requirement under U.S. law that two copies of all published works be deposited with the Library of Congress within three months of publication.

Failure to meet the deposit requirement isn't fatal to your copyright, but it does subject you to some fines and penalties. The statute contemplates voluntary compliance, but the Library of Congress may issue a demand for deposit of copies of published materials at any time. Failure to comply with this demand within three months subjects you to a fine of not more than $250 for each work plus the retail price of the copies. If your refusal to comply is willful or repeated, you can be liable for an added fine of $2,500.

To satisfy requirements for both registration and deposit, send the following in one package to the Register of Copyrights:

- Your two mandatory deposit copies

- A completed application for registration

- A $30 nonrefundable filing fee payable to the Register of Copyrights

If you opt not to register but want to satisfy the mandatory deposit requirement (which may help establish the date of your work), you can send your deposit copies to:

Library of Congress
Register of Copyrights
Attn: 407 Deposits
101 Independence Avenue, SE
Washington, DC 20559-6000

$$ BUSINESS TIP: *Looking for a work that has long been out of print, or have a nagging feeling something may be covered by copyright even though it hasn't been registered? Try the Library of Congress depositories. The Library of Congress doesn't maintain copies of all works deposited, but it is the undisputed largest collection of all types of works subject to copyright in the world.*

FILLING OUT THE FORMS

The sole purpose of copyright registration is documentation. Copyright documents who created what and when they did so. It's not surprising that the process revolves around filling out forms and getting copies of your work to the right place.

> **$$ BUSINESS TIP:** *You can register your individual contribution to a collective work such as a newspaper or encyclopedia.*

HOW AND WHERE TO GET THE FORMS

Copyright forms are free and easy to get, along with informational circulars explaining how to handle issues that may come up. You obtain free forms by doing any of the following:

- Call the U.S. Copyright Office Hotline at (202) 707-9100 and leave a message on their voice mail machine

- Log on to the U.S. Copyright Office Web site at http://lcweb.loc.gov/copyright/

- If you don't know the name of a particular publication, try calling the Copyright Office's prerecorded information line at (202) 707-3000.

COPYRIGHTING SPECIFIC TYPES OF WORKS: WHICH FORMS TO USE

Copyright registration forms are fairly simple to fill out. The tricky part is making sure you've completed the right one. The Copyright Office requires different forms for different types of works, and the materials that you have to send in with the forms varies. Table 10-1 summarizes the required forms and materials for various types of creative works.

TABLE 10-1: *Copyright Requirements for Particular Types of Works*

Type of Work	Requirements for Particular Work	Form to File	Materials to Include
Literary works, computer programs	Literary works may be published or unpublished and include nondramatic textual works with or without illustrations. Computer programs and databases also are considered literary works.	Form TX or Short Form TX	Copies of all material to be registered; $30.00 filing fee
Visual arts	Visual arts are pictorial, graphic, or sculptural works, including two-dimensional and three-dimensional works of fine, graphic, and applied art. "Useful articles," such as furniture, may have copyrightable artistic elements. Some architectural works qualify as visual arts works.	Form VA	Nonreturnable copies of the material to be registered; $30.00 filing fee
Sound recordings	Sound recordings are "works that result from the fixation of a series of musical, spoken, or other sounds, but not including the sounds accompanying a motion picture or other audio-visual work." Common examples include recordings of music, drama, or lectures.	Form SR	Nonreturnable copies of the material to be registered; $30.00 filing fee
Performing arts	Performing arts works are intended to be "performed" directly before an audience or indirectly "by means of any device or process." Included are (1) musical works, including any accompanying words; (2) dramatic works, such as scripts, including any accompanying music; (3) pantomimes and choreographic works; and (4) motion pictures and other audiovisual works. Note: Registering performing arts is not the same as registering a sound recording.	Form PA or Short Form PA	Materials to be included depend on the work; $30.00 filing fee must be included.
Music (compositions)	Sound recordings present special issues. See discussion in this chapter.	To register a sound recording, you should use Form SR. To register a composition you need Form PA. A literary work (such as lyrics) may be registered using a Form TX.	Nonreturnable copies of the material to be registered; $30.00 filing fee
Serials and periodicals	Serial works are issued or intended to be issued in successive parts bearing numerical or chronological designations and are intended to be continued indefinitely.	For single issues, use Form SE or Short Form SE (choose form to use). For a group of issues that meet certain conditions, use Form SE/Group. For a group of daily newspapers or newsletters that meet certain conditions, use Form G/DN.	Nonreturnable material to be registered; $30.00 filing fee

COMPILATIONS, COLLABORATIONS, AND MULTIPLE REGISTRATIONS

Music, lyrics, dialogue, and artistic renditions may all go into a production. Unless the authors intend to merge everything into a joint work, usually each contribution can be registered separately. Suppose you and a friend write a song. You write the lyrics, your friend writes the melody. Each of you may possibly obtain separate copyrights for your contributions to this collaborative effort. Similarly, suppose you and your friend each write chapters of a novel. Each of you can potentially copyright the parts you wrote.

SPECIAL ISSUES FOR COPYRIGHTING MUSIC

Copyright protection for music is automatic, but the issues are far from simple. A song gets copyright protection as soon as it's created and "embodied" in some form.

But the usual form of embodiment, a basic recording of your song, actually includes two copyrights. One copyright consists of the *sound recording* of your musical composition, and the other copyright exists for the *musical composition.*

A sound recording consists of the *actual sounds* embodied on your audiotape, whether these include singing, musical instruments, computer-generated sounds, or exotic animal noises. A musical composition can be purely instrumental or any imaginable combination of lyrics and music. It's also possible to copyright lyrics separately as a literary work.

USING THE COPYRIGHT NOTICE

The tiny little copyright symbol puts the world on notice of your legal rights. This symbol is optional, but it can be worth your while to display it prominently on all of your copyrighted works. Your failure to do so may allow the infringer to assert a defense of *innocent infringement.* This means that an infringer claims he was unaware of your copyright protection. A successful innocent infringement defense can result in a reduction of the monetary damages that you would otherwise receive.

A proper copyright notice, for all works other than sound recordings, consists of three elements:

1. C-in-a circle © or the word *Copyright* or the abbreviation *Copyr.*

2. The year of first publication

3. The name of the copyright owner

> ⚖ **LAWYER'S NOTE:** *While displaying the copyright notice is not required for works published since 1989, it thwarts a defense of innocent infringement.*

For sound recordings, the copyright symbol is actually the letter *P* (for *phonorecord*) in a circle ℗, followed by the year of publication and the copyright owner's name. The Copyright Act does not permit you to spell out *phonorecord.* You have to use the P-in-a-circle.

Immediately following the copyright notice, you should also add the words "All Rights Reserved." This provides special protections in foreign jurisdictions.

> ⚖ **LAWYER'S NOTE:** *The copyright notice should be written in a place that will provide reasonable notice to prospective infringers, such as the cover of your CD or the packaging of your product. Use the copyright notice on all copies of your work, even demos and samples you give to friends. An infringer who gains access to a work through an "unnoticed" copy distributed by or under the authority of the copyright owner can argue "innocent infringement" which may reduce damages to which you are entitled.*

RESEARCHING EXISTING COPYRIGHTS

Receiving a letter that you're being sued for infringement is about as much fun as an IRS audit notice. Research reduces your risk of being sued for infringement. If you do your research, you'll likely be able to dispose of unwarranted infringement claims with a letter of your own. There are three common ways to investigate whether a work is under copyright protection and the scope of the copyright holder's claim.

LOOK FOR THE COPYRIGHT NOTICE

Sometimes the answer to a problem is in plain view and doesn't have to be unearthed by painstaking research. Examine a copy of the work for the copyright notice, place and date of publication, author, and publisher. For example, if the work is a sound recording, examine the disk or tape cartridge. Flip through the pages of a book or manuscript, and make sure you have a complete copy of all the pages that may contain the copyright notice.

SEARCH THE COPYRIGHT OFFICE ARCHIVES

The location of Copyright Office records varies, depending on how far back in time you need to go. The Copyright Office published the *Catalog of Copyright Entries* (*CCE*) in printed format from 1891 through 1978. From 1979 through 1982, the *CCE* was issued in microfiche format.

You can research registrations subsequent to 1982 on the Internet, by accessing the free database located at www.copyright.gov. Simply go to the home page and click the link "Search Copyright Records." You can search the database using the title of the work, the name of the assignee or assignor, or a document number (if you have one).

HAVE THE COPYRIGHT OFFICE SEARCH FOR YOU

Upon request, the Copyright Office staff will search its own records, charging $75 for each hour or fraction of an hour consumed. Based on the information you furnish, the office will provide an estimate of the total search fee. If you decide to go ahead with the search, send the estimated amount with your re-

⚖️ **LAWYER'S NOTE:** *Certified searches are sometimes required to meet the evidentiary requirements of litigation. The office will certify your search request for an extra $80 an hour.*

quest. The office will do its search and send you a written report or, if you request, tell you the results by phone.

The Copyright Office staff will search its indexes covering the records of assignments and other recorded documents as to ownership of copyrights. But the Copyright Office doesn't interpret the content of its documents or their legal effect. You may need a lawyer for that.

> ⚖ **LAWYER'S NOTE:** *Movies are often based on other works such as books or serialized contributions to periodicals or other collective works. Unfortunately, if you need a search for an underlying work, you must specifically request such a search of underlying works and furnish the specific titles, authors, and approximate dates of these works.*

SUPPLEMENTARY REGISTRATION

If you don't get your copyright registration done correctly or completely the first time, you're allowed to amend it later. The amending process is called *supplementary registration.*

Supplementary registration is used when the basic registration is incorrect or incomplete. The law provides for "filing of an application for supplementary registration, to correct an error in a copyright registration or to amplify the information given in a registration."[3] The information in the basic registration record remains unchanged. The supplementary registration is cross-referenced to the record of the original registration.

RECORDING A CHANGE IN COPYRIGHT OWNERSHIP

You can record assignments and transfers of copyright ownership with the Copyright Office. The transfer document must bear the actual signature of the person who executed it, or it must be accompanied by a

---

[3] 17 U.S.C. Section 408(d).

sworn or official certification that it is a true copy of the original signed document.[4]

For more information on the specifics of recording a document, consult the Copyright Office publication, *Recordation of Transfers and Other Documents*. You can find this document at the U.S. Copyright Office Web site located at http://www.copyright.gov/circs/circ12.pdf.

⚖ **LAWYER'S NOTE**: *The U.S. Copyright Office also keeps records of all transfers and assignments of a copyright, so you can tell who owns it at a given point in time.*

---

[4] 17 U.S.C. 205(a).

PART FOUR

....

Practical Patent Concepts

CHAPTER 11 >>>>>

What Can You Patent?

A PATENT OPERATES as a minimonopoly on a technology. Patent holders have the exclusive right to profit from innovations covered by their patents. They also have the right to keep others from selling a product that has only trivial modifications to the product they've patented and is designed to accomplish the same thing. Society has an interest in promoting technology by rewarding and protecting the investment of the creators. However, too many patents in the marketplace can stifle innovation and privatize knowledge that would be of far greater benefit to the world if left in the public domain.

IN THIS CHAPTER YOU FIND OUT:

- What ideas can and cannot be patented

- Why business method patents are so controversial

- The advantages of design patents over copyrights

- How to avoid inadvertently having your work fall into the public domain

IN THE FALL of 1997, Amazon.com files the most controversial patent application of the decade. It's entitled "A Method and System for Placing a Purchase Order via a Communications Network." But most people just refer to it as the as the "1-Click" patent. It describes a now-familiar on-line shopping system where customers enter their credit card number and address just once so that on future visits to the Web site all it takes is one mouse click to make a purchase. On September 28, 1999, two years and one week after filing the application, Amazon.com is awarded Patent Number 5,960,411 for the 1-Click method.

Twenty-two days later, Amazon.com files a lawsuit against Barnesandnoble.com, its largest competitor. Amazon wants to stop Barnesandnoble from using their Express Lane feature, which allows the Barnesandnoble's server to recognize the purchaser and access previously submitted shipping and credit information. Amazon alleges this feature infringes upon its 1-Click business method patent.

On December 1, 1999, the eve of the holiday shopping season, the court issues a preliminary injunction against Barnesandnoble. Barnesandnoble is ordered to remove Express Lane from its Web site. Barnesandnoble appeals this decision and loses. Its Express Lane technology is shelved.[1]

> **CAUTION:** It is difficult to tell by looking at the language of a patent what it may ultimately cover. In an infringement dispute, a court may be called upon to interpret the language of a patent. A court may decide that a patent is either literally infringed based on the language of the claim, or that the allegedly infringing device has such trivial modifications that there is infringement under the doctrine of equivalents. The law in this area is constantly evolving (particularly with respect to the doctrine of equivalents), and it is difficult for even experienced patent attorneys to predict how courts may interpret the language of a specific patent.

Amazon's controversial patent has fueled arguments against overly aggressive patenting practices. One of Amazon's founding programmers, Paul Barton Davis, has publicly stated that Amazon.com's early development "relied on the use of tools that could not have been developed if other companies and individuals had taken the same approach

----

[1] *Amazon.com, Inc., v. Barnesandnoble.com, Inc.*, 239 F.3d 1343 (2001).

to technological innovation that the company is now following." He calls Amazon's 1-Click patent "a cynical and ungrateful use of an extremely obvious technology."

A CONTRACT BETWEEN INVENTOR AND GOVERNMENT

Patents can be viewed as a contract between the government and the patent holder. To encourage private entrepreneurs to undertake all of the research, testing, effort, and expenditure that accompany any new technology, the government agrees to afford a twenty-year monopoly. After the twenty-year period, the invention enters the public domain, where anyone can freely make, use, sell, or profit from it.

CONSTITUTIONAL BASIS: TO PROMOTE "USEFUL ARTS"

The U.S. Constitution specifically authorizes Congress "[t]o promote the Progress of . . . useful Arts, by securing for limited Times to . . . Inventors the exclusive Right to their . . . Discoveries."[2] A patent holder can sue in federal court to enforce the rights granted by Congress.

What exactly are these "useful arts" referenced in the Constitution? This term was originally interpreted to include processes, machines, and manufactured goods. All of these types of patents are known as *utility patents*. In the last few decades, patent law has evolved and expanded to include ornamental design patents, business method patents, and patents of certain types of plants.

Patents protect what an invention *does*, as opposed to how it *looks*. Copyright, on the other hand, has historically protected the aesthetic aspects of an invention. There used to be a relatively clear line between patent and copyright law. But that line is blurring with the recognition of design patents. Innovators, in many cases, may now choose between copyright and design patent protections, or, in some cases, even opt for both.

---

[2] United States Constitution, Article I, Section 8, Clause 8.

WHAT CAN YOU PATENT?

Patent protections are not intended to remove existing knowledge from the public domain. For this reason, patents protect some ideas and exclude others. Case law, statutes, and the U.S. Constitution all limit the scope of what can be patented. The U.S. Supreme Court has observed that patents should not "restrict free access to materials already available" but should "add to the sum of useful knowledge."[3] The Patent Act specifies four categories of patentable subject matter: processes, machines, articles of manufacture, and compositions of matter.

PROCESSES AND BUSINESS METHODS

Processes are a series of useful steps to accomplish a result. They involve some sort of physical or chemical interactions. The popular Scotchgard process for treating carpets, furniture, and clothing so they're more stain resistant is a process. So are methods for taking the caffeine out of coffee or compressing a file on your computer.

In 1980 the U.S. Supreme Court decided whether a method for producing genetically engineered forms of bacteria constituted a patentable process. The purpose of the bacteria was to break down the components of crude oil. The Supreme Court overturned a lower court decision that held that the bacterium was unpatentable because the patentee had discovered "only some of the handiwork of nature." The Supreme Court reversed this decision, finding that "the patentee has produced a new bacterium with markedly different characteristics from any found in nature."[4]

Business method patents are an important outgrowth of the patentability of a process. Processes are a series of steps that collectively accomplish a

> **$$ BUSINESS TIP:** *The recent willingness of the courts to grant broad protection to business methods provides new opportunities for businesses to acquire significant protection against competitors.*

[3] *Graham v. John Deere Co.*, 383 U.S. 1 (1966).
[4] *Diamond v. Chakrabarty,* 447 U.S. 303 (1980).

useful result. A business method can fit within the definition of a process. For example, a process for calculating mortgage rates is entitled to patent protections,[5] and so is the Amazon.com 1-Click method.

MACHINES

A machine such as an engine accomplishes a result through the interaction of its parts. An example of a very simple machine is a yo-yo. It has two interacting movable parts, a string, and a plastic body with a groove. Recently the PTO granted U.S. Patent No. 6,468,125 to cover a yo-yo shaped like a spinning top.

ARTICLES OF MANUFACTURE

An article of manufacture is usually an object without movable parts, such as a chair, a mop, or a pen. There's a lot of overlap in the definitions of machines and articles of manufacture, and consequently neither the PTO nor the courts require you to specifically classify an invention as either a machine or article of manufacture.

COMPOSITIONS OF MATTER

A composition of matter is a combination of chemicals or other materials that can be used to achieve a result. In 1941, a man named Roy Plunkett received a patent for the composition of matter commercially known as Teflon. In 1900, Felix Hoffman received a patent for acetyl salicylic acid, known as aspirin.[6]

---

[5] *State Street Bank & Trust Co. v. Signature Fin. Group, Inc.*, 149 F.3d 1368 (Fed. Cir. 1998).
[6] Subsequent misuse of the trademark name Aspirin resulted in the loss of protection for this trademark, but that's covered in chapter 3.

CHEMICAL AND PHARMACEUTICAL PATENTS

Many drug and chemical patents involve new uses of known sub-stances. The Supreme Court offered the following analysis regarding chemical patents in 1980:[7]

> The number of chemicals either known to scientists or disclosed by existing research is vast. It grows constantly as those engaging in "pure" research publish their discoveries. The number of these chemicals that have known uses of commercial or social value, in contrast, is small. Development of new uses for existing chemicals is thus a major component of practical chemical research. It may take years of unsuccessful testing before a chemical having a de-sired property is identified, and it may take several years of further testing before a proper and safe method of using that chemical is developed.

NEW USES FOR OLD PRODUCTS

Suppose someone uses a hairpin to improve the performance of a car engine. This new use of a hairpin can be patented. The new patent would be limited to that use, and prior patented uses would be unaf-fected. Processes, in particular, don't have to be new to be patented. The Patent Act provides that the term *process* includes a new use of a previ-ously known process.

UTILITY PATENTS: CONCRETE APPLICATIONS VERSUS ABSTRACT IDEAS

Einstein wouldn't have been able to patent his formula, $E = mc^2$. This formula is simply an idea, a theory about a law of nature, and not a spe-cific device or process. Patent law draws a sharp distinction between ab-stract ideas and specific, useful applications. Ideas, like Einstein's theory

---

[7] *Dawson Chemical v. Rohm & Haas,* 448 U.S. 176 (1980).

of relativity or Newton's law of gravity are considered unpatentable laws of nature. But inventions *applying* these theories are patentable.

OVERVIEW: THE FOUR REQUIREMENTS FOR UTILITY PATENTS

Humans shouldn't be able to take credit for the work of nature. This is the basic principle underlying the statutory requirements for patent protection. The statute is intended to separate ideas and laws of nature from actual useful inventions.

Utility patents are the broadest and most common form of patent protection. To qualify for one, the invention must be:

1. Within the classes described by the patent statute

2. Useful

3. Novel

4. Nonobvious

REQUIREMENT #1: THE INVENTION MUST FALL WITHIN A STATUTORY CATEGORY

To be patentable, an invention must fall within one of the categories described by the U.S. Patent Act.

The act provides, "[W]hoever invents or discovers any new and useful **process, machine,** articles of manufacture or **composition of matter,** or any **new and useful improvement thereof,** may obtain a patent therefore subject to the conditions and requirements subject to this title." (Emphasis is added here to the words in the statute.)[8]

A process is a set of steps that achieve a result, and the remaining three categories pretty much represent products that may be brought to market. Machines have moving parts, while articles of manufacture are useful objects like chairs and hairpins. Compositions of matter are chemical inventions and combinations of materials that may come out of labs or are stumbled upon accidentally. New and useful improve-

---

[8] 35 U.S. Sec. 101.

ments include both upgrades and novel applications of technology in the public domain.

REQUIREMENT #2: THE INVENTION MUST BE USEFUL

In the advertising sections of health and fitness magazines you can find advertisements for products that are supposed to burn fat, build muscle, or add inches to a woman's bustline. Since the ads appear month after month, the products probably turn a profit. None of them, however, qualify for patent protection absent a showing that they achieve a useful result.

The use of an invention must be specifically disclosed in the patent application. A patent must specifically demonstrate the functioning application of an idea. If this weren't required, the effect would be to grant a patent on an unknown range of applications, rather than restricting it to the particular application that the inventor has realized. This would be tantamount to allowing patents to encompass ideas rather than demonstrably useful applications, undermining the intent and structure of the patent system.

To be useful, an invention must have a stated purpose, and it must actually work. Fortunately, usefulness is usually the easiest criterion for mechanical and electrical patents to meet, because most inventions of this type are developed to serve a need. (The use can be purely aesthetic, such as waterproof mascara or a fabric that doesn't wrinkle.) However, this requirement can be more difficult to meet in the case of new chemical compounds which are still being tested to ascertain their usefulness.

What about a process that results in a product that's currently useless but might be useful in the future? In 1966, the Supreme Court held that "a patent is not a hunting license."[9] The court considered a patent application for a chemical process that had no discernable utility. The developers argued that because of the importance of ongoing chemical research, they should only have to demonstrate a possible future utility. The majority of the court rejected this approach as having the potential

---

[9] *Brenner v. Manson*, 383 U.S. 519 (1966).

to be too broad a monopoly on ideas. Justice Harlan, writing for the dissent, argued that it was not as important that the process be useful as it was that the process be successful.

Ultimately, courts have moved more toward Justice Harlan's approach. To give pharmaceutical manufacturers some breathing room, courts have held that successful clinical trials on animals demonstrate a probability that the drug will be useful for humans.[10]

A final caveat to the usefulness requirement is that the use must be legitimate. The Patent and Trademark Office will reject applications for products that have only the purpose of deceiving or endangering the public. For example, the office probably wouldn't issue a patent for counterfeiting money or turning back the miles on an odometer. The Atomic Energy Act of 1954 prohibits people from patenting atomic weapons.

REQUIREMENT #3: THE INVENTION MUST BE NOVEL

One of the legally strongest and commercially successful patents of all time is the Polaroid camera patent. Prior to Polaroid, instant imaging simply didn't exist. Consumers had to wait hours, days, or even weeks for their photos to be run through a heavily equipped darkroom. The debut of the Polaroid meant that you could watch your picture develop in minutes, before your very eyes. The Polaroid camera was clearly a novel invention.

In the 1970s, Polaroid was successful in enjoining Kodak from introducing its own instant imaging technology on the market. Kodak's version employed many of the same or analogous chemical processes to achieve a substantially similar result. Kodak was not only required to stop making the infringing camera, it had to turn over all of its profits from the sale of the device to Polaroid.[11]

The Patent Act provides that a patent cannot issue if the invention is known, used, or published by others in the United States or patented

---

[10] See, e.g., *Campbell v. Wettstein*, 476 F.2d 642 (C.C.P.A. 1973).
[11] *Polaroid Inc. v. Eastman Kodak Co.*, 228 USPQ 305 (D.Mass 1985), aff'd 229 USPQ 561 (Fed. Cir. 1986).

in a foreign country prior to the date of invention disclosed on the application.[12]

In deciding whether or not an invention meets the novelty requirement, patent examiners may consider factors such as:

1. What's covered by patents issued anywhere in the world prior to the filing date of the present application?

2. What inventions have been published anywhere in the world prior to the date of the application?

3. What kinds of similar inventions are being sold or offered for sale in the United States?

4. What kinds of similar inventions are being publicly used?

5. What kinds of similar inventions are in the public domain?

6. Has another inventor or manufacturer built or used a similar invention without having abandoned, suppressed, or concealed it?

REQUIREMENT #4: THE INVENTION MUST BE NONOBVIOUS

Nonobviousness would seem to automatically result from novelty, but they're really two distinct requirements. Nonobviousness speaks to the level of creative inventiveness.

Federal law also provides, with respect to novelty, that a patent application be filed within one year of the following events:

• Use or offer for sale in the United States by anyone

• Publication anywhere in the world

Anything that's new is, by definition, novel. Nonobviousness is a requirement that the invention be sufficiently creative so that it's an actual contribution to the field to which it's introduced. Anything less than an

---

[12] 35 U.S. Sec. 102.

actual inventive contribution doesn't justify the grant of the monopoly conferred by patent protection.

Nonobviousness is decided in the context of "prior art." What has been the practice and scope of knowledge prior to the introduction of the invention? What is the difference between the new invention and previously used devices or processes?

In 1941, the Supreme Court held that a device wasn't patentable because it lacked the "flash of genius" normally associated with a nonobvious invention.[13] The court explained that nonobviousness requires a unique insight, which would not be disclosed by simple research. The court subsequently abandoned this requirement.

Combinations of well-known technologies and devices can meet the nonobvious requirement if they're more useful than the mere sum of the components. This is known as the concept of "synergism." A synergistic result provides support for nonobviousness.[14]

The courts also take into account so-called secondary considerations. If a new product takes the market by storm, selling like wildfire, that's a pretty good indication that it's nonobvious.

In 1966, the Supreme Court established the following four-part test for analyzing whether an invention is nonobvious:

1. What is the scope and content of the prior art?

2. What are the differences between the prior art and the claimed subject matter art?

3. What was the level of ordinary skill in the art at the time the invention was made?

4. What secondary considerations, such as commercial success of the claimed innovation, justify the grant of the patent?[15]

---

[13] *Cuno Engineering Corp. v. Automatic Devices Corp.*, 314 U.S. 8 (1941).
[14] *Sakraida v. Ag Pro Inc.*, 425 U.S. 273 (1976).
[15] *Graham v. John Deer Co.*, 383 U.S 1 (1966).

DESIGN PATENTS: INVENTIONS OF AESTHETIC VALUE

Humans long for beauty in their surroundings, and no matter how useful an object is, a pleasant aesthetic appearance increases its value. The Patent Act recognizes this.[16]

Design patents are available for new, original, and ornamental designs for articles of manufacture. They're generally used to protect the shape, ornamental features, and appearance of a functional article. They are a blurring of the distinction between patent and copyright law, since copyrights have traditionally been used to protect the expressive, nonfunctional aspects of an innovation.

WHAT DESIGN PATENTS PROTECT

Design patents cover only the nonfunctional aspects of a product design. For example, consider the design of most chairs; they all function in pretty much the same way. However, chairs can be very different in appearance. It's the aesthetic differences that are protectable by design patents.

In 1958, Eero Saarinen developed the pedestal chair, which consisted of a single piece of molded plastic that formed a chair seat, supported on a pedestal rather than the traditional legs. Mr. Saarinen carefully experimented with different materials and dimensions to make sure the chair would support the weight of the user.

$$ BUSINESS TIP: *Even minor modifications within an existing design trend may fulfill the requirements of a design patent. But does the level of protection you get for those modifications justify the cost and waiting time for the patent?*

In 1968, another designer, Erwine Laverne, applied for a design patent for a pedestal-type chair, but with a differently shaped and molded seat. The PTO initially denied Mr. Laverne a separate patent for his design, because it

---

[16] 35 U.S.C. Sec. 171.

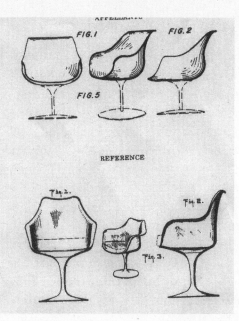

FIGURE 11-1: *The court used these drawings to compare the Saarinen chair (top) and the Laverne chair (bottom).*

varied from Saarinen's only by some modifications to the shape of the molded plastic seat. Mr. Laverne appealed. The U.S. Court of Customs and Patent Appeals, relying on the drawings produced by the PTO, shown in Figure 11-1, sided with Mr. Laverne. (The top row of drawings depicts the Saarinen chair, the bottom row the Laverne one.)

The court acknowledged the overall similarity of the chairs but explained, "One might feel that the two chairs were part of the same style trend . . . but they are in our opinion distinctly different designs within that style trend. The design which initiates a new style does not automatically close the field to all other designs within the same style pattern." [17]

---

[17] *Application of Erwine Laverne and Estelle Laverne*, 53 C.C.P.A. 1158, 356 F. 2d 1003 (1966). (Laverne's design patent covers only the molded seat portion of the chair and not the pedestal.)

REQUIREMENTS FOR DESIGN PATENTS

Not surprisingly, there's no requirement of utility for a design patent.

The requirements of novelty and nonobviousness for design patents are the same as for utility patents, but in addition, the statute substitutes the requirement of *ornamentality*.

To observe that the tests for novelty and nonobviousness are vague is an understatement. Novelty is usually determined by an "ordinary observer" test and nonobviousness to the "ordinary designer"[18] Another equally specific test for nonobviousness is that which would be "non-obvious to the ordinary intelligent man."[19]

The ornamental aspects must be visible in the course of the normal, intended use of the object or at some commercially critical point such as the advertising of the product. For example, the design of a toupee intended to look more natural than prior toupee designs may not be apparent in normal usage but can be made apparent at the time of purchase and in the advertising.

The main restriction of design patents is that they cannot be acquired for an *exclusively* functional design. Design patents protect only the aesthetic appearance of an item, never utilitarian features. For example, a design patent may cover the external appearance of an automobile, but it won't cover the functioning parts such as a newly developed retractable sun roof or specially tinted windows that have the function of minimizing glare if the design aspects of these features were dictated solely by functionality. These aspects of the design would have to be protected by a separate utility patent, if they meet the requirements of usefulness, novelty, and nonobviousness.

DESIGN PATENTS VERSUS COPYRIGHTS

Design patents and copyrights both cover the artistic aspects of an innovation. Where does one begin and the other end? Which innovations are entitled to both types of protection?

Not all elements of design are subject to dual legal protections. The

---

[18] *In Re Nalabandian*, 661 F.2d 1214 (Cust. & Pat. App. 1981).
[19] *Schwinn Bicycle Co. v. Goodyear Tire and Rubber Co.*, 444 F. 2d 295 (9th Cir. 1970).

Patent and Trademark Office won't issue design patents for pictures or mere surface ornamentation (such as an engraved design or logo). Examples of designs sufficiently functional to be patented include the Mrs. Butterworth's syrup bottle (shaped like a plump woman), or the shape of the handle of a lint remover. Purely aesthetic works such as photographs and paintings and nonfunctional sculptures don't qualify for patent protection either.

The Need for Overlapping Protections: Arrow's Paradox

Every grant of patent or copyright protection costs society by taking innovation out of the public domain. Therefore, it seems odd that Congress and the courts allow overlapping protections.

Copyright protection is automatic, but it only protects against outright copying, not the process of creating. Patent protection is more expensive, and the process takes an average of two years to complete, but it can give you more freedom to market your ideas.

Suppose an inventor is in the process of developing a new type of swinging hammock chair that gives the appearance of being suspended without support. The innovator of the chair wants to approach manufacturers with his idea. Unlike a work of authorship, where the manuscript automatically serves as proof of creation and ownership, once the process for creating the chair is described, it can be replicated. The idea itself isn't protected by copyright law. And no manufacturer is likely to invest the resources to produce and market the chair without knowing, with a fairly high degree of specificity, what's entailed in the design. This dilemma—the simultaneous need for secrecy to protect the idea and disclosure to develop it—is known as *Arrow's disclosure paradox*. It's named after an economist, Kenneth Arrow, who identified it.

On the other hand, suppose the inventor has limited resources and feels that obtaining a patent would be too costly. It might be cheaper to design and copyright a prototype chair. The prototype would meet the copyright requirement that the innovation must be in fixed, tangible form. The innovator would be protected against actual copying. However, copyright

> ⚖ LAWYER'S NOTE: Design patents are less expensive and quicker to obtain than utility patents.

protection could be narrower in scope than patent protection, because a patent may cover the marketing of inventions having some minor, nonfunctional changes, whether or not actual copying has taken place. This is called the doctrine of equivalents and is discussed in chapter 13.

Checklist: Choosing Between Design Patent and Copyright Protection

The choice between overlapping patent and copyright protections is economic, strategic, and goal oriented. You need to think about what it's going to take to get your innovation to market initially, as well as what it may take to protect your rights as the market for it expands.

Some of the considerations in the decision are as follows:

⚖️ **LAWYER'S NOTE:** *Design patents are best suited for protecting the shape and appearance of useful objects such as perfume bottles, furniture, cars, and appliances, which have designs that have commercial and economic value. Copyright is best suited for art that appears on functional objects such as a design or ornamentation that is not part of the physical, functional structure of the object.*

• **Cost and timing:** Copyright protection is automatic, once a work is in fixed, tangible form. Registration is optional and can usually be accomplished in six months or less for several hundred dollars, including attorney's and filing fees. Obtaining a design patent, on the other hand, generally can cost thousands of dollars and takes around a year or two.

• **Scope of protection:** Patent protection is far broader. A patent restricts others from commercial use of the idea for the invention and any functionally equivalent invention. A copyright only protects against actual copying of the expression of the idea, not all functionally equivalent commercial uses of the idea.

• **Duration of protection:** Copyright protection is of a much longer duration than patent protection. A design patent lasts for 14 years. Copyright protection generally lasts for the life of the author plus 75 years.

DESIGN PATENTS AND TRADEMARKS

Trademark law offers inventors the opportunity to double dip on intellectual property protections. Unlike patents and copyrights, which can be mutually exclusive, trademark and patent protection usually go hand in hand.

The Coca-Cola Company patented the design of its bottle in 1937, and the appearance of the bottle was also recognized as a protectable trademark. Patent protects the ornamental design of an article of manufacture. Trademark status protects the public identity of the product and prevents confusion and deception.

PATENTING COMPUTER PROGRAMS

Copyright protection is automatic, but it has a distinct disadvantage when compared to patent protection for software: It only protects against outright copying and the creation of derivative works that are identified as such. In contrast, a patent prevents reverse engineering, where competitors may analyze the software product to develop their own functionally equivalent programs. A patent holder has a legal competitive advantage known as the *doctrine of equivalents*. This doctrine protects against products that have only minor variations but perform an identical function. Copyright law offers no protection against a functionally equivalent product obtained through reverse engineering other than copying.

Until the 1980s, it was virtually unheard of to get patent protection for software. Prior to that time, courts uniformly held that computer programs were types of mathematical algorithms, and since mathematical algorithms are laws of nature, patents were not appropriate.

> ⚖ **LAWYER'S NOTE:** *In order to be classified as a patentable process, a software program must affect some hardware or process and produce a useful result. It must be part of an overall process for achieving a result rather than an isolated mathematical algorithm.*

In 1981, the U.S. Supreme Court opened the door for software patents and signaled that it was no longer going to view all programs as simple algorithms. In *Diamond v. Diehr*[20] the court characterized a computer program for regulating the temperature in rubber molds as a process rather than an algorithm. The court reasoned the "process admittedly employs a well known mathematical equation, but [the developers] do not seek to pre-empt the use of that equation. Rather, they seek only to foreclose from others the use of that equation in conjunction with all other steps of their claimed process." The court went on to explain, "Obviously one does not need a 'computer' to cure natural or synthetic rubber," but that using a computer program to enhance or carry out the process did not automatically make the process unpatentable subject matter. This critical case, and the chronology of other cases pertinent to the protection of software, are discussed in detail in chapter 16.

BUSINESS METHOD PATENTS

Business method patents are close cousins to software patents. Both can trace their modern origins to a case that received less media outcry than the Amazon.com case but was far more legally significant.

THE BIRTH OF THE BUSINESS METHOD PATENT

In *State Street Bank v. Signature Financial Group,* the Court of Appeals for the Federal Circuit upheld a disputed patent involving a software system for tracking performance of pooled mutual fund investments for partnerships.[21] Citing *Diamond v. Diehr,* the court viewed the software as a practical application of an algorithm, rather than the algorithm itself. The court included in its opinion language that seemed to be an open invitation to businesses who used similar software-implemented business methods.

---

[20] 450 U.S. 175 (1981).
[21] 149 F. 3d 1368, 47 U.S.P.Q. 2d (BNA) 1596 (Fed. Cir. 1998), cert. denied, 119 S. Ct. 851 (1999).

Since the *State Street* case, the PTO has issued hundreds of business method patents, and has thousands more pending.

SHOULD JANITORIAL TRAINING PROCESSES BE PATENTABLE?

Critics of the business patent boom have argued that the PTO is going too far, issuing patents for trivial claims. For example, U.S. Patent 5,851,117 covers a method for training janitors. The method uses visual displays and systematic steps for cleaning in a safe, thorough, and efficient manner. In 1999, the PTO issued AT&T Corp. a patent for a process of inserting data into a billing field, which met with similar criticism.[22]

NEW PTO STANDARDS OF REVIEW

In response to public criticism and embarrassing press, the PTO announced in March 2000 that it would beef up its scrutiny of business patents.[23] The agency plans to implement new guidelines and meet on a regular basis with representatives from the software industry. Under the new guidelines, when you submit a business method patent, it will be viewed with a heightened level of scrutiny.

The PTO plans to implement a tougher two-tier system of review. After one examiner has conducted a detailed foreign and domestic prior art search, a second-level review will carefully scrutinize the scope of your business method patent claims. This means you can probably expect the process to take longer and generate more challenges to the validity of your patent.

---

[22] *AT&T Corp. v. Excel Communications, Inc.*, 50 U.S.P.Q. 2d 1447, 1443–54 (Fed. Cir. 1999).

[23] "U.S.P.T.O. Business Methods Patent Initiative Action Plan," March 29, 2000. (You can access this document at the U.S.P.T.O. Web site at www.uspto.gov.)

THE LEGISLATIVE OUTLOOK FOR BUSINESS METHOD PATENTS

The flurry of business method patents has not escaped the notice of Congress. The American Inventor's Protection Act of 1999 added a new section to the U.S. Patent Act specifically aimed at stemming the tide.[24]

The act provides a new First Inventor Defense. This defense allows you to avoid liability by proving your prior use of the disputed business process. To prevail on the defense, you must demonstrate that you used the claimed method for more than one year prior to the date the patent application was filed.

There's also pending legislation to make it tougher to get a business method patent. The proposed Business Method Improvement Act of 2000 would prohibit software developers from claiming protection for business methods that were previously implemented manually.[25] Under this standard, inserting data into a billing field might not qualify for a patent because preparing a bill is something that businesses have traditionally done manually.

SHOULD YOU FILE FOR A BUSINESS METHOD PATENT?

Many companies view a business method patent as a good defensive, competitive measure. It makes it harder for a new competitor to enter your market using your methods. A start-up business, short on venture capital, may be deterred by the risk of infringement litigation.

The economics of patenting trivial processes are questionable. Even if you pass the PTO's new heightened scrutiny, your patent may be subject to subsequent costly challenges to its validity.

On the other hand, if your business does employ significant innovative methods and processes, ownership of a business method patent can boost its balance sheet. The patent itself can be a valuable asset. The patent can be an important protection for the investment your company has made in research and development.

----

[24] 35 U.S.C. Sec. 273.
[25] H.R. 5364.

BIOTECHNOLOGY PATENTS: ALTERING LIFE-FORMS

Biotechnology patents are a favorite of the tabloids and are a political and ethical hot topic. Biotechnology is the use of advancements, such as DNA technologies, to create processes that alter biological systems and life-forms.

THE MOUSE THAT ROARED (LEGALLY)

In 1980, amid considerable controversy, on the heels of a decision protecting genetically altered bacteria, the Supreme Court awarded a patent to Harvard University for a genetically altered mouse. The mouse was specially developed to carry cancer cells in its genes and develop tumors quickly.

The Harvard mouse patent was significant, because it was the first to be granted to a new animal life-form. Genetically altered life-forms have since qualified for patent protection as compositions of matter, as well as processes.

IS IT ETHICAL?

Biotechnology patents pose some ethical questions. The Patent Office may not be the place to decide ethical issues. Some hotly debated topics in this area include:

- The economic impact on farmers of having to pay royalties whenever patented livestock are reproduced

- The environmental impact of genetically engineered microorganisms

- Ethical questions surrounding the treatment of animals in producing genetically altered breeds

- Whether genetically altered human materials should be entitled to patent protections

CLONING HUMANS

Once they cloned Dolly, the sheep, no one in the scientific community doubted that human cloning would soon follow. Europe has already adopted legislation denying patents for processes that involve human cloning.

Should the United States follow the European example? Human cloning technologies are clearly patentable. They meet all of the statutory requirements of proper subject matter and utility. Uses include providing an alternative for organ transplantation or allowing individuals who cannot otherwise reproduce to become parents. Anticloning legislation raises the question of whether patent law, which is designed to reward innovation, should prohibit politically undesirable inventions.

CAN A PLANT BE INVENTED?

In 1931, the U.S. Supreme Court granted a patent to Henry Bosenberg for his climbing, ever-blooming rose. This was the first time the Supreme Court had acknowledged the now well-established principle that an inventor of a plant is the first person who "discovers" and reproduces its distinctive qualities by breeding or grafting.

Plants that already exist in a wild or uncultivated state can't be patented. They occur freely in nature, rather than as the product of some sort of scientific discovery.

Plant patents are easier to get than utility patents, but they provide less protection. A holder of a plant patent can't preclude someone from purchasing patented seeds and then legally selling the plants they've grown. However, the holder of a utility patent can claim infringement if the item covered by the patent is sold without permission. The protection afforded by a plant patent is the exclusive right to reproduce the plant.

The requirements for

$$ BUSINESS TIP: *Some plant development processes may qualify for utility patent protection, which is broader than the protection afforded by plant patents. Plant patents do not prevent the sale of plants grown from patented seeds.*

plant patents differ slightly from the requirements for utility patents. Instead of novelty, utility, and nonobviousness, plant patents require novelty, distinctiveness, and nonobviousness. The requirement of distinctiveness is substituted for the requirement of utility.

To meet the distinctiveness requirement, your plant must have been *asexually produced*. This means that the plant is reproduced by a method other than seeds. This usually involves cutting or grafting of plant tissue. This criteria replaces the usefulness requirement of utility patents.

Novelty can be assessed by looking at the characteristics that make the plant different from other plants. Generally, plant patent applications speak to issues of soil composition requirements, color, odor, taste, and durability of the plant. The nonobviousness requirement looks to the extent to which the plant represents an innovation or improvement over existing plants, given the state of the horticultural art.

WHAT RIGHTS DOES A PATENT GIVE YOU?

As a patent holder, your rights can be summed up in a word: exclusivity. As the owner of a U.S. patent you can exclude others in the U.S. from using, offering for sale, and selling what is covered by your patent.

Not only is it an infringement for someone to use your invention, design, or business method, it's an infringement for them to attempt to accomplish the same result using an immaterial variation.

THE TERM OF A PATENT

The "monopoly" granted by a patent is subject to a set term of years, after which time the subject matter of your patent enters the public domain for anyone to use. The years you're allotted depend on the type of patent.

Design patents are granted for a fourteen-year life. Utility patents filed after June 7, 1995 last for twenty years from the date of filing the application. Additionally, a patent holder may be entitled to some extra days, by law, if the Patent and Trademark Office unduly delays taking action on an application.

The duration of a patent can be extended if any of the following types of delays occur:

• **Regulatory review:** Patents may be extended if marketing has been delayed due to regulatory review.

• **Failure of the PTO to examine a new application:** If the PTO fails to examine a new application within fourteen months of filing, the term can be extended.

• **Failure of the PTO to issue a patent within 3 years:** This exception only applies if the applicant didn't cause the delay.

• **Failure of the PTO to undertake certain administrative actions:** An extension will be granted if the PTO fails for more than four months to undertake certain actions necessary to grant the patent.

These extensions to the patent term are subject to a reduction for delays caused by the applicant.

PENDENCY PERIOD AND TERMINATION OF PATENT RIGHTS

The time between the date that a patent is filed and when the patent is issued is called the pendency period. As an applicant, you have no rights under patent law during this period to stop anyone from using or marketing your idea. However, once the patent issues, you have the right to sue to stop any infringing activity. You may also be entitled to seek royalties for the period subsequent to publication, provided certain notice requirements have been satisfied, as discussed following.

Patents are nonrenewable. Once they expire, you can't repatent the same idea. In exchange for the monopoly previously enjoyed, the new technology becomes part of the public domain. It's intended to become a building block for even more advanced technological advancements, which may in turn be the subject of future patents.

THE RIGHT TO PRECLUDE FUNCTIONALLY EQUIVALENT WORKS: DOCTRINE OF EQUIVALENTS

The doctrine of equivalents is what makes patent law the most comprehensive form of intellectual property protection.

Because of this doctrine, patent law not only protects you from the prospect of someone directly copying your invention or design, it protects against the marketing of any invention or design that's functionally or aesthetically equivalent. The doctrine of equivalents is discussed more extensively in chapter 13.

⚖ **LAWYER'S NOTE:** *The doctrine of equivalents does expand a patent's scope beyond what is literally protected. However, claims in patent applications should be drafted to try to maximize what is literally covered.*

THE RIGHT OF SUPPRESSION

Sometimes a patent holder may decide its desirable *not* to market an innovation. The United States doesn't require the marketing of a patented invention, although in other countries the failure to commercialize an invention may result in the loss of patent rights.

The decision not to market a patented invention is distinct from a decision to conceal or fail to patent the invention. The latter may result in the loss of rights to a competing inventor who files for a patent.[26]

LIMITATIONS ON PATENT RIGHTS

One of the most colorful and controversial inventors of all time was Jerome Lemelson. Mr. Lemelson acquired more than 550 patents during his life, and some argued that he "didn't patent inventions. He invented patents." Critics argue that Lemelson built a career on shrewdly predicting trends and emerging technology and acquiring a patent di-

---

[26] 35 U.S.C. 102.

rectly in its path. Lemelson amassed millions of dollars asserting, litigating, and settling claims resulting from patents he acquired this way.[27]

In 1998, customers of two companies that manufactured and sold bar code scanners and related products began receiving letters from Lemelson accusing them of patent infringement. Both companies sued to have Lemelson's bar code–related patents declared invalid. The patents in question were initially filed in the 1950s and were pending for decades. On appeal, the court declared Lemelson's patents potentially unenforceable on the basis of unreasonable delay (under a common law concept called "laches"), noting that Lemelson had legally maneuvered the patent system so that the applications had been pending, but were not prosecuted, for a period of more than thirty years.[28]

An inventor's rights are limited by statutes and by case law. Case law considerations are based on fairness, to protect the interests of the public from inventors who unfairly conceal or misrepresent facts.

ONE YEAR SALE RULE

You can't patent a product after you've offered it to the public for sale for more than a year prior to the date of filing your application. You're barred from acquiring patent protection if you apply for it more than one year after the earliest date the invention is:

- First sold in the United States

- Offered for public use or sale in the United States, or

- Described in a publication printed in any country

Courts have been careful to distinguish between when an invention is offered for sale, as opposed to market testing or experimentation involving the public. In 1998, in *Pfaff v. Wells,* the Supreme Court established a two-part test for determining when the one-year period should start running.[29] The court held that there must first be an offer for com-

---

[27] Nicholas Varchaver, "The Patent King," *Fortune* magazine (May 14, 2001).

[28] *Symbol Technologies, Inc., v. Lemelson Medical, Education & Research Foundation,* 277 F.3d 1361 (Fed. Cir. 2002).

[29] 119 S. Ct. 304 (1998).

mercial sale that isn't related to experimentation. Second, there must be sufficient documentation to demonstrate that the invention is ready for patenting or has been reduced to practice.

CAUTION: *Despite the apparent restrictiveness of the one-year rule in the United States, this a lot more liberal than the standards of some foreign countries. In many countries, any offer of sale or publication within their borders may prevent obtaining patent protection in that country.*

PUBLISHING INFORMATION ABOUT YOUR INVENTION

Whether you're a scientist, entrepreneur, or academician, you may be understandably eager to publish your new findings. Doing so can earn you a lot of well-deserved recognition in your field. It can also operate as a bar to your patent if publication occurs more than one year prior to the filing of your application.

The date of publication, which starts your one-year statutory bar period for patent protection, is the date the publication is first catalogued and made available in any library.

It's not an uncommon request that a submission be treated as confidential. You might consider including a disclaimer such as the following on your manuscript: "This material is submitted solely for the purpose of being considered for publication. The material in this article shall not be disclosed or distributed for any other purposes without the express written consent of the author."

SCOPE OF THE CLAIMS

The rights granted under the patent are strictly limited to the claims set out in it. It's important that the person drafting the application have the expertise to ensure that claims are drafted as broadly as possible to maximize the scope of the protection, yet are specific enough to pass muster with the patent examiner.

The file in the Patent and Trademark Office that contains your patent application is sometimes called the *patent wrapper* or *file wrapper*. All statements, correspondence and supporting documentation pertaining to your patent are placed in the file.

You may be asked by an examiner during an interview to disclaim some elements of your patent during the process. For example, if the patent examiner determines that the tinted glass of an automobile design isn't patentable, the examiner may ask you to relinquish that particular claim.

Subsequently, if you want to sue another automobile manufacturer for infringing your tinted glass design, you're precluded from suing on the basis that the tinted glass is an infringement. This is sometimes called *file wrapper estoppel* or *prosecution history estoppel*.

The attorney that represents the alleged infringer will want to examine the entire file wrapper. Any statements, correspondence, or notes contained in the file can diminish the scope of your claims.

VIOLATIONS OF ANTITRUST LAW AND OTHER MISUSE

The courts have held that violations of antitrust law and other unfair practices may constitute misuse of a patent. For example, in *Morton Salt Co. vs. Suppinger Co.*[30] the court held that it was a violation of antitrust law to require the purchase of an unpatented product in order for a buyer to be permitted to purchase the patented machine. The court held that the defendant, the seller of an infringing patented machine, thus had a successful defense to the infringement action.

---

[30] 314 U.S. 488 (1942).

CHAPTER 12 >>>

Filing a Successful Patent Application

NO ONE KNOWS what the true value of a process to clone a cat or a cow may be worth. The ultimate value of a patent often depends on market factors that are impossible to predict. The patent may soar in value or be rendered worthless by competing and complementary technologies. Its value may even hinge on regulatory issues like FDA approval. Regardless, at the time the application is filed, every inventor has an interest in obtaining a patent having the broadest possible scope.

IN THIS CHAPTER YOU FIND OUT:

- The role of the Patent and Trademark Office

- About hiring attorneys and patent agents to assist with your claims

- The requirements and procedures for filing a patent application

- How to obtain the broadest protection

- What to do if your application is denied

THREE BARNYARD ANIMALS have become central figures in a high-stakes patent war involving the cloning of animals. Dolly, a sheep, undisputedly the first cloned animal to walk the earth, is owned by a company named Geron. However, another company, Infigen, owner of Gene, a cloned cow, claims to have records and documentation to show its use of the cloning technology that produced Gene more that a year prior to Dolly's debut. A third company, Advanced Cell Technology, Inc. (ACT) claims that their George is the real cash cow in the cloning debate, and they hold the patent to prove it.

There's no dispute that ACT won the paper chase, having been awarded patent No. 5,945,577 for the technology that produced George. In European countries, the first to file is the clear winner. If this were the standard in the United States, ACT's claim would trump. However, the U.S. Patent Act provides that a patent cannot issue if the invention is known, used, or published by others prior to the date of filing of the application.[1] Infigen claims detailed lab records support its first use of the technology.

The U.S. Patent Office has agreed to hear Geron's and Infigen's challenges to the ACT patent. The filing and processing of the patent applications is expected to figure prominently in the case. Geron, owner of Dolly, said its patent application was submitted first, then ignored or overlooked by patent clerks, allowing ACT to win. Infigen also claims that the same patent office, in Arlington, Virginia, lost its paperwork.

Currently the three companies involved in this barnyard squabble (ACT, Geron, and Infigen) have more than twenty patents pending between them.

At stake are millions or perhaps even billions of dollars of anticipated revenue from superefficient milk-producing cow clones and clone-derived pharmaceuticals. Not to mention the huge potential market for cloned pets. Genetic Savings & Clone in College Station, Texas has already reported the first cat clone.[2]

Although a patent costs thousands of dollars and takes years to procure, it's the most coveted of all intellectual property protections. The patent prosecution is the unique legal process that has the sole purpose

---

[1] 35 U.S. Sec. 102.
[2] Raja Mishra, "Firms Fight over Lucrative Patent Rights to Animal Cloning," NewsFactor Network, February 20, 2002.

of determining whether something new and useful has been discovered and a patent should issue.

PLAYERS IN THE PATENT PROCESS

A patent prosecution is a rather quirky legal proceeding. It's a unique process where lawyers, engineers, software developers, and scientists come together to hash out what knowledge will be disclosed for the betterment of society. To encourage such disclosure, the patent laws grant the inventor monopoly status for the duration of a patent term.

THE AGENCY: THE PATENT AND TRADEMARK OFFICE

The prosecution process begins in the U.S. Patent and Trademark Office (PTO). The PTO is the federal agency charged with reviewing patent applications and deciding which patents should be granted. The PTO itself is a division of the Department of Commerce and is headed up by the Commissioner of Patents and Trademarks.

You can find the rules that govern the activities and administration of the PTO in the Code of Federal Regulations which is a compilation of regulations passed by Congress to add specificity to federal statutes. The PTO Web site is located at www.uspto.gov. You can also access the following from the PTO site:

- Forms

- Publications explaining how to complete various forms, and how the PTO operates

- Patent statutes

- Patents issued since 1790

- Patent applications filed since March 15, 2001

- A list of FAQs about patents and PTO office procedures

THE ADVOCATES: ATTORNEYS AND AGENTS

You can prepare your own patent application, just as you can prepare your own tax return or handle your own divorce. But the more you feel is at stake financially, the more likely you are to seek the services of a qualified professional. You can hire either a patent attorney or a patent agent, who is registered to practice before the PTO to assist you in the patent prosecution process.

Patent attorneys are sort of a unique breed. Many of them are engineers as well as attorneys. To practice before the PTO, attorneys must have taken science and technical classes and passed an examination that demonstrates they understand U.S. patent laws.

Patent agents don't have law degrees, but they've met the PTO requirements for scientific and technical training and have passed a patent examination identical to that taken by patent attorneys. Patent agents are authorized to help you prepare and prosecute, or process, patent applications.

Whether you hire a patent attorney or patent agent, you must file the correct forms to let the PTO know who's representing you and is authorized to correspond with the office during the patent prosecution. If an attorney is representing you, you need to file a Power of Attorney form with the Patent and Trademark Office. If you're represented by an agent, you need to file an Authorization of Agent form.

$$ BUSINESS TIP: *Both patent agents and patent attorneys are authorized to practice before the PTO. Patent agents may be able to offer you a more reasonable hourly rate, but they can't represent you in any litigation or engage in any activities that amount to the practice of law.*

THE APPLICANTS: WHO CAN OWN A PATENT?

Patent rights are a form of personal property that you can sell, license, transfer, or leave to someone in your will. The actual inventor isn't always the *owner* of a patent. However, a patent application can only be filed by the inventor of the technology.

Ownership issues come up in a variety of contexts:

- **Inventions by employees:** An inventor is generally the rightful owner of his or her invention, even if they are an employee. However, inventions created in the context of the employer/employee relationship are governed by the *workshop doctrine*. This doctrine presumes that an employer has a free, nonexclusive license to practice the patent.

- **Commissioned inventions and consulting agreements:** A commissioned invention is one in which an inventor is paid to develop a technology as an independent contractor rather than an employee. Ownership of the patent is governed by the terms of the contract.

- **Joint ownership of collaborative inventions:** The PTO permits applications for joint ownership of a patent. Joint owners often detail their ownership contributions and obligations in a joint ownership agreement.

- **University-sponsored research:** Most colleges and universities that fund research require faculty to sign agreements assigning ownership of patent rights to the university, and require their faculty members to actively cooperate in the patent prosecution process.

- **Government contracts:** What happens when an inventor's employee is the government? Or when the government collaborates with private industry to develop new technology? Special federal statutes cover inventions made with government assistance.[3] The government can waive some or all of its rights in such inventions. Generally, however, if the government provides monetary support for development, then the government acquires rights for that development.

- **Assigned and licensed inventions:** It's not uncommon for an inventor to lack the capital to bring his idea to market. Inventors may enter into agreements to assign total ownership or license some of their patent rights to manufacturers or other third parties. (See chapter 15.)

---

[3] 35 U.S.C. Sec. 200–11 et seq.

CONDUCTING A THOROUGH SEARCH FOR PRIOR INVENTIONS

If you're convinced you've discovered something novel, you need to see if anyone else may have entertained similar thoughts. The patent application process begins with a *prior arts* search of previously existing technology and inventions.

Although you may undertake a search of PTO records on your own, if you feel something is truly at stake, you may feel economically justified in hiring a certified patent attorney or agent who in turn may hire a professional search firm to undertake the search of previous patents. The attorney or agent initially acts as sort of a paid skeptic, attempting to identify all of the objections, issues, and arguments that may be raised by the PTO in the course of reviewing your patent.

PROFESSIONAL PATENT RESEARCHERS

Your attorney or agent generally doesn't obtain documents directly from the patent office but probably hires a professional research company to undertake a *novelty search*. The professional researcher is usually familiar with the area of technology for which your patent is sought and combs through all of the Patent Office records for potentially relevant documents. Non-patent literature can also be searched, but usually for an extra cost.

Once the patent attorney has located a researcher with the necessary technical expertise in the specific field, it's up to the attorney to formulate a well-defined request. The request should include a thorough description of the invention, a diagram or picture of the invention, and information about any known patents. This information is usually provided to the researcher in the form of a letter, which includes the request to undertake the search.

The researcher ultimately provides your attorney with the results of his or her search, which includes copies of the patents and published patent applications for similar or closely related inventions initially by comparing the abstracts contained within the patents. The abstract is a summary description of an invention. Figure 12-1 contains a sample abstract for a yo-yo.

United States Patent	6,468,125
Nelson	October 22, 2002

Yo-yo structure

Abstract

A **yo-yo** structure utilizing a pair of disks connected by a spindle. The disks form a groove to confine a line connected to the spindle. A cover of soft flexible material fits over at least one of the disks. A shield is fixed in the vicinity of the groove between the disks to prevent portions of the cover from entering the groove when the yo-yo is operating.

FIGURE 12-1: *Portion of patent for yo-yo containing abstract.*

At the conclusion of the search process your attorney can advise you whether or not it appears to be advantageous to pursue the patent, taking into account the legal requirements for the particular type of patent. Utility patents, for example, must be useful, novel, and nonobvious when viewed in the context of prior art or existing technology.

If your attorney concludes the invention has already been invented by another or otherwise disclosed to the public or is an obvious modification of a preexisting invention, he or she will probably advise you not to invest further time and money pursuing the patent. If, on the other hand, the attorney concludes that the invention is sufficiently novel to pass muster in the patent office, you can decide where to go from there.

TIPS FOR CONDUCTING YOUR OWN PRELIMINARY SEARCH ON THE INTERNET

You can get a lot of preliminary information on your own off the Patent and Trademark Web site located at www.uspto.gov.

The Web site allows you to search key terms and download relevant patents from several decades. The problem with the key word search approach is that you generally end up with a large number of irrelevant or marginally related patents to sift through. For faster searching, the PTO Web site contains an abbreviated database containing only the text of each patent, without drawings.

The PTO Web site provides free access to all patents filed since 1790 and for pending applications filed subsequent to March 15, 2001. (For patents prior to 1976 you can only search by patent number and not by key word.)

To search for related patents using a key term (such as *yo-yo*):

1. Go to the PTO Web page, located at www.uspto.gov.

2. Click the Patents button. Several options appear on the screen that follows. Click the "Search Patents" hypertext link on the upper left-hand side. A screen appears offering you the Options of searching for Issued Patents or Patent Applications.

3. Click the link for either the Issued Patents or the Patent Applications database.

4. Click the Quick Search link as it appears in Figure 12-2, and enter your search term.

⚖ **LAWYER'S NOTE:** *Foreign patents can be searched on the European Patent Office Web site at www.epo.org or on the World Intellectual Property organization Web site at www.wipo.org.*

If you want to perform a preliminary Internet search including older patents or foreign patents, you can do so using one of the following fee-based search services:

• **Corporate Intelligence Corporation (www.1790.com):** Contains copies of patents dating back to 1790.

• **Micropatent (www.micropatent.com):** Contains U.S., Japanese, European, and other foreign patents. U.S. and Japanese patents date back to 1976. European patents from 1988 and thereafter are available.

• **LexPat (www.lexis-nexis.com):** This fee-based service offers the capability to search technical journals and magazines (as well as

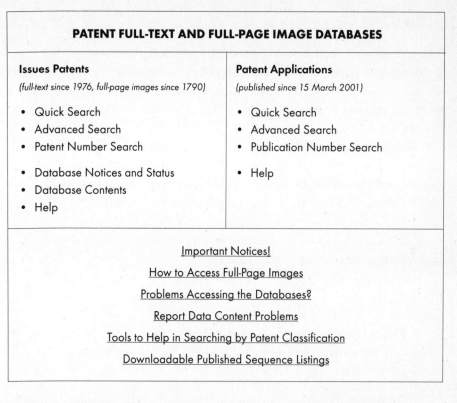

FIGURE 12-2. *This page allows you to search existing patents and pending applications.*

U.S. patents from 1976). This database is especially useful for undertaking prior art searches.

FILING THE PATENT APPLICATION

Filing a patent application is a tough job for an amateur. It requires a skillful drafting style and a precise understanding of the technology involved. The disclosures and representations made in the application and the clarity with which they're made determine the scope of the patent.

INFORMATION SPECIFIED IN THE APPLICATION

The *specification* is the main part of the patent application. In the specification, you're required to adequately describe your invention so that an individual "skilled in the art" can, upon reading the patent, make a working version of the invention without further "undue" experimentation.

The specification has to explain your invention in terms of the *best mode*. The best mode is the most efficient and effective method for implementing the invention known to the inventor. You may know of several alternative ways to create or produce the invention; you're not required to disclose all these alternative methods. However, if you fail to disclose the *best* mode to carry out the invention in the application, this can invalidate your patent rights.

The specification portion of your application must include the following:

- **Title:** The title describes the subject matter of the patent. Examples of titles of patent applications are "High Performance Yo-Yo" and "Circular Flying Disk Toy."[4]

- **Abstract:** The abstract is a summary of the invention. It is only permitted to be one paragraph long. It explains the function of the invention and the technology used to effectuate it in very general terms.

- **Cross-references:** Sometimes an inventor will file a patent for related inventions. If you do so, you must disclose the date and serial number of the related application. If you subsequently receive the patent, you may be able to get the benefit of the filing date of the prior application.

- **Background and summary of the invention:** The background section is an analysis of the prior art, and it explains the need or usefulness of the invention.

---

[4] Patent No. 6,468,125 (yo-yo) and Patent No. 6,322,419 (disk toy).

- **Detailed description of how invention works:** The detailed description requires technical expertise and must be sufficiently specific to allow an individual familiar with the prior art to re-create the invention without research beyond the description provided. Technically, this section must at a minimum include a description of the invention sufficient to enable one of ordinary skill in the art to practice (i.e. make and use) the invention.

- **Drawings of the invention and descriptions of the views contained in the drawings:** Drawings are necessary only to the extent that they're required to convey how the invention works. Drawings are not required, but are customarily submitted with virtually all applications and may include blueprints, three-dimensional computerized representations, sketches, and flow charts.

- **Claims:** Claims are the crux of the patent applications. It's been said that they define the scope of a patent in the same way that the legal description contained in a deed describes the owner's interest in a piece of real estate.

SOME CLAIM DRAFTING CONSIDERATIONS

Claims are the most critical part of your application. They are the portion of your application that defines the scope of your patent rights. Once your patent is issued, you must live with the language of what you've actually claimed and not what in hindsight you wish you might have said.

The Markman Decision

In 1996, a dry cleaner named Herbert Markman brought an infringement suit that forever changed how patent claims would be interpreted in the United States. Mr. Markman sued Westview Instruments for allegedly infringing his patent for a computerized system for managing clothing in a dry-cleaning establishment. The patent claimed a method of "maintain[ing] an inventory total" and "detect[ing] and localiz[ing] spurious additions to inventory."[5]

---

[5] *Markman et al. v. Westview Instruments, Inc., et al.* (95–26), 517 U.S. 370 (1996).

Mr. Markman alleged that Westview Instruments infringed his patent by the way it kept track of invoices and accounts receivable; these, he said, were "inventory" within the scope of his claims.

The jury agreed with Mr. Markman and found infringement. The trial judge overruled the jury, saying that "inventory" meant clothing being cleaned, not invoices and accounts receivable.

In upholding the *Markman* decision, the Supreme Court ruled that the interpretation of patent claims is the duty of the trial judge, not the jury. Federal courts across the country now routinely hold so-called "Markman hearings" prior to trial, before a judge and out of earshot of the jury, to determine how juries should be instructed to interpret patent claims.

Keeping Control of Claim Language by Defining Your Terms

As an inventor, you are free to use claim language of your own choosing and to define the terms describing your invention and the scope of your patent as you please, so long as you clearly set out your definitions within your application. The terms must be sufficiently definite in light of the specification of the patent.

In interpreting your claim language, a court will first look to see if you have defined the disputed term in the specification of your patent application. If the court finds you've done a good job of this, it will usually look no further. You are not, however, required to define all terms. If you don't define a term and the patent becomes subject to an infringement action, a court will set about the task of determining its "ordinary and customary meaning."

How Courts Construe "Ordinary Meaning"

A court is allowed to consult dictionaries, treatises, professional publications, and even listen to expert testimony to determine the "ordinary" meaning of the terms you've included in your claims. The legal standard for ordinary meaning is the meaning that would be understood by "persons of ordinary skill in the art."[6]

The U.S. Court of Appeals for the Federal Circuit has held that, for purposes of determining infringement, when a word in a claim can be

---

[6] *Hybritech Inc. v. Monoclonal Antibodies, Inc.*, 802 F.2d 1367 (Fed. Cir. 1986).

given either of two meanings, the narrower meaning will be used, because that serves the purpose of giving fair notice to competitors. In other words, the benefit of the doubt goes to the accused infringer. Courts take the view that the patent owner could and should have been more specific about what he or she intended to claim.

The Supreme Court has stated:

> Were we to allow [the patent owner] successfully to assert the broader of the two senses of [the claim language in question], we would undermine the fair notice function of the requirement that the patentee distinctly claim the subject matter disclosed in the patent from which he can exclude others temporarily.
>
> Where there is an equal choice between a broader and a narrower meaning of a claim, and there is an enabling disclosure that indicates that the applicant is at least entitled to a claim having the narrower meaning, we consider the notice function of the claim to be best served by adopting the narrower meaning."[7]

YOU MUST DISCLOSE INFORMATION THAT WORKS AGAINST YOU

Being able to explain your own invention is not enough. You also have a duty, in your application, to disclose information about other people's inventions and provide copies of patents and publications that may impact on your claims. In particular, your application must disclose information that may be adverse to the positions you take and the arguments you make in your application. You have a specific duty to inform the PTO about prior art, related foreign and domestic patents, and related litigation.

Generally inventors must file an *Information Disclosure Statement,* or IDS form, within three months of the date of learning of the reference (e.g., patent or publication). If more than three months have passed, in most instances an IDS can and should still be filed, subject to the additional fees and requirements specified under federal law. You can find these at www.uspto.gov. The duty to disclose information in the IDS

---

[7] *Warner-Jenkinson Co. v. Hilton Davis Chemical Co.,* 520 U.S. 17 (1997).

form pertains to all *material* information. Material information is defined as:

- Information that tends to refute or establish a claim or element of a claim.

- Information that refutes or may be inconsistent with any position that you take in your application.

An IDS generally includes a listing of U.S. and foreign patents and applications, publications, and other information relevant to the invention. Copies of the relevant patents and publications are required to be clearly referenced. If these documents aren't in English, you may be required to provide a translation with your IDS.

⚖ **LAWYER'S NOTE:** *Information Disclosure Statements may now be filed electronically for U.S. patents and applications.*

OTHER LEGALLY REQUIRED PAPERWORK

In addition to describing your invention, your application must be accompanied by certain legal housekeeping forms. These documents include the following:

- **Oath or declaration:** This is a signed statement attesting to the identity of the inventors and their belief as to the truthfulness of all of the representations contained in the application. The declaration also requires you to identify any prior U.S. or foreign applications which disclose your invention and which you are using to claim an earlier filing date (priority). The PTO provides a specific Declaration Form that includes all of the legally required information.

- **Power of attorney or authorization of agent:** Only the inventor or his agent or attorney certified by the PTO can prosecute a patent application. These forms let the PTO know who's representing you and should get copies of correspondence. The PTO cannot communicate with your agent or attorney unless this form is on file.

- **Certificate of mailing:** A certificate of mailing is a separate statement certifying the date on which the patent application is being mailed; it may be signed by anyone.

- **Transmittal form:** A transmittal form lists all of the documents being submitted and the total number of pages. It must also include the name of the inventor and title of the invention.

- **Self-addressed return card:** An applicant should enclose a self-addressed postcard for the PTO to verify receipt of the application and accompanying materials.

A checklist of the materials that should be included in a patent application appears in Figure 12-3.

□ Patent Application Transmittal Letter

□ Specification

□ Power of Attorney

□ Declaration

□ Information Disclosure Statement (IDS)

□ Filing Fee

□ Return Postcard

FIGURE 12-3: *Patent application checklist.*

SOME SPECIAL TYPES OF PATENT APPLICATIONS

Inventions and inventors themselves sometimes defy the rigors of classification imposed by the standard patent application. The PTO offers some specialized types of forms to accommodate various issues that can arise with respect to a particular invention.

SAVING SOME MONEY: FILING AN ABBREVIATED APPLICATION

If you find yourself short of time or money but want to protect your idea ASAP, consider filing an abbreviated provisional application. You can file a Provisional Patent Application (PPA), which allows you to establish an immediate filing date for your patent. The PPA allows the applicant to claim patent pending status for the invention, just as you would be able to do with the regular application.

The PPA is a sort of abbreviated interim document. If the regular patent application is filed within one year, the date of filing the PPA, rather than the full application, governs.

The PPA must include a description of the invention and must clearly explain how to make and use the invention. Like the regular application, the PPA must describe the best mode for re-creating the invention. The PPA requires less detail than the full application but must clearly explain how to make and use the invention. Diagrams and other supporting documentation are optional.

There are several advantages to the PPA process, in addition to the expedited filing date and the ability to claim patent pending status.

1. The PPA is less costly to prepare and file than the regular application, allowing you to defer the expense of preparing a more detailed application while you further research your invention or the market for your invention.

2. The PPA allows you to describe the invention with less specificity, which means less research and testing prior to filing.

3. The complicated IDS form (described in the previous section) need not accompany the PPA.

4. The PPA ultimately extends the duration of the patent by as much as one year, the expiration of which is twenty years from the date of the filing of the regular patent application.

If an inventor doesn't file an application within one year, the PPA is abandoned and becomes worthless. If, however, the invention is changed, improved, or further developed, during the time between the PPA filing and the filing of the regular application, an inventor can file additional provisional applications covering the new developments.

ADDING NEW INFORMATION: CONTINUATION APPLICATIONS

Continuation applications are a special type of form that allow you to make certain changes to the claims in your initial application. One use of a continuation application occurs when an examiner allows narrow claims, but rejects the broader claims in the application. An applicant can accept what the examiner has allowed, and then file a continuation application to later pursue the broader claims.

DIVISIONAL APPLICATIONS: SEPARATING MULTIPLE INVENTIONS

Only one invention is allowed per application. If a patent examiner determines that your application contains two or more inventions, he or she may require you to split up your claims and put them into two or more separate applications. You can file one or more divisional applications, in addition to your original patent application, to delineate the claims pertaining to each separate invention. Divisional applications allow you to preserve your original filing date, which means you still get priority over inventors that file after you filed your initial application.

REISSUE PATENTS

Suppose you're successful in getting a patent for your invention, but you realize that there were errors in your application that impact on the scope of your patent. You can attempt to fix your patent by filing a reissue patent.

The reissue patent can also be used as an error correction procedure. For example, if your specifications or drawings were incorrect, you can opt for this procedure or the simpler procedure of filing a certificate of correction.

Reissue patents usually have the effect of narrowing or broadening claims in the existing patent. If your reissue patent would have the effect of broadening your claims, it must be filed within two years of the issue date of the original patent. The expiration date for the reissue patent is the same as for the original patent.

SMALL ENTITY DECLARATION FORM

The PTO gives a price break to certain types of entities. If you're filing on behalf of one of the following, you qualify for a reduced fee:

- Nonprofit organizations, as defined in the Code of Federal Regulations

- Small businesses with 500 or fewer employees

- An independent inventor, i.e., an individual or small business

PROSECUTING YOUR PATENT APPLICATION

After an application is filed, it takes anywhere from eighteen months to five years for the PTO to process your application, with the average being around three years. During the prosecution process, the PTO issues two different types of official determinations called *office actions*.

FIRST OFFICE ACTION: REQUIRED CHANGES AND AMENDMENTS

Almost no one gets it right the first time around. The first office action communicated to you by the PTO usually requires additional clarification, documentation, or amendments to claims. If the examiner determines some of the claims are too broad or aren't justified, the PTO may require you to eliminate or narrow some of them. The initial office action may require additional research.

You're generally given three months, but extensions extending the time frame to as long as six months may usually be obtained by paying an addition fee, to respond to an office action. All amendments, modifications, and additional materials have to be submitted during this period.

You're not permitted to submit *new matter* in the course of altering, amending, or supplementing your application. Just what constitutes new matter can be the subject of considerable controversy, but the general rule is that it consists of anything that doesn't support the originally filed application.

FINAL REJECTION OR OFFICE ACTION:
NOTICE OF ALLOWANCE AND DISALLOWANCE

Usually, but not always, the second action taken by the PTO is labeled "final." If the PTO approves your application, it issues a Notice of Allowance. After you receive a Notice of Allowance, you need to pay a fee known as the issue fee. Once the issue fee has been paid, your patent certificate will be issued. Excerpts from your patent appear in the *Weekly Gazette*. The *Weekly Gazette* is a publication available in most U.S. libraries and on the PTO Web site (www.uspto.gov) that's issued every Tuesday and summarizes patents and certain actions related to patents. (It also publishes patents that have expired due to nonpayment of required maintenance fees, and patents that are reinstated after their owners pay a late maintenance fee.)

If the amendments you've made to the application don't satisfy the PTO, the second office action may be a denial, or Final Office Action. However, a Final Office Action may not truly be final. The applicant has several options, as discussed in the next section of this chapter.

USING THE PATENT PENDING DESIGNATION
FOR YOUR INVENTION

During the pendency period, between the filing and granting of a patent, you're allowed to use the coveted Patent Pending designation on materials pertaining to your invention. This notice informs the public you're applying for a patent. Of course, the public may or may not understand that there's no enforcement capability behind this designation until you actually acquire a patent.

> **CAUTION:** *You may be subject to special civil penalties if you use the Patent Pending designation when you don't actually have an application pending.*

Effective December 2002, patent applicants are actually entitled to some retroactive protection for infringements that occur during the pendency period. Subsequent to 1999 applicants are encouraged to publish notice of their pending application within eighteen months after the first filing date. You can later use the publication to prove an infringer had actual notice of your pending application and of their own infringement.

Oddly, pending applications are published to provide notice to the public, not to facilitate commentary. The public isn't allowed to protest a pending application without the applicant's consent (highly unlikely!). However, the public can submit relevant prior art to be included in the PTO file and considered by the examiner.

> **$$ BUSINESS TIP:** *You can avoid the requirement to publish an application by filing a statement with your initial application that the patent application will not be "published abroad." If you change your mind and decide to publish abroad, you need to give notice to the PTO within forty-five days.*

APPLICATION DEADLINES AND EXTENSIONS

You generally have three months to respond to any *substantive* office action by the PTO, such as a Final Office Action. If the action is for some nonsubstantive matter, such as an administrative issue or clarification of the spelling of someone's name, you're generally given only one month.

If you fail to respond or act within the deadline specified in the office action letter, your application technically becomes abandoned. Abandonment, if not cured, is tantamount to a dismissal or denial of your application.

Not to worry, though; if you miss a deadline, you can revive your application by buying an extension or filing a petition to revive.

BUYING AN EXTENSION

You can literally buy an extension if you miss a deadline to any office action. If you don't send in your reply within the time period designated by the office action letter, you can obtain an extension to send in your reply up to six months after the office action if you pay the prices shown in a special fee schedule published by the PTO and file a form called Petition for Extension of Time along with a Certificate of Mailing.

FILING A PETITION TO REVIVE

There are two reasons that entitle you to file a petition to revive your patent application within two years from the date of abandonment.

The first is that the delay was unavoidable. Unavoidable delays include things like a death or a severe illness. You must specially petition the Patent and Trademark Office and and provide documentation of these extraordinary events.

> ● **CAUTION:** *In computing the six-month maximum period during which you can file a response to an office action, compute it from the date you received the original office action letter, not from the date of expiration. For example, if you received a letter dated February 10, for which the time to reply expired March 10, the maximum time for which you can obtain an extension should be computed six months from the February 10 date.*

But what if you simply dropped the ball? It happens. Fortunately, the second reason that entitles you to file a petition to revive is that the delay was avoidable but unintentional. That covers just about every situation, doesn't it?

Along with a hefty fee (over $1,000), you need to file three documents to revive your petition:

- The reply to the office action that you were otherwise required to file

- The Petition to Revive form

- A declaration statement explaining the reasons for an unavoidable delay, or if the delay was avoidable, stating that it was unintentional

WHAT TO DO IF YOUR APPLICATION IS REJECTED

A Final Office Action denying your claims isn't a happy event, but it's also not a kiss of death. Patent Office rules spell out so many ways to reverse a "final" action, the term hardly seems to apply.

OVERVIEW: WHAT DO THE PTO RULES SAY?

Patent Office Rule Number 113 (the numbering has nothing to do with superstition) dealing with "Final Rejection or Action" provides: "On the second or subsequent examination or consideration, the rejection or other action may be made final, whereupon applicant's response is limited to appeal in the case, or rejection of any claim . . . or to amendment as specified in Rule 116."

In turn, Rule 116 provides: "After final rejection or action (Rule 113) amendments may be made canceling claims or complying with any requirement . . . and amendments presenting rejected claims in better form for consideration on appeal may be admitted." An applicant can also submit arguments, *without* amending or narrowing claims, if he or she believes the examiner's rejection is improper.

Accordingly, a final action is not fatal to your application. You must, however, take one of the following actions in response to the denial:

1. Narrow or eliminate claims in response to the grounds for rejection cited by the examiner.

2. Request that the patent examiner reconsider his grounds for denial (i.e., argue with him or her).

3. File a Request for Continuing Examination (RCE).

4. Appeal to the Board of Patent Appeals and Interferences (BPAI).

5. Petition the PTO Commissioner (for certain types of matters that don't relate to patentability).

6. File a continuation application.

7. Abandon the application.

AMENDING AND NARROWING YOUR CLAIMS

A Final Office Action disallowing your patent is usually a disappointment but not a complete shock. Most likely you've gotten a sense of which claims are causing the problems from the initial office action. If amendments or changes made in response to a first office action don't cure the problem in the eyes of the examiner, the dreaded Final Office Action may issue as a second action. Amendments filed after a Final Office Action are referred to as *after-final* amendments.

Requirements for Filing Amendments After Disallowance

After a Notice of Disallowance, you have three months to bring the application into *condition for allowance status.*

Patent Office rules provide, technically, that generally, after the first office action, amendments aren't permitted without a showing of good reasons as to why they weren't permitted earlier. Fortunately, showing that the amendments would be sufficient to get your claims allowed is considered a good reason.

Tips for Filing Successful Amendments After a Disallowance

Patent Office rules are intended to ensure that you'll know precisely what aspects of your claim displeased the patent examiner. Rule 113 requires: "In making a final rejection, the examiner shall repeat or state all grounds for rejection then considered applicable to the claims in the case, clearly stating the reasons therefore."

A careful reading of the Final Office Action should give you some clues as to how to proceed in amending your claims, and even whether it looks as though it will be possible to do so. Sometimes it's not possible to respond by amending and narrowing your claims without giving up so much of the protection you're seeking that it doesn't make sense to go this route.

⊖ **CAUTION:** *If you decide to amend your claims following a Notice of Disallowance, be sure to file the actual amendments within the three-month deadline, plus any extensions you've bought. You cannot file an after-final amendment for an application that's technically been abandoned.*

The process of narrowing and amending your claims involves three analytical steps:

1. **Make sure you understand the examiner's reasons for issuing the Notice of Disallowance.** If the examiner's rationale is not fully clear

to you, you may correspond with the office through your agent or attorney to elicit further information. Be sure that any amendments or changes to your claims are responsive and specific to the examiner's concerns.

2. Decide whether it's advantageous to amend or narrow the claims to the extent required. You may feel the examiner is requesting that you give up so much of your claims that the patent, even if awarded, would provide dubious protection. You must decide whether the examiner is justified in his or her concerns. Even if you're not in total agreement, it may be expedient to make the requested amendments if the amended patent would still afford you sufficient protection.

3. Make the necessary amendments to your application. If you decide to amend rather than narrow or eliminate problematic claims, you can only do so to the extent the amendment doesn't require new matter, which is any information that materially alters your initial application.

PERSUADING THE PATENT EXAMINER

You certainly don't want to antagonize a patent examiner, but there are times when it's appropriate to advance a polite argument. Patent examiners are, after all, only human and subject to fallibility, such as technical oversights, just like the rest of us.

$$ BUSINESS TIP: *Personal face-to-face meetings or telephone may work better than written communication, since they provide the opportunity for immediate feedback and clarification, which is helpful to the persuasive process. Also, some communication experts believe it's harder to say no to someone in person.*

If you feel the examiner has overlooked a point of law or a technical nuance that differentiates the functioning of your invention from prior art, the process allows you to point this out. Your agent or attorney is free to communicate your arguments in writing, by phone, or in person. If you go this route, be sure to do so at the earliest opportunity, so that you can appeal within the required three-month time frame if your attempts at persuasion are unsuccessful.

APPEALING A FINAL OFFICE ACTION

If you don't think an amendment or narrowing of your claims is justified, you can take the position that the patent examiner is flat-out wrong by appealing his or her disallowance. The PTO has a special staff of judges to handle appeals, known as the Board of Patent Appeals and Interferences (BPAI).

To initiate the appeal process you must file a *Notice of Appeal* stating it's your intent to file an appeal of the disallowance by the patent examiner. The notice must be accompanied by the filing fee and a *Certificate of Mailing* stating the date the document is mailed and what is included with it.

> ⚖️ **LAWYER'S NOTE:** *Appeals to the Board of Patent Appeals and Interferences (BPAI) have about an estimated 35 percent success rate.*

You don't need to state your arguments for the appeal in the notice, but you're required to file a brief detailing your position within two months of the time you file your Notice of Appeal.

The patent examiner must file a responsive brief answering all the arguments in your brief. Sometimes, in the course of doing so, the examiner changes his or her mind and the matter is resolved. However, it's more likely that the examiner will stand firm and file a document called the *Examiner's Answer.* You're entitled to file a reply (in the form of a legal brief) to the Examiner's Answer.

The matter may then be set for *oral argument,* during which you'll have twenty minutes to present your case. The examiner has fifteen minutes to present his or her case.

If you're successful in persuading BPAI, it will issue instructions to the examiner to allow your patent or instructions to take other action. If BPAI agrees with the examiner, as it does about 65 percent of the time, it will issue a written decision explaining why it believes your invention to be unpatentable.

You can appeal an adverse decision by BPAI within sixty days to the

Court of Appeals for the Federal Circuit (CAFC) (or in the D.C. District Court). You can obtain an extension of up to six months from the filing of a notice of appeal by paying the appropriate fee. The CAFC has its home base in Washington, D.C., but it's a sort of traveling court. It sits and hears cases at various locations throughout the year. If the CAFC rules against you as well, you can appeal to the U.S. Supreme Court, although the odds are very slim the court will agree to hear the case. This means, as a practical matter, the CAFC is pretty much your last hope as far as the court system goes.

PETITIONING THE PTO COMMISSIONER
ON NONSUBSTANTIVE MATTERS

Sometimes your controversy with a patent examiner doesn't relate to the patentability of your invention. Perhaps the examiner has refused to enter an amendment because he or she feels it constitutes new matter. Or maybe there's an argument over time periods or filing dates, or as to whether you've submitted all required documentation. These matters are considered nonsubstantive and you can directly petition the Commissioner of Patents and Trademarks.

⚖️ **LAWYER'S NOTE:** *The Commissioner of Patents and Trademarks has the authority to overrule any patent examiner but cannot overrule BPAI.*

Although there are no specific deadlines for appealing an action to the Commissioner of Patents and Trademarks, you're advised to do so ASAP after you become aware of the issue. There is a fee for this appeal process, and you must file a notarized statement explaining the matter you're appealing.

FILING A CONTINUATION
OR CONTINUATION IN PART APPLICATION

A Continuation Application is a way to continue arguing with the examiner after a Final Office Action. It contains further evidence in support of the disallowed claims. It cannot include any new matter but may involve entirely new arguments or claims. The full Continuation Application, because it contains no new matter, has the same filing date as the original application. (Maintaining the original filing date is an advantage in case you need to argue that you have legal priority over someone who later tries to obtain a patent or infringe yours.)

But what do you do if you need to amend a claim to comply with an office action, but realize you can't effectively do so *without* introducing new matter? As you recall, new matter is information that materially alters your initial application. It's not allowed as part of a standard amendment in response to an office action.

The *Continuation in Part Application* procedure solves this dilemma. A Continuation in Part Application is a second application filed for the same invention while the initial application is still pending and includes new matter to correct an error, add previously omitted information, or disclose an improvement. It is often used to seek protection for further development. You can also file a Continuation in Part Application if you discover an improved method or process for carrying out your invention. For example, you might want to substitute a more effective ingredient in a chemical compound or simplify the implementation of a computer program.

> **CAUTION:** *Both the Continuation in Part and Continuing Applications must be filed before the date on which original "patent" application is considered abandoned or issues as a patent.*

The rules governing the filing date for a Continuation in Part Application can be confusing, since there are actually two pertinent filing dates. This dual filing date concept works to your advantage. The filing date for the Continuation in Part Application is the same as the filing date for the initial application, except for any new matter covered. You don't lose any priority with respect to subsequent applications filed by other inventors for material covered in the original application.

ABANDONING YOUR PATENT APPLICATION

Sometimes it's best not to go down with the ship. Despite your best efforts to research the prior art and carefully draft and support your claims, fatal issues may arise in the course of prosecution.

Abandonment occurs when you simply stop prosecuting your patent. Doing so forecloses your right to file any type of Continuation Application as well as many of your appeal rights, and consequently you cannot later claim that the filing date of the original application date applies. If you decide you want to refile in the future, you'll have to file a new application, with an entirely new filing date. This means you won't have priority over intervening prior art developed or published prior to the new application.

SURVIVING THE DREADED PATENT INTERFERENCE PROCESS

As if prosecuting your patent and persuading the examiner to issue it weren't tough enough, the patent rules allow for a special process called a *Patent Interference.* This process allows the Commissioner of the PTO to quite literally interfere in the prosecution of your patent when he or she finds that an existing application would:

- Interfere with an already pending patent application; or

- Interfere with an unexpired patent that's previously been granted

> ⚖ **LAWYER'S NOTE:** A patent applicant can also provoke an interference by "copying" pending claims into their own application.

A patent interference is an adversarial process in which you have about a 1 percent chance of becoming embroiled—that's about how often the Commissioner elects to interfere. It's expensive and time consuming, and is most often used to resolve issues involving the priority of a patent.

The adversaries in this process are referred to as the *junior* and *senior parties.* Generally, in the U.S. the first inventor is entitled to a patent. However, if the inventor is not "diligent" in reducing his patent to practice (i.e., developing it), the rules may change. The senior party is the applicant who filed first. The junior party has the burden of proving one of the following:

- That the junior party reduced the invention to practice before the filing date of the senior party; or

- The junior party both conceived of the invention and reasonably attempted to reduce it to practice before the date of filing of the senior patent.

CARE AND MAINTENANCE OF YOUR PATENT

Once you've prevailed in the patent prosecution process, you can frame your new patent certificate and hang it on your wall. However, it will become a meaningless piece of paper if you forget to pay the periodic fees required to maintain it.

At the time your patent is granted, you're required to pay an initial issuance fee that covers your registration costs for four years. Subsequently, you're required to pay maintenance fees at the following times after issuance: 3½ years, 7½ years, 11½ years. A six-month extension is available for a small surcharge.

A patent can be forfeited for failure to pay the requisite maintenance fees. You can petition to revive a forfeited patent on the basis that the delay was unavoidable. But it's a lot easier to mark your calendar for the due dates.

> **$$ BUSINESS TIP:** *Certain small entities and nonprofit organizations are eligible for a 50 percent reduction in maintenance fees.*

HOW YOUR PATENT RIGHTS CAN BE FORFEITED

Getting a patent is a big step toward protecting your product, but it is no guarantee of perpetual protection. The PTO can invalidate a patent for any of the following reasons:

- **Newly discovered prior art:** The PTO subsequently discovers relevant prior art that wasn't disclosed or discovered during the examination process.

• **Public use or sale:** If the PTO is alerted to transactions showing that you offered the invention for public use or sale prior to the date of the application.

• **Misuse:** If you used your patent for improper purposes, such as to accomplish antitrust violations, the PTO may step in and invalidate it.

• **Fraud:** Obviously, you have an obligation to be truthful to the patent examiner and in all aspects of the patent prosecution process. Evidence of misrepresentation or concealment of facts can result in invalidation of your patent.

ADDITIONAL NOTES ABOUT DESIGN PATENT APPLICATIONS

Although the process for obtaining design patents pretty much follows the procedures outlined in this chapter, there are some specific aspects of the design patent process that are worth noting.

Only one claim is permitted in a design patent application. This sole claim is based on the drawings. Thus, the drawings in a design patent take on much greater importance than for utility patents. The specification portion of the application is generally simpler and less technical. However, the drawings and specifications submitted with your application take on much greater importance.

Usually, amendments are simpler and more straightforward in the design patent process. Also, there are no maintenance fees charged for design patents.

CHAPTER 13 >>>>

Avoiding, Detecting, and Defending
Against Patent Infringement

BEGINNING IN THE 1960s and on through the 1980s, a controversial engineer named Jerome Lemelson acquired between 500 and 700 patents by tracking the development of emerging technologies and simply being first to file for patents on these technologies (although often not the first to invent). Mr. Lemelson allegedly made millions of dollars pursuing infringement litigation against unsuspecting companies who desired to bring products to market that were covered by his patents. One recent publication for the steel industry warns, "[I]f you receive a letter or other notice from the Lemelson Foundation or one of its lawyers stating you have been or are about to be sued for patent infringement, treat it seriously." The publication explains that "[t]he common approach used by the Lemelson Foundation is to name many defendants in a lawsuit, and follow up with a letter to the defendants to negotiate a settlement for royalties to use the Lemelson patents, thereby avoiding expensive litigation expenses (which may exceed $1 million in a lawsuit which goes to trial) with a losing defendant paying the Foundation's (as well as its own) legal fees." Unfortunately, the publication explains, "defendants are given little time to think it over, and are pushed to quickly negotiate or face high expenses and potential damages."

IN THIS CHAPTER YOU FIND OUT:

● How to request that a competitor cease and desist infringing activity

● When to resort to litigation

● What damages courts may award for infringement

● Under what circumstances a government agency can seize infringing merchandise

● What to do when someone else accuses you of infringing on their patent

IN THE LATE 1970s, the Polaroid Corporation receives several patents for its revolutionary instant imaging process, which develops photographs within minutes before the user's very eyes. Four years after the debut and extraordinary marketing success of the Polaroid, which has become a household name for the instant imaging, Kodak, a major competitor in the industry, introduces its own instant imaging camera.

Polaroid promptly files suit, alleging that Kodak has infringed its patents for the SX-70 camera. Kodak responds that the Polaroid patents are invalid and unenforceable, and in any event were not infringed. The Massachusetts Federal District Court disagrees, finding after seventy-five days of trial that seven of ten of Polaroid's patents have been infringed and assesses $909,457,567.00 in damages.

Kodak loses its appeal and is forced to announce that it is ending its foray into the instant imaging business from which it had previously reported a profit of more than $2.7 million in less than one year. Kodak enters into a voluntary exchange program, offering to swap its noninfringing camera for an estimated 16 million infringing ones. Polaroid is reportedly disappointed with the $909,457,567.00 verdict, because it had requested treble (triple) damages but ultimately settles similar litigation against Kodak in Canada.[1]

---

[1] Mazzone, A. D., Judgment in *Polaroid Corporation v. Eastman Kodak Company*, No. 76-1634-MA, United States District Court for the District of Massachusetts (October 12, 1990) (damages phase of trial).

Patent research can be difficult to undertake, and it can be a painstaking process to compare the elements of a claim to determine whether a product is an infringement. It's not surprising that even careful, well-intentioned entrepreneurs can find themselves embroiled in litigation for direct, indirect, or contributory infringement of a patent that appears both obscure and unrelated.

ACTIVITIES THAT CONSTITUTE PATENT INFRINGEMENT

It's a common myth that you can't be sued for patent infringement unless you copy someone else's invention. You can be sued for many activities other than direct copying. You can potentially infringe on a patent by making a product that works differently but does the same thing as someone else's invention. It's also a violation to make an unauthorized improvement to someone else's patented invention.

It's important to understand what activities constitute infringement so you can protect your own patents and avoid being accused of infringing someone else's. This section explores the various types of activities that can get you named as a defendant in an infringement suit.

LITERAL INFRINGEMENT

Literal infringement is the most blatant kind. It occurs when you copy someone else's invention, element for element. Goods that have been literally copied, sometimes referred to as knockoffs, may have been deliberately copied to function or look like the original patented, copyrighted, or trademarked version. They often come from foreign countries that are not a party to the important international trade agreement (GATT) discussed in chapter 4. These goods, if they are identical in function and appearance, literally infringe a patent.

Countries to which the greatest numbers of counterfeit goods and knockoffs are attributed include China, Hong Kong, Taiwan, Korea, and Thailand. In 1992, under heavy international pressure, China revised its patent laws, significantly strengthening them, although enforcement remains weak, and the number of seizures of Chinese counterfeit goods by the U.S. Customs Service remains high.[2]

General Motors has aggressively fought the counterfeiting of its truck parts. In 1990, it announced the success of an undercover sting operation conducted by the FBI and U.S. Attorney that resulted in forty raids in fifteen states for the purpose of seizing counterfeit truck parts. The truck parts included brake pads, wheel covers, floor mats, voltage regulators, and many other patented and nonpatented truck parts.[3]

INFRINGEMENT BY CREATING A SIMILAR DEVICE

Literal copying is easy to detect by an inventor, if not easy to prevent. An inventor may suspect literal infringement simply by looking at a competitor's goods and finding it virtually indistinguishable from his or her own product. A more challenging issue arises when one invention functions the same way as another, subject to some minor modifications.

The Doctrine of Equivalents

Patent protection extends beyond the literal scope of the claims contained within the patent; however, the courts do not interpret the claims literally. Instead, the claims are read by courts to prohibit any invention that achieves substantially the equivalent result in substantially the same way. This is known as the *doctrine of equivalents*.

In 2002, in *Festo Corp. v. Shoketsu Kinzoku Kogyo Kabushiki Co.*,[4] the U.S. Supreme Court reaffirmed the importance of the doctrine of equivalents as providing the necessary certainty and meaningful protection to inventors to encourage their investment in research and development.

The court explained that "[i]f patents were always interpreted by their literal terms, their value would be greatly diminished. Unimportant and insubstantial substitutes for certain elements could defeat the

---

[2] Hak Choi, "Piracy and Economic Development," The Chinese University of Hong Kong, article available at http://www.sba.muohio.edu/abas/1999/choiha.pdf.

[3] John Nahas, "Pirated Parts Create Liability for Distributors and Users Trailer/Body Builders," July 1, 2000, article available at http://trailer-bodybuilders.com/ar/trucks_pirated_parts_create/.

[4] U.S. Supreme Court, *Festo Corp. v. Shoketsu Kinzoku Kogyo Kabushiki Co., Ltd.*, No. 00-1543 (May 28, 2002).

patent and its value to inventors could be destroyed by simple acts of copying."

The Doctrine of Prosecution History Estoppel

The *doctrine of prosecution history estoppel* applies when you take a particular position as to the scope of your claims in the course of prosecuting your patent. You are *estopped,* or precluded from later taking a position that your claim is broader than what you had argued in the course of prosecuting the patent and in making amendments to satisfy the patent examiner.

In an infringement action, a judge or jury must decide whether two inventions have the same purpose and function in pretty much the same way. The court must take into consideration the *prosecution history* of the invention, in particular looking at amendments you made to the claims to satisfy the Patent Office during the prosecution of the patent. Sometimes amendments indicate that it was the intent of the applicant that a particular modification fall within the scope of the doctrine of equivalents, and other times the amendment may make clear an intention that a patent ultimately have a more limited scope.

The theory is that you, as the inventor, had the opportunity to argue for the broadest possible protection during the patent prosecution process. You also have the opportunity to appeal an adverse finding by a patent examiner, rather than narrowing an amendment just to get the patent issued. It is unfair to allow you to argue for broader protection after the prosecution process is over than the positions you took during it.

The *Festo* Facts

In *Festo Corp. v. Shoketsu Kinzoku Kogyo Kabushiki,*[5] the Supreme Court issued a strong opinion, giving attorneys and inventors a lot of guidance as to just how the doctrine of equivalents and prosecution history estoppel are supposed to work.

The plaintiff, Festo Corporation, owned two patents for an indus-

---

[5] U.S. Supreme Court, *Festo Corp. v. Shoketsu v. Kinzoku Kogyo Kabushiki Co., Ltd.,* No. 00–1543 (May 28, 2002).

trial device. During the course of prosecuting one of the patents, the application was specifically amended to provide that the device would contain a pair of one-way sealing rings and that its outer sleeve would be made of magnetizable material. After Festo Corporation began selling its device, the defendants entered the market with a similar device using a two-way sealing ring and a nonmagnetizable sleeve.

A lower court had held that the doctrine of estoppel applied to bar Festo Corporation from asserting the doctrine of equivalents for a claim that had previously been amended. The Supreme Court vacated and remanded the decision, holding that prosecution history of estoppel doesn't automatically apply every time a patent claim is amended. Rather, the court held that all amendments should be considered on a case-by-case basis to determine if they were actually intended to have the effect of narrowing the claim.

The Supreme Court stated, "Estoppel arises when an amendment is made to secure the patent and the amendment narrows the patent's scope. If [an] amendment is truly cosmetic, then it would not narrow the patent's scope or raise an estoppel." This is called the *flexible bar* approach and is the standard that the Supreme Court has now directed lower courts to apply.

UNAUTHORIZED IMPROVEMENTS

Not all improvements are welcome. If you improve someone else's patented invention and market or use the patented device without permission, you may find yourself defending a lawsuit for patent infringement.

You may be able to patent your improvement under a separate application, but this does not give you rights to the original unimproved device. Your options consist of waiting for the original patent to expire, obtaining permission or a licensing arrangement with the original inventor, buying the rights to the original invention outright, or abandoning your improvement.

DESIGN PATENT INFRINGEMENT

Design patent infringements are sometimes obvious just from looking at them. A design patent infringement occurs when a competitor's product is so similar to another patented product that the public can't be expected to tell the two apart. (See chapter 11 for a more detailed explanation of the requirements and procedures for design patents.)

ACTIVITIES THAT AREN'T PATENT INFRINGEMENT: UNFAIR COMPETITION

What if you decide that you want to make an identical copy of a circuit found in a competitor's product to include in your own product? Can you do so?

It's possible that you are allowed to make and use an identical copy of the particular circuit, so long as you don't infringe on any aspects of the product that are subject to the claims of any patent covering the invention. In short, you are generally able to copy certain aspects of someone else's product that aren't subject to patent, copyright, or trademark protection.

However, if you deliberately seek to make your product similar to your competitor's, you may be subject to an action for unfair competition. Unfair competition is a type of civil action that can supplement the usual intellectual property law remedies. The basis for a lawsuit for unfair competition is that someone has deliberately sought to confuse the public as to the identity or origin of a product or service (i.e., trying to capitalize on your competitor's goodwill and make the public think your product is your competitor's).

> **CAUTION:** Although you are free to copy aspects of a product that are not subject to patent, copyright, or trademark protection, you will be subject to an action for unfair competition if your product is so similar to your competitor's that it tends to confuse the buying public.

BEFORE YOU CALL AN ATTORNEY:
IS SOMEONE REALLY INFRINGING YOUR PATENT?

Patent infringement litigation is one of the most expensive types of lawsuits to bring. Not only are you likely to need an attorney who specializes in patent law, you're likely to need costly expert witnesses. Depositions and pretrial discovery alone can cost hundreds of thousands of dollars.

The expense of litigation may be justified, depending on the value of the patent rights you seek to protect. However, few companies can reasonably afford to undertake litigation without the expectation that the other side may ultimately prevail.

Statistically, about 50 percent of all patent infringement suits are ultimately decided in favor of the plaintiff (the person initiating the lawsuit). Before you litigate, you want to do some preliminary analysis to determine whether you can reasonably expect to prevail.

RESEARCH THE SPECIFICS OF THE COMPETITOR'S PRODUCT

Before you even think of calling a lawyer (and start his or her billing clock running), you need to learn everything you can about the competitor's product. An infringer may have had to learn about your product to copy it or may have accidentally and independently developed an infringing product. Regardless, you need to know as much as you can about the development of the infringing product.

> **$$ BUSINESS TIP:** *You can assist your attorney by carefully preparing a list of each and every similarity you note, as well as any aspects of the product or process that differentiate it from yours.*

Sometimes it's possible to examine the product itself and to get the particulars about how it was created. You can gain added insight by getting copies of manuals, advertisements, and information provided by the competitor to its customers.

COMPARE THE COMPETITOR'S PRODUCT TO YOUR CLAIMS

Your patent doesn't necessarily cover every competing product. Product similarity is important, but it's only a superficial starting point. Remember that it's the scope of the claims in your patent application that ultimately determine your rights to stop a competitor from marketing a functionally similar product or process.

An attorney or judge will look first to the claims in your patent application, giving the language a reasonably broad interpretation, listing each claim separately, and looking at all of the elements of each claim. In an action for infringement, you can prevail if any single claim is infringed. You don't need to prove that all of the claims have been infringed.

> ⚖️ **LAWYER'S NOTE:** *If your competitor's product entirely lacks one or more of the elements of your patent claims, it is not an infringing product. If the competitor has made only an immaterial modification corresponding to one of the elements, infringement may have occurred under the doctrine of equivalents.*

For a particular claim to be literally infringed, your competitor's product must contain each and every element of the particular claim you are alleging has been infringed. Compare your competitor's product to each of the elements you've listed. To prevail in an action under the doctrine of equivalents, you must prove that your competitor has made only insignificant modifications to the elements of the claim.

Even if the competitor has added features to the product, if all of the elements of your product are present, the competitor may be infringing by making an unauthorized improvement, as discussed previously in this chapter.

DOES THE DOCTRINE OF EQUIVALENTS APPLY?

The doctrine of equivalents applies when your competitor does not use elements that precisely correspond to your patent claims, but substitutes equivalent elements. An element is equivalent if it performs the same function to achieve the same result.

When you compare any differences between your product and your competitor's, you need to look carefully at what these differences accomplish. For example, if you have included an elastic band and your competitor has included a spring, both may accomplish the same purpose and may be considered immaterial modifications under the doctrine of equivalents.

REMEDIES FOR INFRINGEMENT

If you can prove you are a victim of patent infringement, the courts have a fierce array of remedies. Courts can issue injunctive orders to make the infringer stop their infringing activity and have discretion to order damages equal—or even triple—to the economic losses you've suffered. Courts even have the discretion to order the infringer to pay your attorney's fees, although this discretion is seldom used.

INJUNCTIVE RELIEF

Injunctive relief is sometimes viewed as the brass ring in patent litigation. It means that the court will order your competitors to stop their infringing activity.

An injunction may be preliminary or permanent. A preliminary injunction is issued on a temporary basis while litigation is pending. Depending on the outcome of the litigation, the injunction can be made permanent.

The standards for a court to issue an injunction are high, since a temporary injunction can be a devastating financial blow that can permanently put a competitor out of business.

Generally, a court must determine that all five of the following factors are present before it will issue an injunction.

1. The patent owner must have a *substantial likelihood* of prevailing on the merits of the case at trial.

2. The patent owner will suffer *irreparable harm* if the preliminary injunction isn't granted.

3. The patent owner doesn't have another adequate remedy at law that will keep him or her from suffering the irreparable harm.

4. The threatened harm to the patent owner outweighs the potential harm to the defendant.

5. The granting of a preliminary injunction serves the public's interest.

If a preliminary injunction is granted, there is a strong likelihood the patent holder will prevail at trial and succeed in making the injunction permanent. Indeed, many of the issues that would otherwise be resolved at trial may be effectively decided during the hearing for the preliminary injunction.

DAMAGES

Damages compensate the plaintiff for the costs and economic losses it has suffered as a result of infringement. In cases where the court finds that the infringement was willful, the court can triple the amount of damages.

> ⚖ **LAWYER'S NOTE:** *For utility patents, a patent owner must mark his or her own product with notice of the patent or give actual notice in order to receive monetary damages. This notice requirement is waived for process patents.*

In the famous Polaroid case, where Kodak was found liable for infringing Polaroid's patent with its own instant imaging camera, triple damages were requested. Polaroid expressed disappointment that it received only a $909,457,567.00 damage award, instead of the treble (triple) damages requested.

ATTORNEY'S FEES

You probably shouldn't initiate a lawsuit with the expectation that you'll be reimbursed for your attorney's fees. It's the rare exception, rather than the rule, that courts use their discretion to award attorney's fees to the prevailing party, even in cases of willful infringement.

However, patent owners routinely ask for attorney's fees. Occasionally, a court is so moved by the plight of a patent holder and the egregious nature of a defendant's conduct that such a request is successful.

IMPORTANT CONSIDERATIONS PRIOR TO FILING SUIT

All litigation has risks to the plaintiff as well as the defendant. The plaintiff generally must front the costs of bringing a lawsuit, without any certainty that these costs can be recouped. Also, litigation often breeds more litigation, in the form of civil counterclaims and even actions on the part of the Patent Office to revisit the legitimacy of your original patent.

CAN YOU RECOVER FROM THE DEFENDANT IF YOU WIN?

The most favorable judgment in the most uncertain terms is no guarantee that you will get paid a dime. Many defendants, faced with the devastating impact of combined injunctive relief and heavy damage awards, simply elect to file bankruptcy. Bankruptcy laws afford companies protection from all of their creditors, and there may be a quite a few of them in addition to you.

WHO CAN YOU NAME AS A DEFENDANT IN YOUR LAWSUIT?

Federal law permits an inventor to cast a wide net when it comes to naming defendants in an infringement suit. It's a good idea to take advantage of your wide net, naming as many culpable parties as possible in order to increase your chances of having responsible, financially solvent defendants named in your action that can foot the bill for any ultimate damage award.

Examples of parties you may sue include the following:

- Retailers who sell an infringing product

- Purchasers and end users of an infringing product

- Advertisers who encourage the public to infringe your patent or tell them how to do it

Infringement occurs when one of your three exclusive rights, as a patent holder, is infringed. These rights are using, making, and selling your patented device or process. Included within these rights is the right to import your products into the U.S. Your patented device or process must be infringed in its entirety; there is no cause of action for partial infringement.

There are three types of infringers: direct, inducement of infringement, and contributory. The distinction is important, because ignorance and good faith only constitute defenses if the infringement is contributory.

The Direct Infringers

Direct infringement occurs whenever someone makes, uses, or sells your patented product. Direct infringement can be committed innocently, even if the infringer has no direct knowledge of your patent. In fact, this is often the case. However, the law provides that a patent owner must mark his or her own product with notice of the patent, or give actual notice in order to receive monetary damages.

Inducement of Infringement

Indirect infringement occurs when someone doesn't directly make, sell, or use your product but instead induces someone else to do so. For example, if someone sells information telling the public how to manufacture your patented product or replicate your patented process, the advertiser is liable for indirect infringement.[6]

The Contributory Infringers

Contributory infringement occurs when an infringer knowingly sells a specially adapted component that contributes to the infringement of a patented process or product with an intent to profit from the ultimate infringement. The component may actually be something that's in the public domain.[7] For example, you may be liable for vicarious infringement if you knowingly supply specially adapted tennis shoes to a com-

---

[6] *Fromberg Inc. v. Thornhill*, 315 F.2d 407(5th Cir. 1963).
[7] 35 U.S.C. Sec. 271(b) (liability for inducing infringement); 35 U.S.C. Sec. 271 (liability for contributory patent infringement).

pany that is equipping the shoes with a light, in violation of someone's patent to make a light-up gym shoe.

Your tennis shoe does not in and of itself infringe any patent. However, the contributory infringement statute can actually bring unprotected, unpatentable matter within the scope of the Patent Act.

The law specifies the following three-part test for contributory infringement:

- **Sale:** There must be a sale of the infringing goods.

- **Material component:** The sale must involve a material component of the invention as defined in the claims of the patent.

- **Knowledge:** The defendant must have actual knowledge that he or she is trafficking in infringing goods.

In the early 1960s, Ford Motor Company manufactured hundreds of thousands of convertibles with a popular retractable top. The problem was that Ford somehow neglected to enter into a valid license agreement for the convertible tops. Each manufacturer of the convertibles would have been liable for contributory infringement if it could be proven that they had actual knowledge of the infringement. Since the statute requires "knowing" infringement, the manufacturers were held liable only for the manufacture of convertibles that occurred after they received notification of the invalid license agreement.[8]

> ⊘ **CAUTION:** *If a company is infringing your patent by making goods under a government contract, subject to government requirements, you can't sue the company in your local jurisdiction or get an injunction against it. You can only sue the Court of Claims in Washington, D.C. Your remedies are limited to damages and interest. The government, effectively, has the right to impose a compulsory license arrangement for any patented technology.*

---

[8] *Aro Manufacturing Co. v. Convertible Top Replacement Co.*, 377 U.S. 476 (1964).

Subsequently, in the late 1980s there was a huge black market in the United States for counterfeit General Motors truck parts. Retailers and repair shops who knowingly resold the infringing parts could have been named as defendants in an infringement suit.

STATUTE OF LIMITATIONS AND THE NEED TO ACT PROMPTLY

There's no statute of limitations for patent infringement. However, damages can be recovered only for a six-year period before the filing of the complaint.[9]

Aside from the statute of limitations, there's another important reason to act promptly in contacting the infringer. If you fail to contact the infringer, the court may decide that you allowed the continued infringement and did not act reasonably to minimize your damages. Since damages are at the court's discretion, this may affect the ultimate amount of your damage award.

JURISDICTION AND VENUE

If you do business in New Mexico, you probably don't expect to have to travel to Alaska to defend yourself in a lawsuit under Alaskan law. That is, of course, unless you happen to be soliciting and doing business in Alaska.

Location can dramatically affect the cost, ability to defend, and even the ultimate outcome of a lawsuit. This is the justification for rules pertaining to jurisdiction and venue.

JURISDICTION

Jurisdiction is the legal authority of a particular court to hear a case. Federal courts have jurisdiction over lawsuits involving patents. This is

---

[9] 35 U.S.C. Sec. 286.

because the authority to regulate patents arises under the U.S. Constitution.

The federal courts, however, only have exclusive jurisdiction over disputes that specifically involve the enforcement, infringement, and validity of patents. For example, if there is a contractual dispute involving a patent license agreement, a state court would have the right to hear the matter since state law would govern the contract.

To make matters slightly more confusing, federal courts may still have jurisdiction, even when there are not federal patent questions presented. *Diversity* jurisdiction allows a lawsuit between citizens of two different states to be brought in federal court.

VENUE

Venue is the legal concept that ensures that a Florida defendant doesn't have to travel to Alaska. Venue is the specific geographical location of the federal court where a lawsuit is brought.

The venue statutes pertaining to patent matters require you to choose a court in a district where the defendant lives or has some sort of business-related connection.

If the action is for patent infringement, you can bring your lawsuit "in the judicial district where the defendant resides, or where the defendant has committed the act of infringement and has a regular and established place of business."[10]

Generally, under the Patent Act, you can file suit in the judicial district where:

1. Any defendant resides, if all defendants reside in the same state

2. The majority of the acts giving rise to the lawsuit occurred, or where the property that is the subject of the litigation is located

3. Any defendant can be found, if you can't find a suitable venue using (1) and (2) above[11]

---

[10] 28 U.S.C. Sec. 1400 (b).
[11] 28 U.S.C. Sec. 1391 (b).

If you're a defendant and you think the lawsuit has been brought in an improper venue, you can actually file a motion to dismiss the action. The court can also entertain a motion to transfer venue, which is more common.[12]

YOUR BURDEN OF PROOF

In any lawsuit, the person who files it has a *burden of proof*. A burden of proof is what you must legally establish in order to win your lawsuit. If a defendant brings counterclaims or alleges your patent is invalid, the defendant has the burden of proving these things.

There are different evidentiary standards of burdens of proof that plaintiffs and defendants must meet, depending on the type of action being filed. In an action for patent infringement, as a plaintiff, you must show that the *preponderance of the evidence* points to the conclusion that the subject patent has been infringed. A preponderance of evidence standard means that there is more evidence that the patent has been infringed than that it has not been. It's a fairly lenient standard, compared to some of the other ones courts use.

If a defendant alleges as a defense that your patent is invalid or unenforceable, that defendant has a higher burden of *clear and convincing proof*. The clear and convincing proof standard means that the conclusion drawn from the evidence is highly probable and free from reasonable doubt.

THE NEW ROLE OF JUDGES AND JURIES

Obviously, you want your case decided by the tribunal that's most likely to favor you. Prior to 1996, juries were more likely to favor plaintiffs in patent litigation, issuing decisions finding infringement about 60 percent of the time. However, due to an important U.S. Supreme Court case decided in 1996, the jury may be limited to deciding the issue of damages, with a judge actually interpreting the claims and deciding

---

[12] Fed. R. Civ. P. 12(b)(3).

whether infringement has occurred. In *Markman vs. Westview Instruments, Inc.,*[13] the U.S. Supreme Court decided that juries do not possess the requisite expertise to evaluate claims and that claim construction is the job for a judge to undertake in what is now called a *Markman hearing*.

Different federal jurisdictions implement the Markman decision in various ways, and each district has its own rules as to filing requirements and due dates for various legal documents called *pleadings*. Consider a hypothetical defendant "Infringoman" and a hypothetical plaintiff "Manufacto." Suppose Infringoman is making knockoffs of Manufacto's light-up headphones, and Manufacto brings suit in a federal district court. Here is how the case might progress in a hypothetical district court:

- **Complaint:** Manufacto must file a complaint and allege how Infringo has infringed its patent.

- **Response (including relevant prior art):** Infringo will then have a set number of days to retain counsel and respond to Manufacto's claims; Infringo's response must allege a detailed description of any prior art it believes would limit Manufacto's ability to enforce its patent.

- **Proposed claim construction statement:** After a stated number of days, Manufacto might be required to submit to the judge a document explaining how the claims of its patent should be interpreted and must distinguish any alleged prior art identified by Infringo in its response.

- **Response to claim construction statement:** Infringo must respond to Manufacto's interpretation of its own claims, indicating why it is not infringing.

- **Meeting and settlement discussion:** The judge or relevant rules for the particular jurisdiction may require Manufacto and Infringo to meet to identify the areas on which they agree and disagree, as well as any potential for a voluntary settlement. Both parties will report the results of these discussions to the judge, usually in some sort of joint pleading.

---

[13] *Markman v. Westview Instruments, Inc.,* 116 S. Ct. 1384 (1996).

- **Hearing:** The judge will hold a hearing to construe the language of the claims; typically one or both sides will file a *Motion for Summary Judgment* requesting that the judge rule in their favor (i.e.,

> ⚖️ **LAWYER'S NOTE:** *You need to check the rules of the federal district in which you are filing to determine the procedures and filing deadlines for that particular district.*

there is no material issue of fact) and that the facts can only be construed in their favor, at the end of the hearing.

Because of the *Markman* decision, patent litigation is more streamlined than in the past. Patent litigation can, conceivably, take months instead of years to conclude.

ARBITRATION AS AN ALTERNATIVE

Arbitration can be a more economical alternative to litigation, but both the plaintiff and defendant must agree to use it, and special rules apply for arbitrations related to patents. You must pay an arbitrator, but you save on the cost of depositions, discovery, and pretrial motions. For more information about arbitration, you can visit the American Arbitration Association Web site located at http:www.adr.org.

RESOLVING INFRINGEMENT ISSUES WITHOUT LITIGATION

Prior to filing a lawsuit, you can try simply asking the infringer to stop. Sometimes the infringement is inadvertent, and sometimes a serious threat of litigation causes the infringer to reconsider whether continuing to infringe makes good business sense.

> ⚖️ **LAWYER'S NOTE:** *Consult with a lawyer before sending a letter to a potential infringer. If the letter gives the competitor a reasonable expectation of being sued for infringement, the competitor can go to court to challenge the validity of your patent.*

DRAFTING A COMPLAINT FOR PATENT INFRINGEMENT

A complaint is to litigation what the opening pitch is to a baseball game. It's the initial document filed in a lawsuit and served upon the defendant.

Your complaint must contain the following information:

- Notice to the defendant as to what conduct constitutes basis for the lawsuit, including detailed information about the defendant's conduct that established the necessary elements to prove infringement

- The type of relief you are requesting, such as injunctive relief and damages

- Whether you're requesting a jury trial or want a single judge to decide your case

- Why the court with which you have filed the complaint has the proper jurisdiction and is located in the proper venue to hear your complaint

⚖️ LAWYER'S NOTE: *Sometimes patent infringement is not the only cause of action you're alleging against a defendant. Your complaint may allege other causes of action, such as trademark and copyright infringement in the same complaint.*

- Facts sufficient to establish your ownership of the patent (for example, the patent registration number)

STOPPING FOREIGN INFRINGEMENT: THE CUSTOMS SERVICE

The U.S. Customs Service and International Trade Commission have an official obligation to look out for the interests of patent holders and inventors. These services aren't necessarily alternatives to suing in federal court but can be useful and appropriate under the right circumstances.

You can request that the Customs Service conduct an import survey for the duration of two, four, or six months (ranging in cost from

$1,000 to $2,000). The Customs Service will provide you with the address of any importer whose goods appear to infringe on your patent. Sometimes this procedure has the collateral effect of delaying the importation of the infringing goods. To obtain an application for an import survey, you can write to:

Commissioner of Customs
Attention IPR Branch, Room 2104
U.S. Customs Service
1301 Constitution Avenue
Washington, D.C. 20229

If your patent is particularly valuable and you need to take steps to stop its infringement on a global scale, you can bring a proceeding before the International Trade Commission. This type of proceeding can be expensive, but it is very powerful. It enables you to have the importation of the device stopped and quarantined at the U.S. port of entry.[14]

INSURING YOUR PATENT

Patent litigation is some of the most expensive litigation there is, in part because it usually requires specially certified lawyers and expert witnesses on the clock.

Because of the high cost of patent litigation, a number of companies write insurance policies to cover the costs of protecting valuable patents from infringement. Some companies that specifically offer this coverage are Lloyds of London (www.lloyds.com) and Intellectual Property Insurance Services (www.infringeins.com).

> **$$ BUSINESS TIP:** *If you're sued for patent infringement, you may be covered under the terms of your general business liability policy.*

---

[14] 19 U.S.C. 1337(a).

HOW TO AVOID BEING SUED FOR PATENT INFRINGEMENT

There's nothing more exciting to an entrepreneur than the discovery of a new market niche. Unfortunately, an unfilled need in the current marketplace doesn't mean that no one has ever thought of your idea. The previous inventor may have simply lacked the wherewithal or initiative to bring the invention to market or may have hesitated to manufacture it because the timing simply wasn't right.

IS A COMPETING PATENT CURRENTLY IN FORCE?

The first thing in manufacturing a new item or process, from a legal standpoint, is determining whether there's an existing patent in force. Unfortunately, a search of existing patents doesn't give 100 percent certainty, because there's currently no way to effectively search all pending patent applications. Not all patent applications are required to be published, as explained in chapter 12.

If you want to manufacture an item similar to one that's already on the market, the first thing you should do is examine the item and any instructions or documents accompanying it to see if the manufacturer discloses an existing patent number and date.

If the patent is subject to publication requirements, you can download a copy of the patent application, including all of the claims, from the PTO Web site locate at www.uspto.gov. (The procedure for a patent search is discussed in chapter 12.)

After you've obtained a copy of the patent, you want to determine when it expires. Utility patents are good for twenty years from the filing date. Design patents expire after fourteen years.

If you find that there is a current patent in force, you need to figure out if it covers the product currently manufactured. Very often the claims of the original patent application don't provide very much protection at all.

What if the product you want to manufacture is simply marked "Patented" and has no number? You have two options. One option is to contact the manufacturing company, but the company is not obligated to respond to a possible competitor.

Your other option is to do a search of all the patents issued covering classes and subclasses of the product. This is more expensive but offers you greater assurance. However, this type of search won't disclose pending patents. Accordingly, if the device or process you want to copy is fairly new, you should proceed very cautiously, since it may very well be the subject of a pending patent application.

> **$$ BUSINESS TIP:** *Although you can run a search of patents issued to a particular company, this may not be successful because the manufacturer may not actually own the patent. They may be a licensee.*

GETTING AROUND AN ENFORCEABLE PATENT

Finding out that the device or process is covered by someone else's patent isn't necessarily the kiss of death to your new line of business. If you want to manufacture a device or process that's subject to a current patent, you have several options:

• **You can wait for the patent to expire.** Patents are nonrenewable. When a patent expires, the technology goes into the public domain for anyone to use. If a patent is close to the end of its term, you can wait for it to expire. Patents (other than design patents) are currently issued for a twenty-year term. Design patents have a fourteen-year term.

• **You can purchase the patent.** This is often a cheaper route than litigation to acquire patent rights.

• **You can try to design around what's covered by the patent claims.** It's a common misconception that a valid patent allows the owner to preempt an entire area of technology. A patent covers only the technology embodied in the claims. It's often possible to substitute dissimilar, improved technology for elements of the claim. You may also find that key elements of the product design are in the public domain and not covered by the claims of the patent. You are free to copy aspects of the product or process that are not subject to patent protection.

> **CAUTION:** *In trying to design around someone else's patent, you walk a tightrope with the doctrine of equivalents, discussed earlier in this chapter, which precludes you from marketing a substantially identical product with only insignificant modifications.*

• **Cross-licensing.** This sort of swap is an increasingly popular option in the computer technology industry. Basically this is how it works: If the company that holds the patent on the desired technology wants to use some of your patented technology, you negotiate a trade via license.

• **You can attempt to enter into a licensing agreement with the rightful owner of the patent.** Although many patent owners see the business sense in this arrangement, others may view you as unwanted competition. After being denied a license, you're at the disadvantage of having alerted the patent owner to the possibility that you may be attempting to design around the patent. The patent owner knows to look out for your product and is alerted to the possibility of bringing litigation.

• **You attempt to break the patent.** You can challenge the enforceability of the patent using the reexamination process discussed in the next section, or by having an attorney search for flaws in the patent itself.

CHALLENGING THE VALIDITY OF A PATENT

If you want to break someone else's patent, you're going to want a hired gun. Challenging a patent is precisely the type of adversarial process for which lawyers are best suited.

You can begin the process of challenging the patent by hiring a professional patent search firm to do a comprehensive patent search. You also want to order a copy of the patent office's file, created during the patent prosecution process. This file will have a complete record of office actions and actions taken to clarify, narrow, or abandon claims. The records, notes, and correspondence included in the prosecution file can give you insight as to weaknesses and possible bases to challenge the patent.

You can ask the PTO to reexamine any patent to determine whether any prior art that you call to its attention affects the validity of the patent. You must file a request setting forth the patent number, explaining what you consider to be the prior art, and pay a rather substantial fee. If the PTO considers the prior art you've identified to be relevant, it will conduct a reexamination. If it thinks the prior art is irrelevant, the PTO may refund a portion of your fee.

After the PTO completes its reexamination process, it issues a *certificate of patentability* or *unpatentability*. If the Patent Office decides on the side of unpatentability, you've successfully challenged the patent. If, however, the PTO issues a certificate of patentability as the result of the reexamination, you've effectively reinforced the validity of the patent. The certificate of patentability can help a patent holder who subsequently decides to sue *you* for infringement.

DEFENDING YOURSELF IF YOU'RE ACCUSED OF INFRINGEMENT

Suppose your morning mail brings a letter notifying you that you may be infringing on someone else's patent and asks you to cease and desist producing your profitable product line. Suppose further that you've been manufacturing the allegedly infringing product for years.

If you believe your product is clearly distinct and dissimilar to any other, your first impulse may be to take a wait-and-see approach. A plaintiff must meet a heavy burden of proof to prevail in an infringement action. However, it's in your interest to quickly assess the potential impact on your business and to consider which of the following positions you're going to take and how you are going to respond to that letter in your morning mail.

POSITION #1: "I HAVEN'T INFRINGED YOUR PATENT"

After taking a good look at your product and your competitor's patent, you may decide that they are not the same at all.

You may be able to distinguish your product from what's covered in your competitor's patent. You can get a copy of the patent off the PTO

Web site (www.uspto.gov). (The patent date and number may have been included in the "cease and desist letter you received, or you can write back and request it from the patent owner.)

In order to prevail in a lawsuit, the patent holder doesn't need to show that you've infringed every claim, only that you've infringed one or more of them. Generally it requires a skilled patent attorney to look at the elements of each claim and compare your device or process to the elements in the claim to determine the degree of similarity.

> 🚫 **CAUTION:** *The doctrine of equivalents, discussed earlier in this chapter, may still apply. (The doctrine of equivalents is discussed in more detail on page 236.)*

POSITION #2: "SORRY, YOUR PATENT IS INVALID"

The owner of a patent can place himself at risk by sending you a cease and desist letter. You, as the recipient of such a letter may act offensively and challenge the very validity of the patent.

You can challenge the enforceability of a patent in the following ways:

- **Initiating a Reexamination Process:** You can ask the PTO to reexamine your competitor's patent in view of prior art that was not considered at the time of the initial application but which you've now identified. The cost of the process is fairly substantial, but it can be cheaper than defending a lawsuit for infringement.

> ⚖️ **LAWYER'S NOTE:** *In the face of a new prior art reference the Patent Office may be more inclined to maintain the validity of a patent than a court.*

- **Provide evidence that the product or process was sold or used one year prior to the issuance of the patent:** A patent is unenforceable if the device or process has been sold or used one year prior to the filing of an application, so you can have the patent invalidated. You should comb your files for advertising, customer contracts, records of manufacturing costs, and other documentation that provides evidence of sale or use one year prior to the issuance of the patent.

• **Demonstrate that the patent holder committed a fraud during the patent process:** It is considered a fraud sufficient to invalidate a patent application if the patent owner failed to disclose relevant facts during the patent process. Relevant facts omitted may include prior art or other pertinent activity known to the applicant, information about previous patents, or the best mode, discussed earlier in this chapter on page 212.

• **Show the PTO that the invention described doesn't work, or the explanation of the invention is incomplete.** The patent application must describe a working implementation of the invention, and the description contained in the application must be sufficient to fully describe to someone skilled in the art how to make the invention. If you can demonstrate that the patent owner has failed to do this, the PTO may declare the patent invalid.

• **Provide evidence of misuse of the patent.** If the patent holder has misused the patent, the PTO will invalidate the patent retroactively. A finding of misuse is rare and has most frequently involved antitrust violations. However, a showing that the patent owner has used his invention for any illegal purpose may, theoretically, be used to invalidate the patent.

POSITION #3: "YOUR PATENT IS VALID, BUT IT'S UNENFORCEABLE"

A perfectly good patent can be rendered unenforceable for a variety of legal faux pas.

Here are a few of the ways a patent holder can shoot himself in the foot:

• **False marking:** False marking is incorrectly marking patented products with numbers that don't cover the patent granted. You are required to mark your product materials to put the public on notice of your patent. Failure to do so, with an intent to deceive, can negate your right to damages. Including an incorrect number is an instance of false marking that can render the patent entirely unenforceable, absent a showing that the false marking was due to inadvertent error or otherwise in good faith.

• **Unreasonable delay in bringing a lawsuit.** The law frowns upon a patent owner who ignores infringing activity. Suppose you watch a manufacturer develop, market, and sell a product for a decade, then decide to sue just when the product line catches on and begins turning a profit. The defendant can argue you have been aware of the infringing activity for years, have taken no action, and therefore should be estopped from enforcing the patent.

• **Patenting an invention that doesn't actually work:** If your device or process doesn't work, your patent may be unenforceable against a competitor who develops a working implementation.

PART FIVE

....

Issues for Entrepreneurs

CHAPTER 14 >>>

Trade Secret Protection

PUBLISHED PATENT AND copyright applications are matters of public record that your competitors can peruse on the Internet to see exactly what you have done and how. Trade secret law provides a mechanism to keep valuable knowledge from your competitors when other areas of intellectual property law require public disclosure of the very information you're trying to protect.

IN THIS CHAPTER YOU FIND OUT:

- The advantages of trade secret protection over patent and copyright
- How to identify information that should be afforded trade secret status
- How you can inadvertently lose a trade secret
- How to protect and defend trade secrets from misappropriation

THE ORIGINAL FORMULA for Coca-Cola was concocted by a pharmacist named John Pemberton in 1886, using mysterious equipment and ingredients in his own backyard. He dubbed the formula 7X and kept it locked up in a bank security vault in Atlanta. Had Mr. Pemberton instead opted to patent 7X, that patent would have expired more than 100 years ago, and the formula would have been marketed by competitors once it entered the public domain. Instead, Mr. Pemberton's 7X remains subject to trade secret protection and is the exclusive property of The Coca-Cola Company to this day.

Krispy Kreme donuts are made out in the open for the public to see, but their precise recipe is a closely guarded trade secret.

The Kellogg Company, at one time, stopped tours of its facilities because it feared corporate spies posing as tourists would gain access to valuable breakfast cereal formulas.

Nearly every business has a customer list that warrants consideration of trade secret protection.

WHY DO WE HAVE TRADE SECRET PROTECTION?

Information requires investment of money, technology, and skilled human capital to research and produce. It can be the most valuable asset your business owns, but it can instantly become worthless if disclosed to your competitors. Trade secret law recognizes that proprietary information is a unique form of intellectual property. As with other forms of intellectual property, it's in the interest of society to promote the research and development that leads to advancements.

Generally registration of a copyright requires public exposure and publication, which is exactly the opposite of what you want for intellectual property you're trying to keep confidential. Patents require disclosure

⚖️ **LAWYER'S NOTE:** *Software enjoys an exception to the general rule of public exposure and publication for copyright protection. Software can be both registered for copyright protection and maintained as a trade secret. The portions subject to trade secret protection can be omitted from the submission to the Copyright Office.*

of information sufficient to replicate your invention. Your patent application is freely available to your competitors on the PTO Web site.

SPECIAL LAWS PROTECTING TRADE SECRETS

Both federal and state governments favor the development of commercial and industrial knowledge that place businesses within their borders at a competitive advantage. Both federal and state statutes provide the necessary cloak of secrecy to foster this research and development.

STATE STATUTES: UNIFORM TRADE SECRETS ACT AND RESTATEMENT OF TORTS

Most states have their own statutes covering trade secrets, but many, if not all, have co-opted the basic concepts and language from three well-known sources: common law, the Uniform Trade Secrets Act, and the Restatement of Torts.

Common law is law developed by courts rather than congressmen. It consists of legal rules and precedents established by court decisions, rather than statutes. Often statutes are developed to codify prior common law decisions as laws, which are more concise and easier for the public to access. Most state and federal trade secret statutes are based on common law principles.

Some state statutes are based on the *Uniform Trade Secrets Act,* which is a model act created by a collaboration of judges, lawyers, and scholars in various states. About half of the states have adopted the Uniform Trade Secrets Act in some form, which is based largely on common law principles.

In addition to the Uniform Trade Secrets Act, the *Restatement of Torts* is a guide used by most states. It summarizes common law principles pertaining to trade secret protection and has also been adopted by most states that have codified some form of the Uniform Trade Secrets Act.

The Uniform Trade Secrets Act was created in 1979 and was significantly amended in 1985. In those states where it's been adopted, it's deemed to preempt any previously established common law (except that law included in the Restatement of Torts, if it's been adopted).

FEDERAL LAW: ECONOMIC ESPIONAGE ACT OF 1996

In 1996, President Clinton signed the Economic Espionage Act into law. The act makes it a federal crime to steal a trade secret or to receive or possess trade secret information if you know that it's been stolen. As you might imagine, a major target of the act is high-tech theft of information over the Internet.

The act provides criminal penalties, with jail terms up to ten years and fines of up to $500,000 for individuals. Corporations or organizations can be fined up to $5 million.

Stricter penalties apply if a trade secret benefits a foreign entity. Maximum prison terms shoot up to fifteen years. Corporations can be fined up to $10 million for stealing secrets for foreign entities.

The act also provides mechanisms to the U.S. government to seize property obtained as a result of trade secret theft and to dismantle entities and networks facilitating the theft of trade secrets.

WHAT IS A TRADE SECRET?

Because something is secret doesn't necessarily mean it is valuable. Trade secrets must possess both confidentiality and have value. Whether the particular information has value is a matter highly specific to industry context.

DEFINITION OF A TRADE SECRET: THE UNIFORM TRADE SECRETS ACT

The Uniform Trade Secrets Act promotes uniformity primarily by providing a standard definition as to what constitutes a trade secret. This definition is so central to the statutory scheme of the majority of states that it warrants some scrutiny. The act provides:

A trade secret is information, including a formula, pattern compilation, program, device, method, technique or process that:

> (i) derives independent economic value, actual or potential, from not being generally known to, and not being readily ascertainable by proper means, by other persons who can obtain economic value from its disclosure and use, and
> (ii) the subject of efforts that are reasonable under the circumstances to maintain its secrecy.

From this definition, it's apparent that there are certain elements information must possess in order to be characterized as a trade secret. Although trade secret protection may differ slightly from state to state, you can assume that a trade secret in any jurisdiction must be all of the following:

- **Nonascertainable:** The information must not be generally known or ascertainable to the members of the general public through legitimate means. Information disclosed in marketing materials and presentations, customer seminars, trade journals, and other nonconfidential marketing materials is considered readily ascertainable.

- **Valuable:** To be classified as a trade secret, information must have actual economic value. Value can be proven by showing that revenue is derived as a result of using the information.

- **Maintained with discretion:** The owner of a trade secret must use reasonable efforts to maintain its secrecy, or the information loses its status as a trade secret.

SOME EXAMPLES OF TRADE SECRETS

A good test for determining whether something is a trade secret is to ask yourself whether your business would be damaged if your competitors got hold of it.

Examples of information you might want to protect as trade secrets include:

- Formulas and procedures used for creating and delivering your product or service

- Marketing strategies

- Customer lists and valuable knowledge obtained about the needs of your clients

- Research pertaining to new product formulations

- Research pertaining to rejected or abandoned product formulations

- Specialized training materials developed to train employees in methods specific to your company

- Designs and specifications for your manufacturing facility and equipment

- Specialized modifications made to commercial software products

COMPARING PATENT AND TRADE SECRET PROTECTIONS

Occasionally an inventor or entrepreneur will opt for trade secret protection rather than going to the trouble and expense of applying for a patent. The two protections are sometimes mutually exclusive, since the patent process requires public disclosure in the patent application, while trade secret protections require that confidentiality be maintained. This means that an entrepreneur can lay down their money on one but not on both of these types of protection.

ADVANTAGES OF TRADE SECRET OVER PATENT PROTECTION

Trade secret protection is much cheaper and faster to obtain than patent protection. Patents can require well upwards of $10,000 and many years to prosecute (the average is around three years), with no guarantee that the patent will ultimately be granted. Other potentially more important advantages of trade secret protection over the long term include:

- **Perpetual protection.** Utility patents expire after twenty years. Trade secret protection, like the Coca-Cola formula, can be maintained in perpetuity

- **Broader protection.** Patents must be narrowly drawn and cannot cover elements of your business know-how unless they are proven to be novel and nonobvious. Thus, patent protection may not cover many aspects of your business process. Trade secret protection can be used to protect processes and information in their entirety.

- **Timely and automatic protection.** Trade secret protection is automatic if your information falls within the statutory definition. You aren't at the mercy of the Patent Office to grant your application and do not need to endure the average eighteen-month waiting process.

- **No proof of novelty required.** You are not required to prove that your information constitutes novel technological advancement as is the case with patented inventions.

LIMITATIONS OF TRADE SECRET PROTECTION

Trade secret protection can be tenuous in many areas. The following considerations might induce you to apply for a patent:

- **Reverse engineering:** Anyone is free to discover your trade secret by legitimate means. This is called reverse engineering, and it is strictly prohibited by the patent process, which gives you a virtual monopoly to make, sell, and use the technology claimed. Reverse engineering is the reason trade secret protection is not useful for most computer software, which can be reverse engineered using computers called decompilers.

- **Loss of protection:** Trade secret protection is immediately lost if you fail to maintain confidentiality or the information becomes known through any legitimate means whatsoever.

- **Someone else can patent your trade secret:** The fact that you have decided to protect your innovation or process as trade secret, and have acted properly to do so, does not prevent someone else from developing the technology by legitimate means and patenting it.

SECURING YOUR TRADE SECRETS

Trade secret protection can literally be lost overnight if your competitor gets the information through legitimate means. This can occur if the competitor somehow independently develops the information or if you are sloppy or ineffectual when it comes to taking reasonable precautions to maintain its confidentiality.

THE CLEAN ROOM DOCTRINE

To demonstrate that a company developed information through "proper means," a company must demonstrate that it developed it independently. This can include deliberate reverse engineering.

Under the *clean room doctrine,* a figurative clean room exists when a company demonstrates that its own engineers and analysts have developed the information independently, using publicly available technology. Companies who are actively engaged in reverse engineering of trade secrets usually maintain careful documentation to show how the information was developed and that only publicly available resources were consulted, or that they obtained the information through other legitimate means.

YOUR DUTY TO MAINTAIN CONFIDENTIALITY: WHO HAS ACCESS?

Trade secrets that have been maintained for decades can be lost overnight by a single breach in confidentiality. The law is surprisingly unsympathetic, even when the secrets are discovered by unethical or unscrupulous means. A stray file, a misdirected E-mail, or a disgruntled employee can be the kiss of death for a trade secret.

Once you've determined information has value as a trade secret, you need to be careful about who has access to it. You also need to document policies and procedures calculated to keep it confidential. Failure to exercise such controls can lead to a finding by a court that you haven't really kept the information secret at all.

What do your employees need to know to do their jobs? Can their duties be defined so that no employee is fully aware of all of the elements of the secret? What do your suppliers know? When employees transfer from one department to another, will they learn enough about making the product in each department to replicate it? What do your suppliers need to know?

Coca-Cola has several suppliers provide parts of their formula, but final mixing is done under direct secure company control. Many companies immediately cut off the access to facilities and computer systems by terminated employees.

EMPLOYEE CONFIDENTIALITY AGREEMENTS

The biggest threat to company confidentiality can come from within your own ranks. Your employees may have knowledge of your company's manufacturing processes, proprietary formulas, trade secrets, and customer outlets. Employees are likely to be an integral part of your marketing and development strategy.

> **$$ BUSINESS TIP:** *Customer lists and specifications can be viewed as a form of trade secret.*

It's good preventative medicine to have employees routinely enter into confidentiality or nondisclosure agreements. These agreements put employees on notice that they are under an obligation to keep mum about the details of your daily operations, particularly where competitors are concerned. Without a formal agreement and the discussion that accompanies it, an employee would assume that anything he or she learns on the job is theirs to claim on a résumé, regardless of how sensitive or integral that information may be to your business.

Unfortunately, in the absence of an express written agreement, a disgruntled employee who blabs to your competitors may have the stronger legal position in court. By the time you get to court, your trade secrets may have long since lost their secrecy. For example, everyone on your customer list may already have been contacted.

To avoid this scenario, the confidentiality agreement into which you enter with your employees should establish the following:

- **The scope of the confidentiality:** The agreement should specifically define what information is to be kept confidential and is considered proprietary by the employer.

- **Ownership of innovations or creative work developed in the workplace:** The agreement should make clear that the employer is the owner of innovations and creative work product that is related to employment and is developed during the course of employment.

- **The existence of valuable consideration:** In order for any contract to be binding, *both* parties must receive something of value. The legal term for this is called *consideration*. If the agreement is signed at the beginning of the employment relationship, the employment opportunity may serve as legal consideration to the employee. If the agreement is entered into later, bonuses and raises may serve as consideration. The consideration given to the employee should be specifically identified in the agreement.

Suppliers, consultants, and even investment bankers can all pose a hidden threat to your trade secrets, depending on how much they need to know to assist your business and do their jobs. Confidentiality agreements for third parties have become relatively commonplace. Generally, if your supplier wants your account, it will have no problem signing such an agreement. Investment bankers and financial professionals consider them routine. A sample third-party nondisclosure agreement is included in appendix B.

LITIGATING TO PROTECT YOUR TRADE SECRETS

Trade secret litigation can proceed under two theories. The first is the breach of a contractual obligation to maintain confidentiality. The second is an established cause of action of misappropriation by improper means.

To prevail on a contract theory, you must have an enforceable agreement that the material was to be kept confidential. Agreements can be oral, but a written agreement puts you in a stronger position.

The Uniform Trade Secrets Act defines misappropriation as the acquiring of information by unauthorized means by someone who knew or should have known they had a duty to maintain it. A common defense is that the information was not secret. To prevail on a theory of misappropriation, you have the burden of proving that you took reasonable measures to secure the information and maintain its confidentiality.

⚖️ **LAWYER'S NOTE:** *The Uniform Trade Secrets Act has a three-year statute of limitations, but states that have not adopted the act may have different limitations periods.*

CHAPTER 15 ⋙

Getting Your Idea to Market:
Licensing and Other Arrangements

RADICAL IDEAS ARE often met with scorn until they're properly marketed. Silly Putty, Teflon, Liquid Paper, the tampon, and disposable diapers all required initial pubic acceptance. The success of these ideas, which have now become familiar to millions of households, could not have been possible without the involvement, capital, and expertise of someone other than their inventors to bring them to market.

IN THIS CHAPTER YOU FIND OUT:

- What options you have for marketing an idea without relinquishing all control of it

- The difference between assigning versus licensing your idea

- How to protect the confidentiality of an idea while attempting to market it

IN 1930, AN unknown toy salesman approached Walter Elias Disney with a proposition to allow the use of the image of the already-famous Mickey Mouse on a pencil case. This type of agreement, now known as a license, was, at the time, unprecedented.

Shortly thereafter, realizing the potential of licensing, Walter Disney hired toy entrepreneur Herman Kamen to promote and manage all of Disney's licensing arrangements with third parties. In 1933, the worst year of the Depression, Kamen began to enter into agreements with retailers across the nation to develop marketing campaigns based on Donald Duck, Snow White, Pinocchio, and other characters to promote everything from children's clothing to orange juice. Under Kamen's skillful management, Disney's licensing revenue soon outpaced its cartoon and movie revenues and spawned the Disney merchandising dynasty that has lasted seven and a half decades.

Today licensing agreements are a commonplace legal arrangement. The licensing of ideas has generated billions of dollars in global commercial activity and has made possible the development of technologies that might not otherwise have been made accessible to consumers. Walt Disney used his licensing profits to finance artistic productions that remain classics and are still enjoyed by the public today.[1]

OVERVIEW: MAKING IT TO MARKET

Starting up your own business to market your invention ensures you maintain control of it. But it also means you assume all the financial risks and headaches of any start-up business. Not everyone has the investment capital or desire to do this.

Fortunately, you can enter into a number of legal arrangements and agreements that transfer the financial risk and responsibility for marketing your invention to a third party. Under these types of agreements, you receive payment in exchange for relinquishing some of your proprietary rights.

---

[1] *The Master of Marketing,* Robert Heide & John Gilman (November 1, 2002).

ASSIGNMENT AGREEMENTS

Assigning your rights means that you legally transfer them to a purchaser or other assignee. Assignments usually are executed in connection with some sort of outright sale of intellectual property. For example, if you sell your business, you would typically assign all of your rights in any trademarks associated with your business.

The U.S. Patent and Trademark Office and the U.S. Copyright Office keep track of who owns intellectual property. For this reason, you're required to record assignments with the appropriate office.

An assignment agreement usually contains a provision obligating you to execute any other agreement that's necessary to give the assignee the contractual rights set forth in your agreement. For example, you may be required to execute the forms for notifying the Patent and Trademark Office or the Copyright Office to record the assignment, or notifying a lien holder of the transfer.

LICENSING AGREEMENTS

A license allows you to retain more rights than an outright sale or assignment of your idea. Licenses typically involve royalty payments based upon a percentage of sales.

WHY ENTER INTO A LICENSING AGREEMENT?

Licensing involves the transfer of less rights that an outright sale or assignment of your idea. Reasons you might want to enter into a licensing agreement are:

- **A need to raise capital to get your innovation to market:** The licensee finances and orchestrates the marketing initiative and pays you a portion of the profits in the form of a licensing fee.

- **A need to penetrate new markets:** Entering into a license agreement may enable you to sell your innovation to a segment of the market you would not otherwise be able to reach. This might include a geographically remote market or a market in which you would lack credibility or recognition if not for your association with the licensee.

• **A desire to associate your product with that of the licensee:** Perhaps you've invented a technology that enhances the functionality of someone else's invention. You may want to enter into a licensing arrangement to have the two products jointly marketed or to eliminate concerns that your product may infringe on the patent, copyright, or trademark of the preexisting product.

> ⚖ **LAWYER'S NOTE:** *An assignment usually refers to selling the rights for one lump sum payment, but it's not uncommon for an assignment agreement to also include royalties. The difference between an assignment and a license is that an assignment generally involves a transfer of title to the intellectual property.*

LICENSING AGREEMENTS AND THE UNIFORM COMMERCIAL CODE

The Uniform Commercial Code (UCC) is a set of commercial statutes that forms the basis of most state regulations relating to sales and commerce. Despite its name, however, the UCC can be anything but uniform, since states often adopt a modified version of its provisions. The UCC applies to sales and licenses of goods.

The UCC provides a set of standardized warranties, called implied warranties, that apply to all goods and services unless they're specifically waived. Licensors are allowed to include provisions in license agreements

> ⚖ **LAWYER'S NOTE:** *Goods sold under the Uniform Commercial Code carry the warranty that the item will do what it is intended to do, that it is fit for a particular purpose, that the product does not infringe third-party rights, and that the seller has proper title to sell the item.*

requiring licensees to waive the UCC's implied warranties, but they have to make sure they do it right. The UCC is extremely picky about warranty waiver provisions. The waiver provisions have to include very specific language and even have to be a specific font size.

MANUFACTURING AGREEMENTS

If you don't happen to own your own plant or a factory, you might find it expedient to enter into a manufacturing agreement with a third party. These agreements typically provide that the manufacturer will be paid a specified amount that's not directly tied to the marketing success of the product.

It's critical that your manufacturing agreement address issues of both confidentiality and competition. The manufacturer of your product, by definition, knows how to create and replicate it. The manufacturer may even have knowledge of all of your customers and marketing outlets. This puts an unscrupulous manufacturer in the ideal position of being able to make a knockoff of your product and directly compete with you!

JOINT VENTURES AND OTHER TYPES OF HYBRID AGREEMENTS

Joint ventures, as their name implies, are a collaborative effort between two or more companies. Typically these companies will enter into an agreement under which they form a third, separate legal entity for the purpose of launching a specific marketing endeavor. Joint ventures can involve any number of combinations of assignment and license provisions, effectively creating a sort of legal hybrid.

Joint ventures are not the only type of hybrid agreement you'll find in the marketplace. Many agreements do not fall neatly within the category of license or assignment but contain elements of both. For example, an assignment agreement that effectively transfers all of the rights in a patent may still provide for payment in the form of ongoing royalties similar to those you typically find in a license agreement.

PROTECTING PROPOSED IDEAS FROM BEING STOLEN

How do you keep someone from stealing an idea you include in a proposal or a manuscript that you submit to them? Your ideas can be vulnerable to appropriation by others as you attempt to market them. Such ideas generally don't rise to the level of trade secrets, since the very act of their submission results in a loss of confidentiality. However, you can enter into an enforceable agreement that regulates the disclosure and use of the material you are submitting.

In the early 1980s, a comedian named Art Buchwald submitted an idea for a movie to Paramount Pictures. Buchwald and his producer were savvy enough to insist upon and enter into a written agreement that provided if Paramount Pictures ever made a movie based upon Buchwald's submission, Buchwald would receive a portion of the profits.

In 1988 Buchwald recognized his own idea in the plot of the movie *Coming to America,* starring Eddie Murphy. The movie was about an African king who suffers amnesia and begins working in a restaurant in America. Buchwald was ultimately successful in suing the studio for a portion of the movie's profits.[2]

In the absence of the written agreement, the presumption is that there is no protection. As explained in chapter 7, copyright law protects only the expression of ideas and not the ideas themselves.

THIRD-PARTY CONFIDENTIALITY AGREEMENTS

The need for confidentiality can collide with the realities of marketing. In order to market your product or idea, you may need to tell third parties quite a bit about it. This may include consultants who help you produce a prototype of your product or banks that you approach in search of venture capital.

It's not unreasonable for you to routinely request third parties to which you convey such information to enter into a confidentiality or nondisclosure agreement. The agreement should identify the information that you deem to be confidential and the specific purposes for which you authorize its use. Appendix C contains a sample confidentiality agreement.

---

[2] *Buchwald & Assoc, Inc. v. Rich,* 723 N.Y.S.2d 8 (1st Dep't 2001).

CHAPTER 16 >>>>

Software Savvy

THE PTO HAS recently become more flexible in extending patent protection to software. This liberalizing trend has met with resistance from a surprising source—the software industry itself. Many prominent and vocal software developers seem, at first glance, to be taking positions strangely at odds with their own financial interests. Chat rooms, bulletin boards, and on-line industry publications are ablaze with opinions as to whether and how patents should apply to the software industry.

IN THIS CHAPTER YOU FIND OUT:

- When and how you can protect software with patents and copyrights
- How to protect software as a trade secret
- When your software screens and icons can be trademarked
- Which types of legal protections work best for software
- About the direction of future legal trends for software protections

LESS THAN TWO years after the controversial Amazon.com 1-Click patent, the PTO is flooded with objections to Patent No. 6,430,602. The patent covers Active-Buddy software which creates "bots" (short for robot). Bots, which are also called interactive agents, are software components that work with instant messaging services to allow a user to ask questions in plain text and receive an automatic response from a server. For example, if an employee wants to know how many times a customer has ordered a certain part, the employee could simply type the question in plain text, rather than running through a series of commands.

Instant messaging is expected to be the workplace successor to traditional E-mail, having already earned the loyalty of a huge (mostly teenage) market. The patent promises to be very lucrative for ActiveBuddy.

The ActiveBuddy patent is greeted with an industry outcry that bots are prior art; developers cite examples of products already on the market such as Wirebot and Runabot. Many experts concur that a programmer named Aryeh Goldsmith developed a bot technology called the Net::AIM module, which was time stamped on the Internet nearly two years prior to the ActiveBuddy patent.[1]

ActiveBuddy's CEO, Tim Kay, aggressively maintains, "We invented interactive agents. Anybody using his or her own tools (to make bots) is obviously using our technology without paying us. . . ." However, if ActiveBuddy attempts to enforce its patent with a lawsuit, the defendant can request a reexamination of the patent, with the risk of placing the ActiveBuddy patent among the ranks of several dozen software patents that have recently been invalidated amid claims of prior art.

Meanwhile, in India a bot technology is announced that can make computers accessible to millions of poor, illiterate Indian residents who speak only Hindi. The technology interacts and responds to the user in their native Hindi language. However, the company introducing the technology fears that the ActiveBuddy patent may have foreclosed the field.[2]

ActiveBuddy founder Tim Kay continues to defend his company's decision to seek a patent against the spate of negative publicity, arguing, "Any company such as ours that is venture-funded has to protect itself. It's standard procedure to file for patents when you invent something. This simply allows us to build a business."[3]

---

[1] Ryan Naraine, "ActiveBuddy Turns to Developers," http://www.internetnews.com/dev-news/article.php/1459901 (September 10, 2002).

[2] Reported at AI Depot, "Chatbot Mania, Patenting & Hindu Speech," http://ai-depot.com/Applications/665.html (August 28, 2002).

[3] As quoted by Ryan Naraine, "ActiveBuddy Turns to Developers," http://www.internetnews.com/devnews/article.php/1459901 (September 10, 2002).

By definition, the process of issuing patents is law chasing technology. But software technology seems to be moving at a breakneck speed, with the PTO, the courts, and the legislature frantically trying to keep up. The software industry is critical of the PTO's evolving understanding of software issues.

BAD LAWS OR JUST BAD PATENTS?

Neither patent nor copyright protection provides a perfect fit for software. Law school professors and academics have, for several years, suggested that Congress pass legislation to create a unique category of legal protection for software, a sort of hybrid with characteristics of both patent and copyright law. (This is what was done for mask protection and semiconductor technologies.)[4]

But software developers don't seem to think that a bad fit between software and patent law is the problem. They suggest the problem is just "bad patents."

San Francisco–based BustPatents, which acts as a legal resource for software/technology patents, suggests the PTO is simply undermanned and overworked. "One of the reasons so many bad software patents issue . . . is that patent examiners do not have enough time and library resources to do their jobs." BustPatents adds that "strained conditions under which patent examiners do their jobs . . . lead to many patents of questionable quality being issued."[5] The Web site www.bustpatents. com lists dozens of software patents that have been invalidated either by the USPTO during a patent reexamination or by courts charged with reviewing them.

Some of these ex-patents include:

- Patent No. 5,960,411: Method and system for placing a purchase order via a communications network

---

[4] For a terrific discussion of *sui generis* protection for computer technologies, see Lemley, et al., *Software and Internet Law* (Aspen Law and Business, 2000).

[5] "Why Many Invalid Patents Are Being Issued by the Patent Office," BustPatents Web site, www.bust patents.com.

- Patent No. 5,333,184: Call message recording for telephone systems

- Patent No. 4,205,780: Document processing system and method

- Patent No. 4,169,290: Utility meter date recording method and apparatus

- Patent No. 4,057,829: Communications TV monitoring and control system

One software CEO, Jeff Bone, whose company holds a number of software patents, argues, "The problem with patents like the Active-Buddy patent is [they] . . . undermine the legitimacy of the entire patent system. They turn the patent system into an incredible waste of time, money, and effort on the part of anyone who seeks to obtain protection on true inventions." Bone contends, "[S]ince patents are granted without apparently any substantial due diligence [by the PTO], no inventor who receives a patent on something is in any way assured that his invention is protected." Bone advocates a total overhaul of the software patent system.[6]

THE CHRONOLOGY OF SOFTWARE PATENT CASES

A software developer has an interest in protecting *more* than computer code. As an individual, the developer has a keen economic interest in protecting as much of the functionality of the software as possible. But over the long term, the software industry as a whole is hurt by an over-proliferation of patents that can be roadblocks to future innovations in the field. Innovators may be preempted from using or improving upon software that has already been deemed as proprietary. Ultimately, overly broad protections in the industry can stifle rather than foster innovation.

In the courts, software patent cases reflect the tension between the need to encourage innovation by individual developers and the need to

---

[6] Jeff Bone, "Bad PTO: Activerse, ActiveBuddy, and Prior Art," http://www.oreillynet.com/pub/wlg/1836 (August 15, 2002).

foster growth in the industry as a whole. Both the PTO and federal courts have been attempting to achieve balance in this area for nearly three decades.

THE 1970S: A DISMAL OUTLOOK FOR SOFTWARE

Prior to the early 1980s, the prospects of patent protection for the infant software industry looked pretty dismal. In 1972, in *Gottschalk v. Benson*,[7] the Supreme Court considered the novel issue of whether a program converting decimal numerals into binary numerals was patentable. (This type of conversion made it possible for a digital computer to perform a lot of high-level tasks and functions.) The court denied patent protection to the program, reasoning that the patent "would wholly preempt [a] mathematical formula and in practical effect would be a patent on the algorithm itself." An algorithm is a set of steps to achieve a desired result. Since virtually all software programs contain some sort of algorithm, after *Gottschalk*, the outlook for extending patent protection to software looked grim indeed.

Subsequently, in 1978, in *Parker v. Flook*,[8] the Supreme Court issued another blow to the software industry, holding that a method for updating alarm limits during catalytic conversion processes could not qualify for patent protection. The court reiterated that a patent could not issue for any patent claim based on an algorithm. This certainly seemed to spell doom for software patents.

THE DOOR OPENS WITH THE DOT.COM BOOM

In 1981, coinciding with the start of the dot.com business boom, the judicial tide turned, and the sun began to shine on software patents. In *Diamond v. Diehr*,[9] the U.S. Supreme Court specifically held that a software program was patentable. The court limited the earlier prohibition on patenting algorithms of the *Gottschalk* case to mathematical algo-

---

[7] 409 U.S. 63 (1972).
[8] 437 U.S. 584 (1978).
[9] 450 U.S. 175 (1981).

rithms. More importantly, for the first time, the Supreme Court had actually provided developers with a road map for patenting software!

A few months later, in *Diamond v. Bradley*,[10] the Supreme Court affirmed the distinction between mathematical and other types of algorithms. The court upheld a claim for a program containing an algorithm directing data transfers between registers and memory. In *In re Pardo*, decided one year later,[11] the court stated that that the applicants' use of the term *algorithm* to describe the invention is not an admission of nonpatentable subject matter.

In 1982, the Court of Appeals for the Federal Circuit (CAFC) was recognized as the sole appellate court authorized to hear all patent cases. The CAFC continued on the course of liberalizing patent protection.

The effect of these cases was to convey a sense of security to software developers as to their ability to obtain patent protection. Subsequent to the *Diamond* cases, it appeared that claims for software patents would be allowed unless they simply involved the use of mathematical formulas to calculate and display numbers.

RECENT CASES

Today, the patentability of software is a fact of life. In 1994, in *In re Alappat*,[12] the CAFC decided that the software patent application presented proper "useful" statutory subject matter, even though the patent claims were merely for a series of physical "elements" within a machine to perform the functions.

More recently, in 1998, in *State Street Bank v. Signature Financial Group*,[13] the CAFC ruled that a patent should issue for a data-processing system that allowed related mutual funds to pool their assets into an investment portfolio with numerous similar funds. The software "invention" made several calculations on a daily basis related to each fund's percentage share of the investment's assets and expenses. The *State Street* case is often quoted by attorneys and courts for the proposition

---

[10] *Diamond v. Bradley*, 450 U.S. 381 (1981).
[11] *In re Pardo*, 684 F.2d 912, 916 n.6 (C.C.P.A. 1982).
[12] 33 F.2d 1326 (Fed. Cir. 1994).
[13] 149 F.3d 1368 (Fed. Cir. 1998).

that software algorithms are patentable when applied to accomplish a specific task.

CURRENT PTO GUIDELINES

The U.S. Patent and Trademark Office (PTO) takes great care to educate its own examiners as to when claims for patenting software should and should not be allowed. In 1996 the PTO prepared a manual titled "Examination Guidelines for Computer-Implemented Inventions" to assist its patent examiners and the public in prosecuting software patents.

Examples given in the current PTO guidelines as to when computer programs are considered "practical applications in the technological arts" under the Patent Act include the following:

- Methods for controlling transfer, storage, and retrieval of data between cache and hard disk storage devices so that the most frequently used data is readily available

- Methods for controlling parallel processors so that the processors can simultaneously perform several computing tasks to maximize computing efficiency (commonly called multitasking)

- A method of making a word processor by changing the state of the computer's arithmetic logic unit

- A digital filtering process for removing noise from a digital signal

HAS PATENT PROTECTION GONE TOO FAR?

Has the patent pendulum swung too far? Critics of the Amazon.com 1-Click patent case (discussed in chapter 11) and of the ActiveBuddy patent argue that it has. Many key players in the software industry claim that the PTO is now far too liberal in granting patents to preexisting or obvious software technologies, foreclosing the field to future innovation. Others argue that aggressive patents are necessary for their businesses to thrive.

Regardless of their position on the correct level of innovation that should be required for a patent, software industry leaders seem in agreement that patents will play a major role in the future of the software industry. The PTO currently has thousands of software patent applications pending.

CRITICAL SOFTWARE COPYRIGHT CASES

Copyright never treads on the toes of patent law. You cannot copyright ideas that are functional, as opposed to merely expressive, because that is the purview of patent law.

Copyright doesn't cover procedures, processes, systems, methods of operation, concepts, principles, or new discoveries embodied in the program. Copyright does protect all forms of original expression, economically and expeditiously. Copyright protects developers from the copying of their code, prevents the distribution of copies, and prevents the preparation of derivative works. These are all very valuable rights, since software is so easy to copy and distribute on a disk or over the Internet.

THE WATERSHED *WHELAN* CASE

An early significant case extending copyright protection to software was *Whelan Associates, Inc. v. Jaslow Dental Lab.*[14] In this case a consultant created a functionally similar program to a proprietary one she had been hired to create for someone else. At issue was whether the structure, sequence, and organization of the two programs were so similar that the second one was a violation of the proprietary patent rights. The Court of Appeals for the Third Circuit held that "the manner in which the program operates, controls and regulates the computer in receiving, assembling, calculating, retaining, correlating, and producing information either on a screen, print-out or by audio communication" was protected.

---

[14] *Whelan Associates, Inc. v. Jaslow Dental Laboratory, Inc.*, 797 F. 2d 1222 (3d Cir. 1986).

AFTER *WHELAN*: WHICH FEATURES ARE COPYRIGHTABLE?

Since the *Whelan* case, courts have cautiously extended copyright protection to "look and feel" as well as software code. The standard of originality from protecting the distinctive appearance and feel is high. Words used to describe software actions or features that are commonly used or intuitive terms are not protected. In *Lotus Development Co. v. Borland International, Inc.,*[15] a federal district court held that menu structures and the appearance of the menus were not capable of copyright protection. Copyright protection only extends to elements of a program that are dictated by expressive rather than functional considerations.

THE COMPUTER ASSOCIATES TEST

In 1992, in *Computer Associates v. Altai Associates International, Inc.,* the Court of Appeals for the Second Circuit developed a rather complicated three-part test for determining whether software is infringed under the copyright laws.[16] This test is known as the "abstraction/filtration/comparison" test, and it is frequently used by other courts.

In the first step, called abstraction, the court looks at the functions the program performs, without regard to the specific code. In the second step, filtration, the court decides what aspects of the computer program are dictated by functional, as opposed to expressive considerations. The functional elements are "filtered out," since only the expressive elements are protected under copyright law. In the third step, the comparison step, the court looks hard at the elements of the program that have *not* been filtered out, which are the elements of the computer code that are actually subject to copyright protection. In this fi-

⚖ **LAWYER'S NOTE:** *There is no centrally designated appeals court for copyrights as there is for patents. Thus, the scope of copyright law protection may vary among the jurisdictional boundaries of various circuit courts of appeals.*

---

[15] *Lotus Development Co. v. Borland International, Inc.,* 799 F. Supp 203 (D. Mass 1992).
[16] *Computer Associates Int'l. v. Altai, Inc.,* 982 F.2d 693 (2d. Cir. 1992).

nal step the court compares the protectible elements of both programs to see if copyright infringement has occurred.

PATENTS VERSUS COPYRIGHTS: WHICH ONE WORKS BEST?

The commercial life of even the most useful software program can be cruelly short, and eighteen months to get a patent can seem like an economically ruinous eternity. Copyright protection has the advantage of being automatic, since it applies to any work in fixed, tangible form, whether registered or not. However, other considerations may make patent protection well worth the wait.

PATENTS PROTECT AGAINST REVERSE ENGINEERING

Suppose one of your competitors hires experts who don't have access to your computer code to analyze how your software works, but they independently write the code. This is called *reverse engineering*.

Patents protect you against reverse engineering. If you hold a patent, your competitor cannot make a functionally identical work. Copyrights protect only against actual copying. In *Stac Electronics v. Microsoft Corp.*,[17] Stac Electronics received a $120 million patent infringement award against Microsoft when Microsoft created a functionally equivalent data compression program.

THE EASE OF OBTAINING COPYRIGHT PROTECTION

Patents are generally viewed as the Cadillac of software protection. Although they generally provide much broader legal protection than copyrights, patents always cost upwards of $10,000 and take an average of eighteen months to two years to obtain. During this time you can't assert any patent rights, and the software may even be technologically surpassed by other products introduced into the marketplace.

---

[17] *Stac Electronics v. Microsoft Corp.*, No. C-93-0413-ER (C.D. Cal. 2000).

In contrast, copyright protection automatically exists in software upon its fixation in a tangible form. This means that the protection is immediate and free. Registration of your copyright is necessary to bring a suit to obtain statutory damages and attorneys' fees. (See chapter 7.)

CLAIMING BOTH COPYRIGHT AND PATENT PROTECTION FOR SOFTWARE

Patent and copyright protections aren't mutually exclusive. In fact, the two can mesh very nicely. Copyright protects expressive elements and precludes literal copying. Patent protects against functionally similar uses of the technology you've patented, including derivation, independent development, or incorporation of protected functional aspects of your program. The fact that copyright protection is immediate can be invaluable to you while you're waiting out the lengthy approval process for your patent application.

TRADE SECRET PROTECTIONS FOR SOFTWARE

Unlike copyright and patent protections, which can readily coexist, there's an uneasy tension between trade secrets and the need to disclose information in patent and copyright applications.

TRADE SECRETS AND PATENT APPLICATIONS

Patent law requires that the inventor disclose the invention "in such full, clear, concise and

exact terms as to enable any person skilled in the art to which it pertains . . . to make and use" it.[18] The *best mode,* or most efficient way of
carrying out the invention, must be disclosed in the application.

Is it necessary to include code in a patent application? Recent cases
indicate you may be able to get away without it. In *In re Sherwood,*[19] a
federal court found that it was unnecessary to disclose code to satisfy
the best mode requirement because the developer had provided a very
detailed outline of the methodology used. On the other hand, in *White
Consolidated Industries v. Vega Servo-Control, Inc.,*[20] a patent was invalidated because key software considered a trade secret was not included in the application. In the *White* case, the developers did not
attempt to comply by including a detailed outline, as the developers had
done in the *Sherwood* case.

Generally, you can assume
that detailed code is not required
to satisfy statutory disclosure requirements in software patent
applications. Algorithms and
techniques need only be described in general terms. These
descriptions may include sum-
maries, diagrams, or flow charts.

> **$$ BUSINESS TIP:** *Patent, rather than
> trade secret protection, is more suitable for
> software that can easily be reverse-engineered
> using computers called* decompilers. *Patents
> protect against reverse engineering, but
> trade secret laws do not.*

CONFIDENTIALITY FOR COPYRIGHTED SOFTWARE

Unlike pending patent applications, which can be perused on the Internet, copyrighted code need not be registered immediately. You must register your copyright prior to bringing an infringement action, but you
have several different options for depositing materials with the Copyright Office, depending upon your need for confidentiality. These options include:

---

[18] 35 U.S.C. § 112 (first paragraph).
[19] *In re Sherwood,* 613 F.2d 809 (C.C.P.A. 1980), *cert. denied,* 450 U.S. 994 (1981).
[20] 713 F 2d. 788 (Fed. Cir. 1983).

- Filing the first twenty-five and last twenty-five pages of source code with portions containing trade secrets blocked out

- Filing the first ten and last ten pages of source code alone, with no blocked-out portions

- Filing the first twenty-five and last twenty-five pages of object code plus any ten or more consecutive pages of source code, with no blocked-out portion

$$ BUSINESS TIP: *For copyright applications, the goal is to include enough information to be able to prove copying, while giving away as little trade secret information as possible.*

- For programs fifty pages or less in length, filing the entire source code with trade secret portions blocked out

TRADEMARK PROTECTION FOR SOFTWARE

Trademark registration can be used to protect screens generated by computer code, even though these screens may be separately and automatically protected under copyright law. If you use icons that are to serve as identification of a source of goods, these, too, may be entitled to trademark protection. For more information about what visual elements of your program may be entitled to trademark protection, see chapter 3.

SOFTWARE LICENSING AGREEMENTS

When you purchase some new software and click, click, click through the contractual terms, you may not realize you're actually entering into a licensing agreement with the manufacturer of the software. What are the implications of these legal agreements that are so commonplace that many computer users barely pay attention to the fact they're entering into one?

ARE "SHRINK-WRAP" AGREEMENTS VALID?

When you click the "I Accept" button, most states now recognize the existence of a legally binding agreement with the software vendor. These agreements generally address the issues of making copies of the software or using it in a manner that infringes on the intellectual property rights of the developer. They may give the vendors special remedies, such as the right to sue you in a particular jurisdiction.

Regardless of the extent to which a shrink-wrap agreement is recognized in a particular state, they offer some benefit to the manufacturer under federal law. They make it more difficult for an infringer to claim that their infringement was "innocent" or inadvertent under federal copyright law.

AGREEMENTS FOR CUSTOMIZED SOFTWARE

Customized software is now critical to the functioning of many businesses. It represents a major investment for the business. Review of software development agreements has turned into a profitable sideline for many attorneys.

Customizations need to be spelled out in an agreement. At a minimum, a software customization agreement should contain provisions specifying the following:

- Customizations, interfaces, or integration of the software

- A description of the final software functionality deadlines

- Testing

- Conditions for acceptance

- Installation

- Any ongoing maintenance and technical support to be offered by the developer

- Whether the licensee or licensor owns the customized version of the software

- Conditions for termination of the agreement
- Conditions and milestone dates that must precede payment
- Conditions for terminating the agreement
- Liability limits
- Updates and upgrades
- Indemnification
- Any duty of confidentiality by the licensee
- Whether the licensee is permitted to make backup copies

SOFTWARE PIRACY ISSUES

The Business Software Alliance's "Nail Your Boss" mail campaign encourages employees to blow the whistle on employers that use unauthorized copies of software. The U.S. Naval Academy recently seized 100 computers from U.S. midshipmen in a crackdown on on-line piracy.

Noncompliance with copyright law is an easy trap for most businesses, particularly where software is concerned. To protect against civil and criminal liability, companies need to adopt specific policies and procedures to ensure employees are not violating copyrights.

A company should take two commonsense precautions to insulate itself from potential liability for software copyright infringement. First, the business should maintain a software inventory that tracks what software each computer is running with what it's licensed to have running. Second, a company should clearly communicate its policy about unauthorized software copying to its employees in writing. If you are a developer seeking damages for infringement, it's likely that a jury will be swayed by an infringing company's failure to undertake these reasonable measures.

> **$$ BUSINESS TIP:** CDs and other storage media containing software that can be copied should be secured. Programs are available that can help your organization figure out what software is running on your network, and who is running it.

CHAPTER 17 ❯❯❯❯

Protecting and Promoting Your Web Site

THE INTERNET MAKES it possible for a start-up business with a virtually nonexistent advertising budget to reach millions with a Web site. However, the World Wide Web can be a source of worldwide liability for a company that is careless in accessing, publishing, and appropriating information that's owned by others.

IN THIS CHAPTER YOU FIND OUT:

- Sound legal policies and practices for administering your Web site

- How to link to other Web sites without legal liability

- How to avoid infringing someone else's copyright on your site

IN JANUARY 1999, Ticketmaster Corporation sues Microsoft Corporation for unauthorized linking with Ticketmaster's Web site. Ticketmaster's complaint identifies Microsoft's use of a practice known as deep linking, which creates a link to a specific page in the Ticketmaster site that offers tickets to specific events. Ticketmaster al-

leges that the deep link bypasses Ticketmaster's home page and the sequence of pages leading to its ticket ordering page. This allows users linking from the Microsoft site to skip much advertising on bypassed Ticketmaster pages. Ticketmaster seeks damages and a permanent injunction against Microsoft. It seeks to enjoin Microsoft "from making any commercial use of Ticketmaster's name, marks or Website in connection with its seattle.sidewalk Website or with any advertising sold or sponsored by Microsoft." The litigation is closely watched by attorneys all over the world, but the case is settled out of court before the court has an opportunity to rule on the novel questions in the case and establish anxiously anticipated precedent.[1]

Web master is the grandiose term commonly used for someone who administers a Web site and regulates what goes on it. If you take on this task for your business or organization, this chapter contains a few steps to help you avoid being served with a lawsuit that threatens to establish a legal precedent with your company's name on it.

ASSUME EVERYTHING IS PROTECTED

Operate under the assumption that any material you want to co-opt for your site is subject to somebody's trademark and copyright protections, unless you have very good reason to believe the material is subject to one of the exceptions discussed in chapter 7.

Find out who owns the copyright or trademark, either by checking the PTO and Copyright Office databases on the Internet or by writing the likely owner directly. Examine the materials you want to use carefully for the copyright notice or the name of an individual or company that may have a copyright interest even if they haven't bothered to display the notice. (Remember: displaying the copyright symbol is optional.)

GET PERMISSION—IT'S USUALLY EASIER THAN YOU THINK

Getting permission to use copyrighted material can be easier than you think. The first step is locating the holder of the intellectual property

---

[1] *Ticketmaster Corp. v. Microsoft Corp.*, No. 97-3055 (CD CA, complaint filed April 28, 1997).

and contacting them by phone or mail to explain your request. The copyright owner won't necessarily require you to pay to use the material if it results in positive exposure for the owner. That type of exposure may have value to the owner.

In your letter or inquiry you should explain:

- What portions of the material you want to use on your site

- How the material will be displayed

- What benefit there is to the copyright owner from having exposure for his or her work on your site

- If possible, how many users you expect to visit your site (owners of copyrighted material often want to know this)

Although verbal consent is valid, if a dispute arises, it may be difficult to prove you got it, and memories may fail as to what it actually encompasses. Written consent is clearly the desired course. A sample letter requesting permission to use copyrighted material appears on page 159. You may opt to rely on an oral consent initially if you're on a deadline, to be followed up with written consent. That strategy poses the obvious risks that you may need to revise your site if the written permission, encompassing everything you need, isn't forthcoming.

> ⚖ **LAWYER'S NOTE:** *Don't assume you can freely use someone else's work simply because it has been posted on the Internet without a copyright or trademark notice.*

LOOK FOR FREE MATERIALS

Many companies offer artwork, photos, and other materials for free reuse. This type of material goes under a variety of names, such as free clip art, shareware, or freeware.

If you're lucky enough to find materials that you may freely use without permission, don't assume that these materials can be distributed or copied without limitation. Examine the terms and conditions in the "Click to Accept" agreements, rather than just clicking the "I Accept" button without reading. Failure to adhere to the terms of shareware or free clip art can earn you the status as a party in a lawsuit for illegally distributing the work. This is especially true if you are profiting from its use.

DON'T LINK TO A LAWSUIT

Technology not only offers lots of visually appealing choices for displaying materials on your site, it allows users to access information on other sites from your site. Linking, framing, and inlining are common methods of connecting to the information at other Web sites, and all carry the potential for an accusation that you're infringing someone else's copyright or trademark.

⚖️ **LAWYER'S NOTE:** *Lawsuits are most likely to arise if you modify or display material from someone else's Web site in a way that either confuses the public about the origin of the material or effectively bypasses the paid advertising on the other site.*

HYPERTEXT LINKING WITHOUT LIABILITY

When Ticketmaster Corporation sued Microsoft Corporation, Ticketmaster's main objection was the Microsoft site's direct link to specific events on the Ticketmaster page. The "deep link" bypassed Ticketmaster's home page and lots of other pages, which allowed Microsoft linkers to skip lots of advertising.

Ticketmaster sought damages and a permanent injunction against Microsoft "from making any commercial use of Ticketmaster's name, marks or Website" in connection with Microsoft's own Web site. Unfortunately, because the case settled and was dismissed, the court had no opportunity to rule on the novel questions of law and issue some guiding precedent in the case. However, until the law is clearly settled in this area, you should carefully consider the risks of establishing deep links that bypass someone else's advertising without obtaining their consent to do so.

FRAMING FAIRLY

In contrast to a traditional hypertext link, where the user jumps from the original Web site to the linked site, framing displays the content of the linked Web site back in the original Web site. In other words, the linked site is framed by the original site. Since it involves displaying someone else's content on your site, it poses some obvious permission issues. Most attorneys will advise you to obtain written permission for materials you display by framing on your Web site.

At least one court has held framing to be a copyright infringement. Another more publicized case involving framing was settled. In *Washington Post Co. v. Total News Inc.,* the *Washington Post* and five other media companies, including CNN and Dow Jones, sued TotalNEWS, Inc. At issue was TotalNEWS's practice of framing other Web sites within a site with TotalNEWS's advertising.[2] The case was never decided by the court because the parties settled, with TotalNEWS agreeing to discontinue framing. The publicity fallout and issues raised by this case have changed the legal trend to one of obtaining prior written permission, despite the fact that no actual precedent was set.

In a similar suit, CNN sued a news Web site that framed its content. Under the terms of a settlement agreement, the news Web site agreed to stop framing and instead use hypertext links to the CNN site. This settlement indicates that a legal distinction is evolving between framing and linking.

INLINING ISSUES

Inlining is sometimes referred to as *mirroring.* It's similar to framing in that it involves displaying graphics from one site on another. United Media, the copyright owner of the *Dilbert* comic strip, used the threat of litigation to deter a Web site from the practice of inlining daily comic strips taken from the United Media Web site.

---

[2] *Washington Post Co. v. Total News, Inc.,* No. 97 Civ. 1190 (PKL) (S.D.N.Y. complaint filed February 20, 1997).

DON'T OVERUSE FAIR USE

Fair use is an established copyright law doctrine that holds that the public should be entitled to freely use portions of copyrighted material for certain purposes. These purposes generally include commentary, criticism, or parody, as discussed in chapter 8.

The problem with relying on fair use is that courts are fickle in finding it, and there's no way to guarantee that Web content use will actually qualify as fair use. If you believe that your use qualifies and the copyright owner disagrees, the result may be litigation. And even if you ultimately persuade the court that your use was fair, is the expense of the litigation worth it?

REMOVE POTENTIALLY INFRINGING MATERIAL WHEN NOTIFIED

If someone credibly complains that you're using material on your Web site without proper authorization, your policy should be to immediately remove it. This is not to imply that you should cave in to baseless complaints, but failure to remove infringing material when notified to do so is just not a sensible course of action. Judges and juries are favorably moved by prompt action and are aggravated by defendants who ignore clear notification by the copyright holder.

The Digital Millennium Copyright Act[3] provides that an Internet service provider that hosts the Web site on its computer server can mitigate liability by speedy removal of the offending material.

DISCLAIM CONFUSING AFFILIATIONS

A lawsuit involving Estee Lauder Cosmetics against iBeauty.com Inc. and Excite Inc. got downright ugly in an attempt to stop the search en-

---

[3] DMCA (Digital Millennium Copyright Act), October 20, 1998. Signed into law October 28, 1998, as Public Law 105–304.

gine company from using certain Estee Lauder trademarks as keywords and triggers to display iBeauty's banner ads. Another company had the nerve to launch a Web site with the address amazo*m*.com, selling none other than books. With all of the traffic generated by Amazon.com, this retailer figured it could capture a healthy share of the market just by waiting for people to misspell the Amazon.com address. U.S. Bancorp sued USABancShares.com Inc. to stop it from using the Internet address www.usabanc.com.

A disclaimer is a statement denying that you're endorsing something or affiliated with it. If you link to another site that sells products or services that may be confused as being related to yours, consider a statement disclaiming your affiliation. You should also disclaim an affiliation with a company when it has a name that is similar to yours and may create confusion. For example, if you are AAA Boat Repair, you may be wise to disclaim any affiliation with the famous AAA car and road service, the American Automobile Association.

DON'T IMITATE THE APPEARANCE OF ANOTHER WEB SITE

Both copyright and trademark law have been playing catch-up in the world of e-commerce. Not only is the domain name itself protected, but the overall appearance or look and feel of your Web site can be protected as a form of trade dress.

The U.S. Copyright Office now permits copyright registration of both graphical and textual elements of a Web site. Since copyright protection belongs to the creator, the amalgamation of materials and collaboration that often go into creating a Web presence can pose many interesting legal issues.

LAWYER'S NOTE: *If you have an outside firm create any part of your Web site, be sure to have a written agreement that you retain the copyright to any creative Web site content.*

CHAPTER 18 >>>>

From Brain to Balance Sheet: Tax Considerations

ALBERT EINSTEIN ONCE said that "the hardest thing in the world to understand is income tax." Fortunately, most successful innovators can hire accountants.

IN THIS CHAPTER YOU FIND OUT:

- The advantages of expensing intellectual property rather than amortizing it

- When intellectual property can qualify for favorable capital gains tax rates

- How disclosure can jeopardize trade secret deductions

DUPONT PAINT COMPANY maintains that certain paint formulas are trade secrets. Dupont takes the position that the trade secrets are a form of intellectual property, and consequently, the company should be permitted to take amortization deductions for the asset. However, the IRS denies these deductions. Dupont appeals, and the court upholds the IRS determination, based on the fact that

Dupont failed to maintain secrecy, and therefore the formulas can't be treated as trade secret assets. Since there is no asset, there can be no deduction.[1]

The intellectual property area is replete with unexpected tax consequences. However, careful planning can control many results and turn the tax situation to your advantage.

SOME CORE TAX PLANNING CONCEPTS

The biggest single expense individuals and businesses usually incur is taxes. If intellectual property—patents, trademarks, copyrights, and trade secrets—are significant line items on your balance sheet, you can benefit from understanding how the IRS views and treats them. Tax planning for these intangibles involves both careful drafting of agreements for transactions involving them and correct treatment and classification of the assets and transactions.

Some expenses in developing your intellectual property may be deductible in full in the year you incur them, while others must be deducted a little bit at a time over a prescribed period of years, or may not even be deducted at all until the asset is fully developed and sold. Thus, it helps to have a broader sense of how the Internal Revenue Code works and what tax planning goals you are working toward. Some core concepts of tax planning are summarized in this Section.

DEFER INCOME, ACCELERATE DEDUCTIONS

An almost universal tax planning objective is paying later rather than sooner. Money that you can legitimately hold onto at tax time can be put to good use in your business or invested for a profit until it comes due.

Deferring income means recognizing it in the latest tax year possible. This may mean waiting to sell an asset until after the close of the tax year or taking other actions that cause the income to be taxed to

---

[1] *Dupont vs. U.S.*, 288 F.2d 904 (Ct. Cl. 1961).

you in a subsequent year. On the other hand, when it comes to deductions, you want to take them as soon as you can, keeping the current tax bill as low as possible. This gives you more cash to invest in developing and marketing your idea.

AMORTIZING INTELLECTUAL PROPERTY ASSETS

Amortization is a concept similar to depreciation, except that it applies to intangible assets, such as intellectual property. Intangible assets are amortized over their useful life. An amortization deduction can be taken each year over the useful life of the asset. The useful life of certain types of assets are specified by the Internal Revenue Code.

Section 197, when applicable, allows you to amortize the costs of acquiring an asset over a term of fifteen years. This period begins on the first day of the month after you acquire the asset, and the deduction is prorated when you acquire or sell the asset during a tax year.

Assets that may be covered under Section 197 of the Internal Revenue Code may include:

- Copyrights

- Trademarks and trade names

- Trade secrets

- Formulas

- Processes

- Designs

- Patterns

- Know-how

- Formats

- Package designs

- Computer software

- Contracts for the sale or use of other Section 197 assets

- Interests in films, sound recordings, video tapes, books, "or other similar property"

Not all patents, copyrights, and other intellectual property assets listed above are covered by Section 197. Generally, Section 197 covers only patents that are acquired or purchased as part of the sale of trade or business, and consequently, are amortized over the fifteen-year period provided in Section 197. (There are exceptions relating to certain types of contracts for the sale of business). Patents acquired separately, and not as part of the sale as a trade or business may be eligible for amortization under Internal Revenue Code Section 167, which provides for a longer, twenty-year recoverable period.

EXPENSING IS USUALLY BETTER THAN AMORTIZING

If you have a choice between taking the entire cost of an asset as an expense deduction in the year that you buy it or amortizing it over its useful life, which would you choose? Expensing the whole thing the first year is usually preferable, since you're accelerating the amount of your present deduction.[2] You are permitted, for example, to expense certain types of research and development costs under Internal Revenue Code Section 174.

However, there are some situations where it may be in your interest to amortize, if you're permitted to do so. For example, if you own all the shares in a certain type of small business corporation known as an S corporation.

If the S corporation takes the deduction on its corporate income tax return, the deduction is passed through to your individual income tax return. Those particular expenses (not just the deductions) might have to be added back to your income for purposes of computing your alternative minimum tax (if you're subject to it). The amount added back could increase your personal income tax, wiping out the benefit

---

[2] Research and experimental expenditures may be deducted currently, rather than capitalized under section 174(a) of the Internal Revenue Code. Computer software development expenses are considered research and experimental expenses. Trademark development costs are not, and must be amortized over a fifteen-year period under section 197. See section 197(e)(3) (excluding software developed in-house from "section 197 intangibles"), and 197(d)(1)(f) (including trademarks).

of the deduction on the corporate return. However, if you elect to amortize the expenses over ten years, there's no add back on your personal return.

CAPITAL GAINS RATES ARE LOWER THAN ORDINARY INCOME TAX RATES

Assets held for investment like equipment, trucks, stocks, bonds, and real estate (as opposed to inventory or supplies) are considered capital assets. Intellectual property, such as patents, trademarks, copyrights, and trade secrets are all forms of capital assets.

If you are an individual or a business entity other than a corporation, you may get a more favorable tax rate on capital gains. When you sell a capital asset you have owned for more than one year for a profit, that profit is taxed at a lower capital gains tax rate, as opposed to the "ordinary" income rate charged on other income your business may earn. (You don't have to pay tax on a capital gain until you sell the asset.)

Capital assets can be either *long-term* or *short-term*. Long-term capital assets are assets held for more than one year. Long-term capital gains tax rates are generally lower, favorable rates, reflecting a national policy of encouraging Americans to invest in the nation's businesses for the long haul. Short-term capital gains are taxed at ordinary income rates.

⚖️ **LAWYER'S NOTE:** *Corporations currently pay taxes at the same rate on capital and noncapital transactions.*

If you hold a capital asset for at least a year and a day before you sell it, you're entitled to the special capital gain rate. In most cases, this rate will be 20 percent (10 percent if your total taxable income falls within the 15 percent bracket). There are exceptions for certain types of assets.

CREDITS CUT TAX LIABILITY

A tax credit is an immediate and simple tax benefit. It's often the best type of tax benefit to get on a return.

A credit, as its name implies is a direct reduction of your tax liability. For example, if you owe $20,000 in taxes, are entitled to a $3,000 tax credit, your liability is reduced to $17,000. The credit is simply subtracted from the amount of tax due. Unlike deductions, which have a benefit proportional to your tax rate, credits confer a direct, 100 percent, dollar-for-dollar reduction.

In the context of intellectual property transactions, a credit may be available for "qualified research." Qualified research is defined in Section 41(d) of the Internal Revenue Code as activity that is "undertaken for the purpose of discovering information that is technological in nature, and the application of which is intended to be useful in the development of a new or improved business component of the taxpayer."

A tax credit, rather than a deduction, is awarded for qualified research because it is deemed beneficial to society for companies to expand knowledge in technological areas. Ultimately, consumers benefit from expanded and improved product offerings. In keeping with this objective, Section 41(d)(4) generally excludes activity from eligibility for this credit for any research conducted after the product or technology has gone into commercial production. The credit is also unavailable for improvements or enhancements to existing products, except in the case of certain types of software developments.

IRS CLASSIFICATIONS OF LICENSES: A TRAP FOR THE UNWARY

Transactions involving the sale and licensing of intellectual property rights can erupt in a volcano of tax consequences. How they are treated by the IRS depends on a variety of factors, including (but by no means limited to) the following:

- Is the transaction appropriately classified as a license or lease transaction?

- Are you the original creator of the property, or did you purchase it from someone else?

- Is the property a capital asset?

This section looks at how these considerations apply to specific types of intellectual property.

PATENT LICENSES

Suppose your company enters into an agreement to license a patent it owns to someone else. The agreement entitles the licensee to make and sell a patented product for ten years. Even though the agreement between you and the licensee may be specifically titled "License," the transaction may be deemed a sale by the IRS.

The IRS uses preestablished criteria from the Internal Revenue Code to determine whether the transaction is a sale. The IRS's main concern is whether the patent owner is essentially transferring all useful interest in the patent and whether the patent rights will have any value that reverts to the patent owner at the end of the license agreement. The IRS will give considerable weight to the issue of whether license rights were acquired in connection with the acquisition of a substantial part of a trade or business, which makes it more likely that the transaction will be treated as a sale.

If the IRS concludes the transaction is a sale, the Internal Revenue Code requires you to amortize the acquisition costs ratably over fifteen years or to depreciate the cost over the remaining useful life of the patent. This is less advantageous than taking larger lease expense deductions over the ten-year period of the agreement.[3]

On the other hand, if the IRS determines the license agreement is truly a license transaction, the tax treatment is more favorable. Payments under the agreement can be deducted in full as they are actually incurred.

One factor that weighs heavily in favor of treating the transaction as a license is whether the license is nonexclusive. In other words, whether the licensee receives less than an exclusive right to use the patent. Nonex-

---

[3] Internal Revenue Code Sections 197(e)(4); 167(f)(2).

clusivity indicates that the patent holder has retained some significant rights, and the transaction looks a lot less like a sale for tax purposes.

TRADEMARKS

Trademark licenses are a little trickier and may also be deemed sales subject to amortization rules. In the case of a trademark license, the IRS permits you to deduct your payments as you make them (instead of amortizing) only if the payments are (a) contingent on the productivity, use, or disposition of the mark, (b) payable at least annually, and (c) substantially equal in amount or payable under a fixed formula. Otherwise, the IRS requires you to amortize the trademark license payments over a fifteen-year period.[4]

TRADE SECRETS

Trade secrets, if you can prove they exist, are an asset, like other types of intellectual property.[5] The IRS takes the position that if the information hasn't been kept confidential, it doesn't rise to the level of trade secret and thus can't be an asset.[6] Sales of trade secrets are usually treated as capital gains transactions.

COPYRIGHTS

A copyright that you use in your trade or business can be the source of some welcome tax deductions. Copyright development costs are generally deductible over the useful life of the copyright.[7]

Sales of copyrights can result in taxable gain. Unfortunately, such sales by the person who created the work can never qualify for capital gains treatment.[8] However, copyrights you've purchased from some other person or entity can be resold as capital assets.

---

[4] Internal Revenue Code Sections 1253(d)(1) and 2.
[5] Internal Revenue Code Section 197.
[6] The language of Internal Revenue Code Section 197 specifically includes business information and know-how as a "section 197 intangible." This language is often the basis for taxpayers challenging the IRS position in the courts.
[7] Treas. Reg. section 1.167(a)-6(a).
[8] Internal Revenue Code Section 1221(3).

Appendix A

SAMPLE TRADEMARK APPLICATION

TRADEMARK/SERVICE MARK APPLICATION FORM WIZARD

TEAS
Version 2.11: 11/02/2003

To file the application electronically, please complete the following steps:

1. Answer each question below to create an application form showing only sections relevant to your specific filing. Although we strongly recommend that you use this Form Wizard, you can skip by clicking on Standard Form.

2. For more information regarding any of the questions, go to Help or click on the underlined word. While the different sections of the form may appear straightforward and easy to fill out, we strongly suggest that you read the Help instructions very carefully for each section prior to completing it. Failure to follow this advice may cause you to fill out sections of the form incorrectly, jeopardizing your legal rights.

3. After answering all wizard questions, click the Next button at the bottom of the wizard.

4. Once in the actual form, complete all fields for which information is known. Fields with a red * symbol are mandatory fields for filing purposes and must be completed.

5. Validate the form, using the button at the end of the form. If there are errors, return to the form to enter corrections. A warning may be corrected or bypassed.

6. Double-check all entries through the links displayed on the Validation page.

7. You may save your work for submission at a later time by clicking on the Download Portable form button at the bottom of the Validation page.

8. When ready to file, use the Pay/Submit button at the bottom of the Validation page. This will allow you to choose from three (3) different payment methods: credit card, automated deposit account, or electronic funds transfer.

9. After accessing the proper screen for payment and making the appropriate entries, you will receive a confirmation screen if your transmission is successful. This screen will say SUCCESS! and will provide your assigned serial number.

10. You will receive an e-mail acknowledgement of your submission, which will repeat the assigned serial number and provide a summary of your submission.

Once you submit an application, either electronically or through the mail, we will not cancel the filing or refund your fee, unless the application fails to satisfy minimum filing requirements. The fee is a processing fee, which we do not refund even if we cannot issue a registration after our substantive review.

NOTE: This form has a session time limit of sixty minutes. A session begins once you create and enter the form via the Form Wizard. If you exceed the sixty-minute time limit, the form will not validate and you must begin the entire process again. Therefore, you should have all information required to complete the form available prior to starting your session.

1. What is your filing basis?
NOTE: More than one basis may be selected, but do **NOT** claim both §§1(a) and 1(b) for the **identical** goods or services in one application. If claiming a Section 1(a) basis, it is **NOT** necessary or appropriate also to claim a Section 1(b) basis for the same goods or services, simply to indicate an intent to *continue* using the mark for those goods or services—the Section 1(a) basis covers this.

Intent to Use (Section 1(b))
◉ Yes   ○ No

Use in Commerce (Section 1(a))
○ Yes   ◉ No

Right of Priority based on Foreign Application (Section 44(d))
○ Yes   ◉ No

Foreign Registration (Section 44(e))
○ Yes   ◉ No

2. Are your Goods and/or Services in more than one class?
○ Yes   ● No
If the answer is Yes, enter the number of classes [1 ▼]

3. Do joint applicants own the mark?
○ Yes   ● No
If the answer is Yes, enter the number of owners [1 ▼]

4. Is there one applicant but more than one signatory?
○ Yes   ● No
If the answer is Yes, enter the number of signatories [1 ▼]

5. Is an attorney filing this application?
● Yes   ○ No

6. Do you want to appoint a Domestic Representative?
○ Yes   ● No

7. Do you need to enter an additional statement?
○ Yes   ● No

8. What signature approach do you want to use? Choose one from below.
● Sign electronically directly on this application
○ E-mail text form to second party for electronic signature
○ Handwritten pen-and-ink signature
○ Submit application *unsigned* (a signature *must* be supplied later)

| NEXT | CLEAR |

PRIVACY POLICY STATEMENT

The information collected on this form allows the PTO to determine whether a mark may be registered on the Principal or Supplemental Register, and provides notice of an applicant's claim of ownership of the mark. Responses to the request for information are required to obtain the benefit of a registration on the Principal or Supplemental Register. 15 U.S.C. §1051 et seq. and 37 C.F.R. Part 2. All information collected will be made public. Gathering and providing the information will require an estimated 12 or 18 minutes (depending if the application is based on an intent to use the mark in commerce, use of the mark in commerce, or a foreign application or registration). Please direct comments on the time needed to complete this form, and/or suggestions for reducing this burden to the Chief Information Officer, U.S. Patent and Trademark Office, U.S. Department of Commerce, Washington, D.C. 20231. Please note that the PTO may not conduct or sponsor a collection of information using a form that does not display a valid OMB control number.

Appendix B

SAMPLE EMPLOYEE CONFIDENTIALITY AGREEMENT

1. Know-It-All Corporation ("KIT") located at [BUSINESS ADDRESS], possess valuable proprietary and confidential information regarding [DESCRIBE PRODUCT] entitled [NAME OF PRODUCT].

2. KIT is interested in consulting with and obtaining the professional services of [THIRD PARTY] located at [ADDRESS].

3. Both parties acknowledge that [PRODUCT] has/has not been introduced into the marketplace and all information concerning [PRODUCT] (the "Information") is not generally known to the public, and that if the Information becomes known to the public it can economically damage KIT.

4. KIT requests that [THIRD PARTY] agree to maintain in complete confidentiality all information pertaining to [PRODUCT] in confidence, including any evaluations, conclusions, or consultations provided by [THIRD PARTY].

5. [THIRD PARTY] agrees that any information acquired in connection with [PRODUCT] shall be held in confidence for a period of two years or until the Information becomes generally available to the public.

6. [THIRD PARTY] to use the Information only for the purpose of evaluating the [PRODUCT].

Agreed to and accepted:

KIT INC.

By:

      (Signature)

Name:

      (Type or Print)

Title:

      (Type or Print)

Date:

Appendix C

SAMPLE EMPLOYEE NONDISCLOSURE AGREEMENT

Between
Know-It-All, Inc.
and
_____ "Employee"

1. Employee recognizes that KIT's business involves confidential and proprietary knowledge and information; including but not limited to methods, processes, tecniques, financial data, customer lists, specifications, methods designs, and skills ("Information") and that Employee may acquire or become aware of such information in the performance of Employee's duties or otherwise as a result of Employee's employment relationship with KIT.

2. Employee acknowledges that any disclosure of Information would substantially injure the economic and commercial interests of KIT business, impair its investments and goodwill, injure the business of KIT's representatives, and/or jeopardize KIT's relationships with its representatives, suppliers, and customers.

3. Employee will not, except for the performance of Employee's duties for the duration of Employee's employment with KIT, use or disclose or communicate to any third party, or to any of its employees who do not need to know in the performance of their duties, any information received from KIT, except with the prior written permission of KIT.

4. Upon the termination of Employee's employment with KIT, employee will surrender to KIT any and all originals, copies, data, drawings, notes, or other records of, or concerning, KIT's Informatioin. Employee agrees to use its best efforts to compile and return any such materials to KIT.

5. Information received by Employee from KIT during any employment negotiations prior to the date of execution of this Agreement, or subsequent to the termination of Employee's employment is subject to this Agreement.

6. Employee agrees that Information obtained by Employee during Employee's employment with KIT shall be presumed to be confidential and proprietary unless Employee is specifically notified, in writing or otherwise.

7. This Agreement shall be interpreted under the laws of the State of _____.

8. In the event that any provision of this Agreement is found to be void or unenforceable, no other provision of this Agreement shall be affected.

KIT INDUSTRIES, INC.   EMPLOYEE

_____   _____
Signature   Signature

_____   _____
Date   Date

Index

(Page numbers in italic indicate illustrations; those in bold indicate tables)

Abandoned patents, 222, 229–30
Abbreviated patent applications, 217–18
Abstract (specification, patent application), 212
"Abstraction/filtration/comparison" test, software, 288–89
Abstracts, patents, 208, *209*
Access issue, copyrights, 121, 148
ACPA (Anticybersquatting Consumer Protection Act), 92
Act for the Encouragement of Learning, by Vesting the Copies of Printed Books in the Authors or Purchasers of Such Copies, During the Times Therein Mentioned, An statute, 5
Actual damages, copyright infringement, 115, 155, 164
Actual use, filing trademark on basis of, 73–74
Adjectives vs. nouns, trademarks used as, 44
Advertising, as nonservice, domain names, 93
Affiliation issues, Web sites, 300–301
After-final amendments, patents, 225
Aimster, 136, 137–38
Amendments and changes
    patent applications, 220, 225–26, 232
    trademark applications, 82
Amendment to Allege Use form, trademarks, 75, 80
American Arbitration Association, 251
American Inventor's Protection Act of 1999, 194
American Society of Composers, Authors and Publishers (ASCAP), 112, 157
Amortizing assets, 304–6
Amount and significance of copied material (fair use), copyrights, 127, 129–30, 150–51
Andrews, Chris, 4
Anticybersquatting Consumer Protection Act (ACPA), 92
Antitrust law violations, patents, 202
Appealing Final Office Action, patents, 227–28
Application information (section 1, trademarks), 70
Application process
    copyrights, 166–68, **167**
    patents, 203–32
    trademarks, 69–85, 311–13
Arbitrary trademarks, 36, 38, 39, 54, 60, 61, **61**
Arbitration, patent infringement, 251

Arrow, Kenneth, 189
ASCAP (American Society of Composers, Authors and Publishers), 112, 157
Aspen, Marvin, 137
Assigned inventions, patents, 207
Assignment agreements, marketing, 276
Assignments of copyrights, 171–72
Attorney's fees, awarding
    copyright infringement, 155, 164
    patent infringement, 243–44
Attribution and integrity of visual works (first sale), copyrights, 140
Attribution right, copyrights, 112–13
Audio Home Recording Act of 1992, 135–36
Audio works (first sale), copyrights, 140
Authorization of Agent, patents, 206, 216
Authorship vs. ownership, copyrights, 5–6
Automatic protection
    copyrights, 108
    trade secrets, 269

Background (specification, patent application), 212
Bankruptcy impact on patent infringement, 244
Bargaining chip, intellectual property as, 14–15
Basis for filing trademark application, 73–75
Bates, John D., 17
Berne International Copyright Convention, 109
Biotechnology patents, 195–96
Board of Patent Appeals and Interferences (BPAI), 224, 227–28
Bone, Jeff, 283
Bosenberg, Henry, 196
BPAI (Board of Patent Appeals and Interferences), 224, 227–28
BSA (Business Software Alliance) "Nail Your Boss," 13–14, 294
Buchwald, Art, 279
Burden of proof, patent infringement, 249, 257
Business methods patents, 178–79, 181–82, 192–94
Business secrets, 11–12, 263–73, 309, 314
Business Software Alliance (BSA) "Nail Your Boss," 13–14, 294

CAFC (Court of Appeals for the Federal Circuit), 228, 285
Capital gains, 306
Capitalizing trademarks properly, 45
Carlson, Chester F., 7
Catalog of Copyright Entries (CCE) (Copyright Office), 170
Caxton, William, 5
CCC (Copyright Clearance Center), 157
CCE (Catalog of Copyright Entries) (Copyright Office), 170
Cease and desist letter, copyright infringement, 153–54
Certificate of Mailing, patents, 217, 222, 227
Certificate of patentability/unpatentability, 257
Certificate of Registration, trademarks, 80, 85
Certification marks vs. trademarks, 34, 84–85
Certified searches, copyrights, 170
Challenging patents, 256–57, 258–59
Character of use (fair use), copyrights, 126, 127, 129, 149–50, 150
Chin, Denny, 43
Claims (specification, patent application), 213–15
Clean room doctrine, trade secrets, 270
Cloning, 203, 204
Collaborative inventions, 207
Collective marks vs. trademarks, 34, 84–85
Commercial use requirement, trademark application, 29, 73
Commissioned inventions, 207
Commissioner of Patents and Trademarks, petitioning, 228
Common law, 28, 62, 265
Company policies for trademarks, 45
Company's investment protected by trademarks, 27
Competitor's product, researching, patents, 240–41
Complaint, patent infringement, 252
Compositions of matter protected by patents, 179, 181–82
Computer programs. See Software
Confidentiality agreements, trade secrets, 271–72, 273, 314
Confidentiality, software, 291–92
"Confusingly similar" trademarks, 40–41
Consideration, trade secrets, 272
Consistent use of trademarks, 45
Consulting agreements, patents, 207
Consumer Project on Technology (CPT), 21
Consumers and trademarks, 26–27
Continuation Application, patents, 218, 228–29, 230
Continuation in Part Application, patents, 229
Contributory patent infringement, 245–47
Control of nature and quality of goods and services, trademark application, 74
Co-opting for spam prevention, copyrights, 15–16
Copyright Act of 1976, 7–8, 100–101, 108, 109, 112, 114, 115, 126
Copyright Clearance Center (CCC), 157
Copyrights, 95–118
    Business Tips, xii, 102, 103, 117, 121, 156, 164, 165, 166
    Cautions, xii, 109
    concepts of, 95–118
    infringement of copyrights, 142–60
    law, history of, 5–8, 104
    Lawyer's Notes, xii, 99, 100, 106, 108, 113, 117, 151, 160, 169, 170, 171, 172
    limitations of copyrights, 119–41
    patents vs., 125–26, 145, 188–90
    registering and researching copyrights, 161–72
    requirements, 167
    software, 7, 13–14, 140, 167, 191, 282, 287–90, 292
    tax considerations, 309–10
    Web sites and, 296
Counterfeiting trademarks, 47
Court of Appeals for the Federal Circuit (CAFC), 228, 285
CPT (Consumer Project on Technology), 21
Creation date, public record of, copyrights, 163
Creative expression of ideas, protected by copyrights, 99–101, 145–46, 160, 287
Creativity (fair use), copyrights, 127, 129, 150
Credits, tax credits, 307
Criticism and commentary (fair use), copyrights, 132, 150, 160
Cross-licensing, patent infringement, 256
Cross-references (specification, patent application), 212
Culture impacted by intellectual property law, 13–21
Customized software, 293–94
Cyberspace
    domain names, 50, 85, 88–94
    Web sites, 295–301
Cybersquatting, 92

Davis, Paul Barton, 176–77
Deadlines for patent application, 222
Declaration Form, patents, 216
Decompilers, 269
Dedicated works (public domain), copyrights, 146
Deductions, accelerating, 303–4
Defendants, wide net of, patent infringement, 244–47
Defending against patent infringement, 257–60
Defensibility of trademarks, 54
Deferring income, 303–4
Denny, Regis, 150–51
Deposit requirement, copyrights, 165
Derivative works, copyrights, 110–11
Description
    patent application, specification, 213
    trademark application, section 2, 71
Descriptiveness, domain names, 94
Descriptive trademarks, 37–38, 39, 59, 60, 61
Designing around patents, 255
Design patent infringements, 239
Design patents, 186–91, 187, 197, 232
Digital Millennium Copyright Act of 1998, 8, 17, 19, 113, 134, 143
Dilution of trademarks, 46–47
Direct patent infringement, 245
Disclosure of trade secrets, 11–12, 264

Disney, Walter Elias, 274–75
Displaying trademarks, 29–30
Distinctiveness, degrees of, trademarks, 59–61, **61**
Distribution right, copyrights, 110
Diversity jurisdiction, patent infringement, 248
Divisional applications, 218
Doctrine of equivalents, patents, 189–90, 191, 199,
    236–37, 241–42, 256
Doctrine of fair use, copyrights, 7–8, 119, 126–39,
    148–52, **150**
Doctrine of first sale, copyrights, 139–41
Doctrine of independent creation, copyrights, 120–
    23
Doctrine of prosecution history estoppel, patent in-
    fringement, 202, 237
Doctrine of utility, copyrights, 123–26, *125*
Documentation purpose of registering copyrights,
    166
Domain names, 50, 85, 88–94
Dot.com impact on software, 284–85
Drawings
    patent application, specification portion, 213,
        232
    trademark application and, 76, 77, *77*
Duration of
    copyrights, 114, 190
    patents, 190, 197–98

Economic Espionage Act of 1996, 266
Edison, Thomas, 8
Einstein, Albert, 302
Electronic Privacy Information Center (EPIC), 16–17
Employee confidentiality agreements, trade secrets,
    271–72, 273, 314
Employee ownership issues, patents, 207
Encoding/encryption right, copyrights, 113
English Parliament and copyrights, 5
Entertainment industry, copyrights, 19, 140–41, **167**
Entrepreneurship, xi. *See also* Intellectual property
    law
EPIC (Electronic Privacy Information Center), 16–17
Equivalents, patents, 189–90, 191, 199, 236–37,
    241–42, 256
European Patent Office, 210
Examiner's Answer, patents, 226–27
Expensing vs. amortizing, 305–6
Expired copyrights (public domain), 146
Expired patents, 255
Expression of ideas, protected by copyrights, 99–
    101, 145–46, 160, 287
Extensions, patent application, 222

Facts, not subject to copyright protection, 101–2,
    144, 145–46, 150
Fair use, copyrights, 7–8, 119, 126–39, 148–52, **150**
Fair use, overuse of, Web sites, 300
False connections or origins, trademarks, 50, 55
False marking, patent infringement, 259–60
Falwell, Jerry, 89, 128, 129, 130
Fanciful trademarks, 36, 38, 39, 60, 61, **61**
Federal Law, trade secrets, 266

Federal registration, trademarks, 28, 31, 62, 63–64
Federal Trademark Dilution Act, 46–47
Fee-based trademark database, 68
Festo Facts, patents, 236–37, *237–38*
File swapping on Internet, 16–18
File wrapper, patents, 201, 202
Filing Receipt for Trademark Application, 79
Final Office Action, patents, 221, 223–28
Final Rejection, trademarks, 83
First Amendment, 46, 126
First Inventor Defense, patents, 194
First sale, copyrights, 139–41
Fixation requirement, copyrights, 106–8, 144–45
Flexible bar approach, patent infringement, 238
Ford, Gerald, 139
Foreign application/registration, intent to use based
    on (trademarks), 75
Foreign patent infringement, 252–53
Foreign treaties and trademarks, 29
Forfeited copyrights (public domain), 146
Forfeiting patents, 231–32
Framing issues, Web sites, 298, 299
Franken, Al, 42–43
Franklin, Benjamin, 14, 113
Fraud, 10, 232, 259
Free materials, Web sites, 297–98
Free preliminary search, trademarks, 65–68

Gabriel, Peter, 18
General Agreement on Tariffs and Trade (GATT), 52,
    235
Generocide, trademarks, 36–37, **37**, 44–45, 54, 55,
    60, **61**
Geographical factors and trademarks, 31, 32, 74
Goldsmith, Aryeh, 281
Goods and services identification (section 3, trade-
    marks), 72–73
Goodwill from trademarks, 27
Government contracts, patents, 207
Government works (public domain), copyrights,
    146
Gutenberg, Johannes, 5

Hague Conference, 21
Hand, Learned, 102–4, 147
Harlan, Justice, 183
Harrison, George, 122–23
Hemings, Sally, 121
Hilfiger, Tommy, 58, 65
Hoffman, Felix, 179
Hybrid agreements, marketing, 278

ICANN (Internet Corporation for Assigned Names
    and Numbers), 90–91
Ideas
    applications vs. ideas, patents, 180–85
    expressions vs. ideas, copyrights, 100–101, 102–
        4, 145–46, 160, 287
IDS (Information Disclosure Statement), patents,
    215–16, 218
Immoral trademarks, 49–50, 55

Implementing invention, best mode for, 212, 259, 260
Importation protection, copyrights, 164
Improvements, unauthorized, patent infringement, 238, 241
Incontestability, trademarks, 64
Independent creation, copyrights, 120–23
Indirect patent infringement, 245
Information Disclosure Statement (IDS), patents, 215–16, 218
Infringement
    copyrights, 142–60
    patents, 233–60
    Web sites and, 300
Injunctions, copyright infringement, 117
Injunctive relief, patent infringement, 242–43
Inlining (mirroring) issues, Web sites, 298, 299
Innocent copyright infringement, 168, 169
Insuring patents, 253
Integrity right, copyrights, 113
Intellectual Property Insurance Services, 253
Intellectual property law, xi, 1–21
    Business Tips, xii, 20
    culture impacted by, 13–21
    domain names, 50, 85, 88–94
    marketing ideas, 274–79, 315
    stealing ideas, 4, 5, 7, 8, 278–79
    tax considerations, 302–10
    technology impact on, 4, 5, 7, 8, 63, 108, 118, 133–38, 143
    trade secrets, 11–12, 263–73, 309, 314
    Web sites, 295–301
    See also Copyrights; Patents; Software; Trademarks
Intellectual Property Rights Branch (IPRB) of U. S. Customs Service, 53, 164
Intent-to-use application, trademarks, 30–31, 73, 74–75
"Interactive" Web sites, 20–21
International protections, trademarks, 51–53
International Trade Commission, 252, 253
Internet
    copyrights, researching, 157–58, 170
    domain names, 50, 85, 88–94
    intellectual property law and, 16–18, 20–21
    patents, researching, 209–10, 211
    trademarks, researching, 67–68
    Web sites, 295–301
Internet Corporation for Assigned Names and Numbers (ICANN), 90–91
Inventor and government, contract between, patents, 177
IPRB (Intellectual Property Rights Branch) of U. S. Customs Service, 53, 164
Issue fee, patents, 221

Jefferson, Thomas, 6, 121
Joint ownership, patents, 207
Joint ventures, marketing, 278
Judges/juries, new role in patent infringement, 249–51
Junior parties, 230–31
Jurisdiction, patent infringement, 247–48

Kamen, Herman, 275
Kay, Tim, 281
Knock-offs, 47–49, 164
Koons, Jeff, 151–52

Laches, 200
Land, Edwin, 8
Lanham Act, trademarks, 28, 52
Laverne, Erwine, 186, 187
Leibovitz, Annie, 131
Lemelson, Jerome, 8, 199–200, 233–34
Library of Congress, 165
Licensed inventions, 207, 256
Licenses, tax considerations, 307–10
Licensing agreements
    marketing, 274–75, 276–77
    software, 292–94
Limitations of
    copyrights, 119–41
    patents, 199–202
    trade secrets, 269–70
Linking issues, Web sites, 298
Literal patent infringement, 234–35
Litigation
    copyright infringement, 109, 152, 155–56, 163
    patent infringement, 242–51
    trade secrets, 273
Long-term capital assets, 306
Look of a trademark, registering, 62
Love, James, 21

Maaherra, Kristen, 98
Machines protected by patents, 179, 181–82
Madison, James, 6
Madrid Protocol, trademarks, 52–53
Maintaining
    patents, 231, 232
    trademarks, 42–56
    trade secrets, 267, 269, 270–71
Malcolm, John, 18
Manufactured articles protected by patents, 179, 181–82
Manufacturing agreements, marketing, 278
Manufacturing industry, 9
Marketing ideas, 274–79, 315
Material accompanying trademark application, 76–78, 77–78
Material information, patents, 216
Material protected by
    copyrights, 5–8, 99–101, 104–8, 144–47, 160, 167, 301
    patents, 175, 178–80
    trademarks, categories of, 33–34, 60–61, 61
Mirroring (inlining) issues, Web sites, 298, 299
Misappropriation, trade secrets, 273
Misuse
    patents and, 202, 232, 259
    trademarks and, 37, 37, 43–51, 56
Mitchell, Margaret, 120
Monetary damages
    copyright infringement, 115–16, 155–56, 164
    patent infringement, 243

Moore, Robert, 19
Multiple inventions, separating, patents, 218
Music industry
    copyrights, 111–12, 122–23, 135–38, 140, 143, 157, **167**, 168
    intellectual property law, 6, 7, 16–18

Napster, 17, 136–37, 143
Neale, Cindy, 15
New information, adding to patents, 218
News reporting (fair use), copyrights, 138, 149, **150**
New uses for old products protected by patents, 180, 181–82
Nonascertainable characteristic of trade secrets, 267
Nondisclosure agreements, marketing, 279, 315
Nonobviousness requirement (utility patent), 184–85
Nonsubstantive matters, patents, 228
Notice of Allowance, 30–31, 74, 80, 221
Notice of Appeal, patents, 227
Notice of Disallowance, patents, 225–26
Notice of Publication, trademarks, 79–80
Novelty requirement (utility patents), 183–84, 269
Novelty search, patents, 208–9, *209*

Oath, patents, 216
Office actions, patents, 220–21, 222
Official Gazette (PTO), 70, 75, 77, 80
Ogden, Perry, 122
One year sale rule, patents, 200–201, 258–59
Optional registration process, copyrights, 109, 162
"Ordinary meaning" of terms in claims (patents), 214–15
O'Reilly, Bill, 43
Originality requirement, copyrights, 105–6, 144–45
Ornamentality requirement for design patents, 188
Overlapping protections, patents, 189–90
Owner of copyright, finding, 156–58
Ownership issues, patents, 206–7

Paraphrasing vs. quoting, copyright infringement, 160
Paris Convention, trademarks, 51–52
Parodies (fair use), copyrights, 130–32, 149, 150, 160
Passing off goods and services, trademarks, 47–49
"Passive" Web sites, 20–21
Patent agents, 206, 208
Patent attorneys, 206, 208
Patent Interference, 230–31
Patent Pending designation, 221–22
Patent prosecution, 204–7
Patents, 173–202
    Business Tips, xii, 178, 186, 196, 206, 222, 226, 231, 240, 253
    Cautions, xii, 176, 201, 221, 223, 225, 229, 239, 246, 256, 258
    concepts of, 173–202
    copyrights vs., 125–26, 145, 188–90
    infringement of patents, 233–60
    law, history of, 8–10
    Lawyer's Notes, xii, 189, 190, 191, 199, 210, 216, 227, 228, 230, 241, 243, 251, 252, 258

licenses, 308–9
limitations of patents, 199–202
software, 9–10, 191–92, 282–87, 289, 290–91
trademarks vs., 27–28, 191
trade secrets vs., 268–69, 270
Patent wrapper, 201
Pemberton, John, 264
Pendency period, patents, 198
Permission to use copyrighted material, 156–60
Permission to use material, Web sites, 296–97
Perpetual protection, trade secrets, 269
Personal computer impact on copyrights, 8
Petition, filing with commissioner (trademarks), 83
Petition for Extension of Time, patents, 222
Petition to Revive, patents, 223
Pharmaceutical industry, 9, 180
Phonetic spellings, trademarks, 61–62
Photocopying impact on copyrights, 7–8
Physical association for use, trademarks, 29
Piracy issues, software, 294
Planning taxes, 303–7
Plant Patent Act of 1930, 9
Plant patents, 196–97
Pleadings, patent infringement, 250
Plunkett, Roy, 179
Plural use of trademarks, avoiding, 44
Policing copyrights, 152–53
Possessive use of trademarks, avoiding, 44
Power of Attorney Authorization, trademarks, 78
Power of Attorney, patents, 206, 216
PPA (Provisional Patent Application), 217–18
Precedents and trademarks, 28
Preregistration considerations, trademarks, 58–64, **61**
Presumption of validity, copyrights, 163
Preventative practices
    copyright infringement, 160
    patent infringement, 254–57
Principal Register of PTO, 39, 59, 64, 66, 80–82, 84
Printing press impact on copyrights, 5
Prior arts search, patents, 208–11, *209, 211*, 231
Prior local usage, trademarks, 32, 54, 63, 81
Privacy on campus, 16–17
Processes protected by patents, 178–79, 181–82
Product configuration (trade dress), 35
Product identification from trademarks, 27–28, 29, 33
Professional trademark search report, 68–69
Prosecution history estoppel, patent infringement, 202, 237
Prosecution process, patents, 220–23
Proving copyright infringement, 144–52
Provisional Patent Application (PPA), 217–18
PTO. *See* U. S. Patent and Trademark Office
Public display right, copyrights, 112
Public domain works, 105, 106, 146–47, 177
Publicity and trademarks, 42–43
Public performance right, copyrights, 111–12
Public use or sale of invention, patents, 232
Publishing industry, 5–7, **167**

Publishing information about invention, patents, 201, 204
Purchasing patents, 255

"Qualified research" tax credit, 307
Quality assurance from trademarks, 26

Randall, Alice, 120
RCE (Request for Continuing Examination), patents, 224
Recordation of Transfers and Other Documents (Copyright Office), 172
Recording Industry Association of America (RIAA), 16, 135–36, 137, 138, 143
Reexamination Process, patents, 257, 258
Registering
    copyrights, 161–72
    trademarks, 57–87
Reissue patents, 218
Rejection to applications, responses
    patent application, 223–30
    trademark application, 80, 82–83
Remedies for
    copyright infringement, 6, 15–16, 115–18, 155–56
    patent infringement, 242–44
Renewing trademark registration after ten years, 86
Request for Continuing Examination (RCE), patents, 224
Request to Divide Out form, trademarks, 75
Researching
    copyrights, 169–71
    patents, competitor's product, 240–41, 254–55
    patents, prior inventions, 208–11, *209, 211,* 231, 235, 254–55
    trademarks, 54, 57, 58, 64–69
Restatement of Torts, trade secrets, 265, 266
Retail industry, 19–20
Reverse engineering, 4, 134–35, 191, 269, 289
Reviving patent applications, 223
RIAA (Recording Industry Association of America), 16, 135–36, 137, 138, 143
Rosen, Gary, 138

Saarinen, Eero, 125, *125,* 186, *187*
Scandalous trademarks, 49–50, 55
Scholarship and research (fair use), copyrights, 133–39, 149, 150
Scope of claims, patent infringement, 201–2
Scope of patent, 203, 211, 213
Secondary meaning for descriptive trademarks, 37–38, 39, 59, 84
Secrets, business, 11–12, 263–73, 309, 314
Section 8 & 15 Affidavit, trademarks, 86
Securing trade secrets, 270–72
Seizure of infringing merchandise, 117–18
Self-addressed return card, patents, 217
Senior parties, 230
Separating multiple inventions, patents, 218
Service marks vs. domain names, 93
Shareware, Web sites, 297–98

Shayler, David, 21
Short-term capital assets, 306
Shrink-wrap agreements, software, 293
Similar devices, patent infringement, 236–38
Similarity of copied to protected work, copyright infringement, 147–48
Similar trademarks, 54–55, 67
Slogans, trademarking, 26, 50
Small entity declaration form, patents, 219
Smith, Madeline, 147
Software, 280–94
    "abstraction/filtration/comparison" test, 288–89
    Business Tips, xii, 290, 291, 292, 294
    confidentiality, 291–92
    copyrights, 7, 13–14, 140, **167,** 191, 282, 287–90, 292
    customized software, 293–94
    dot.com impact, 284–85
    Lawyer's Notes, xii, 288, 290
    licensing agreements, 292–94
    patents, 9–10, 191–92, 282–87, 289, 290–91
    piracy issues, 294
    reverse engineering, 289
    shrink-wrap agreements, 293
    trademarks, 292
    trade secrets, 290–91
Sonny Bono Copyright Term Extension Act of 1998, 114
Sound recording and bootlegging, copyrights, 113
Spam prevention, 15–16
Specification, patent application, 212–15, 232
Specimen, requirement of (trademarks), 72, 76
Spielberg, Steven, 97
Standard trademark application, 70–75, 311–13
State law and trademarks, 29
Statement of Use form, trademarks, 75
State registration, trademarks, 31, 62, 63
State statutes, trade secrets, 265–66
Statute of limitations
    copyright infringement, 155
    patent infringement, 247
Statutory damages, copyright infringement, 115–16, 155–56, 164
Stealing ideas, 4, 5, 7, 8, 278–79
Stopping copyright infringement, 153–56
Stowe, Harriet Beecher, 6–7
Strong vs. weak trademarks, 36–39, **37,** 48
"Stylized or special form," trademarks, 77–78, *77–78*
Subliminal associations, capitalizing on, trademarks, 59–61, **61**
Suggestive trademarks, 38, 39, 60, 61, **61**
Summary (specification, patent application), 212
Supplemental Register of PTO, 59, 66, 80, 81–82, 83, 84, 85
Supplementary registration, copyrights, 171
Suppression right, patents, 199
Surnames
    domain names, 94
    trademarks vs., 85
"Sweat of the brow" argument, copyrights, 101–2, 145–46

Symbol for intellectual property protection
   copyrights, 108–9, 162, 168–69
   trademarks, 44, 55, 64, 82, 86–87

Tarnishment of trademark's reputation, 11, 45–46
Tax considerations, 302–10
Technology impact on intellectual property law, 4, 5, 7, 8, 63, 108, 118, 133–38, 143
Telephone numbers, trademarking, 50–51
Temporary injunctions, copyright infringement, 117
Termination of patents, 198
TESS (Trademark Electronic Search System), 65–68, 82
Third-party nondisclosure agreements, 279, 315
Thompson, Josiah, 138
Timing requirement, trademarks, 74
Title (specification, patent application), 212
Token use, trademarks, 30
Tomikin, Dimitri, 162
Trade dress concept
   trademarks, 10–11, 34–36
   Web sites, 301
Trademark Electronic Search System (TESS), 65–68, 82
Trademark Revision Act of 1988, 30–31, 73
Trademarks, 23–41
   application process, 69–85, 311–13
   Business Tips, xii, 61, 65, 75, 94
   categories of, 33–34, 60–61, 61
   Cautions, xii, 30, 33, 69, 77
   certification marks vs., 34, 84–85
   collective marks vs., 34, 84–85
   concepts of, 23–41
   copyrights vs., 27–28
   domain names vs., 93
   law, history of, 10–11
   Lawyer's Notes, xii, 27, 29, 31, 39, 47, 60, 66, 71, 81
   licenses, 309
   maintaining trademarks, 42–56
   patents vs., 27–28, 191
   registering and researching trademarks, 57–87
   service marks vs., 30, 33–34
   software, 292
   strong vs. weak trademarks, 36–39, 37, 48
   surnames vs., 85
   trade names vs., 33
   Web sites and, 296
Trademark Trial and Appeal Board (TTAB), 83
Trade secrets, 11–12, 263–73, 309, 314
Transfers of copyrights, 171–72
Transmittal form, patents, 217
Treaties for international protections, trademarks, 51–53
Treaty for Trade-Related Aspects of International Property Rights (TRIPS), 52
Treble damages, trademarks, 64
TRIPS (Treaty for Trade-Related Aspects of International Property Rights), 52
TTAB (Trademark Trial and Appeal Board), 83

UCC (Uniform Commercial Code), 277
UDRP (Uniform Dispute Resolution Policy), domain names, 91, 92
Unauthorized improvements, patent infringement, 238, 241
Unenforceability of patents, 259–60
Unfair competition, patent infringement, 239
Uniform Commercial Code (UCC), 277
Uniform Dispute Resolution Policy (UDRP), domain names, 91, 92
Uniform Trade Secrets Act of 1979/1985, 265–66, 266–67, 273
United States Constitution and intellectual property law, 6, 8–9, 14, 177
University-sponsored research, patents, 207
Unpublished work (fair use), copyrights, 139
Upgrading from Supplemental to Principal Register, trademarks, 81–82, 84
U. S. Copyright Office, 106–7, 108, 166, 167, 170–72, 276. See also Copyrights
U. S. Customs Service, 53, 55, 56, 64, 252–53
U. S. Department of Justice, 18
Use for acquiring trademarks, 29–30, 31, 55
"Useful arts" promoted by patents, 177
Usefulness requirement (utility patents), 182–83
U. S. Patent and Trademark Office (PTO)
   domain names, 92–94
   marketing ideas, 276
   patents, 205, 210, 211
   Principal Register of PTO, 39, 59, 64, 66, 80–82, 84
   publication by PTO, 70, 75, 77, 80
   software, 286
   Supplemental Register of PTO, 59, 66, 80, 81–82, 83, 84, 85
   trademarks, 31, 37, 39, 44, 49, 61, 65
   See also Application process; Patents; Trademarks
Utility, copyrights, 123–26, 125
Utility patents, 177, 180–85, 197

Value characteristic of trade secrets, 267
Value effect destruction (fair use), copyrights, 127, 128, 130, 151–52
Venue, patent infringement, 248–49
Violence associated with trademarks, 26

Washington, George, 6
Web sites, 295–301
Webster, Noah, 6
Weekly Gazette, 221
Willfulness of copyright infringer, 116
Workship doctrine, patents, 207
World Intellectual Property Organization (WIPO), 52

Xerography impact on copyrights, 7–8

Zapruder, Abraham, 138